D1609664

SISTERWRITEREATERS

Edited by
Claire LaZebnik and Ann Brown

Griffith Moon

Printed in the United States of America
First Printing, 2017

Creative Direction: Kimberly Brooks
Interior Design: Sara Martinez

Published by Griffith Moon
Santa Monica, California
GriffithMoon.com

ISBN 978-0-9981686-8-5
Library of Congress Control Number: 2017938808

For Ann. She completes me. And by "completes," I mean she makes me laugh every single day and gives me the best parenting advice I've ever not paid for. So, really, it has nothing to do with completion. The point is: this wouldn't have been fun without her.

– Claire LaZebnik

For Claire. She did all the work. And by "all," I mean she carefully edited each one of the essays. I tried to make myself useful by giving her parenting advice and making her laugh. There is no one better than Claire as a partner in writing or in friendship.

– Ann Brown

TABLE OF CONTENTS

INTRODUCTION...ix

WAKE UP AND EAT..1

Valentine's Day Dinner with Cubette   2
By Claudia Reilly
Warm Cinnamon Rolls for the
Broken-Hearted

Breakfast At Morenci Lane   10
By Cathy Ladman
May Ladman's French Toast

Mustard's Last Stand   16
By Davis Alexander
Mom's Secret (Mustard) Scrambled Eggs

No One Begs Me To Cook Chicken
and Vegetables   20
By Kim Allen-Niesen
Banana Chocolate Muffins

Thursday's Child Is Full of Crepes   23
By Nell Scovell
Dessert Crepes

A Friend Indeed   27
By Kathy Bidus
Crumb Cake

THE SANDWICH
GENERATION..31

Hello, Sexy Gorgeous   32
By Marcie Smolin
Robyn's Tuna Guacamole Melt

Butter Sandwiches   36
By Liane Kupferberg Carter
Butter Sandwich

Melting, a poem   41
By Annie LaZebnik

Sex, Lies and Tuna Sandwiches   42
By Ann Brown
The Best Tuna Sandwich Ever

RX: SOUP..47

Inheritance   48
By Amy Wang Manning
Pork "Turnip" Soup

Frankincense and Leeks   55
By Lunaea Weatherstone
Christmas Eve Potato Soup

Bachelors   59
By Ellen Twaddell
Chicken Soup à la Bachelor

Song of Soup   63
By Alice Scovell
Gram's Vegetable Soup

CARBS, SCHMARBS (SO LONG
AS YOU'RE HAPPY).......................................69

You Are What You Eat   70
By Anna Winger
Jörg's Pasta with Potatoes

Ravioli, a poem   72
By Annie LaZebnik

Savory Bitch   73
By Sarah Thyre
Savory Bitch Ramen

It Was Jelly!   77
By Carolyn Omine
Insanely Good Stuffing

Strong to the Finich (Thanksgiving 2016)   84
By Ann Brown
Spinach Pie Roll-Ups

Bloat Sweet Bloat   89
By Asmita Paranjape
Sabudana Khicidi

While Cooking Spaghetti   93
By Liza Donnelly
Spaghetti Carbonara

FISH, FOWL, AND MEAT
(THE OTHER VEGETABLES)........................99

Sales at Loehmann's   100
By Kimberly Brooks
Kimberly's Famous Santa Monica Salmon

Steve's Salmon   104
By Jeb Sharp
Steve's Salmon

I'm My Own Grandma   107
By Susan Senator
Gefilte Fish à la Grandma Esther

A Meal For All Seasons   114
By Lisa Grace Lednicer
Chicken and Shells

The Terrified Chef   118
By Laurie Sandell
Chicken Pot Pie

Mom's Tacos   120
By Valerie Breiman
Mom's Tacos

The Thing In The Freezer   124
By Maiya Williams
Roasted Opossum

Comfort Jiaozi   129
By May-lee Chai
Jiaozi

Funeral Casserole   138
By Kate Fuglei
Funeral Casserole

SPREAD 'EM (AND SAUCE 'EM)................143

Liquid Smoke   144
By Bernadette Luckett
Uncle Benny's Barbecue Sauce

Family Recipe   148
By Wendy Kout
Not Lena's Pimento Cheese Dip, But Close

The Pesto Chronicles   154
By Nina Laden
Pesto

MULTIPLE COURSASMS................................163

The Elephant in the Room   164
By Claire LaZebnik
Mustard Fish
Roasted or Grilled Vegetable Medley
Green Salad
Flourless Chocolate Cake

Toddlers and Tortillas   172
By April Salazar
Blender Salsa
Pinto Beans
Tortillas
Tamales

WHO DOESN'T LIKE COOKIES?........181

My Life In Six Cookies   182
By Nell Minow
Ammonia Cookies

The Prince And The Peanut Butter   187
By Caissie St.Onge
Prince-Inspired Crispy Peanut Butter Bars

Andy's Cookies   192
By Laura Shumaker
35-Second Chocolate Chip Cookies

A World without Cookies   196
By Merrill Markoe
Merrill's Guilt-Free Cookies and Cake

SWEETS TO THE SWEET * 203
(*but not in the creepy Ophelia's grave
Shakespeare way)

Something Jelled   204
By Claire LaZebnik
Rainbow Gelatin Cake

Barbara Jeane   210
By Norma Safford Vela
Barbara Jeane's Sheath Cake

Apples and Orange Polyester Castles   217
By Becky Hartman Edwards
Apple Pie

31 Flavors Of Inspiration   221
By Michele Willens
Michele's Baked Alaska

Bittersweet and Nuts   224
By Leslie Greenberger
Ima's Chocolate Walnut Cake

HOT DRINKS FOR COLD TIMES 229

Spring   230
By Leah Krinsky
Saffron Hot Chocolate

I Heart 1,3,7-
TRIMETHYLXANTHINE   234
By Barbara Horowitz
The Perfect Coffee Moment

Bread and Tea, a poem   238
By Annie LaZebnik

BIOS 241
ACKNOWLEDGMENTS 251
RECIPE INDEX 252

Introduction

Family and food. Movies and food. Celebrations and food. Anxiety and food. Boredom, alcohol, hunger . . . everything goes with food.

But nothing goes better with food than stories.

So we reached out to writers we admired and asked them to share both their stories and their recipes with us. Then we created a secret, all-girl Facebook group to talk about the project and to get to know each other.

We dubbed ourselves the "Sisterwritereaters."

Our group includes some bestselling authors and a few less-bestselling authors, award-winning television writers, lauded graphic artists, illustrators, photographers, well-known magazine contributors, sitcom writers, journalists, stand-up comics, TED Talkers, playwrights, bloggers, recovering anorexics, secret eaters, healthy eaters, and boring eaters. A few of us are gluten-free; others are lactose-intolerant, vegetarian, carnivorous and Kosher. Three of us are actual sisters. None of us is a chef, and a few of us can't cook at all. Some of us have prizewinning recipes; others have favorite take-out joints. We are fat and skinny, middle-aged and youthful, motivated and lazy, confident and insecure, self-indulgent and disciplined.

Many of us eat too much junk.

Some of us enjoy a nice cocktail in the late afternoon.

One of us keeps a bong in the pantry next to the Doritos.

In these pages are essays, drawings, photos, poems, and recipes—recipes that remind us of the dinners we've prepared for ourselves and our families, the holiday feasts we lingered over, the leftovers we gulped standing over the kitchen sink, the elaborate dishes we hoped would seduce a lover, the strange and familiar foods of our cultures that sustained, embarrassed and delighted us, and the meals that we ate with relatives who are no longer here to enjoy another meal with us.

All of the recipes have been through a rigorous testing process.*

(Disclaimer: NONE of the recipes has been through a rigorous testing process. Or, really, any testing process at all. The point is: don't sue us. Please.)

(If you have to sue someone, sue Ann. She's the strong one.—CSL)

(Claire's the rich one. —AB)

We kept the writing assignment as loose as possible. "A personal essay that brings in food in some way," was our only guideline. We wanted a wide range of stories, and that's what we got, but we noticed some patterns. Like:

1.   We like cookies.
2.   All kinds of cookies.

These are recipes that take you to the writer's heart. This is a cookbook with emotional baggage.

So come, sit with us. Here, have a cookie. Have two.

We're human. And we're hungry.

Love,
Claire & Ann

WAKE UP AND EAT

Warm Cinnamon Rolls for the Broken-Hearted

May Ladman's French Toast

Mom's Secret (Mustard) Scrambled Eggs

Banana Chocolate Muffins

Dessert Crepes

Crumb Cake

Valentine's Day Dinner with Cubette

by Claudia Reilly

On an icy February night in 1976, my college boyfriend GG burst into my apartment two hours late with glittering, glazed, gray eyes and a white-toothed, sexy smile. Oh, that smile made my heart hope. With him was a gorgeous woman passionately clutching his shoulder as if he were her knight in shining armor and she his damsel in distress. The woman's raven hair curled down to her waist. She was wearing a dazzling red cape dotted with snow. I'd never seen anyone so beautiful other than on a magazine cover. Her blue eyes seemed to shine almost purple. Both she and GG were trying not to giggle the giggle of ravishing gods being greeted by a mere mortal in a homemade pink velvet dress who resembled Tricia Nixon.

"Happy Valentine's Day," GG said, kicking off his snow-covered cowboy boots. "Sorry I'm late, but I found my old friend Miriam with her car stuck in a snow bank, so I told her to come here. Miriam, Claudia. Claudia, Miriam."

I wanted to be angry with GG, but I was a twenty-year-old undergrad, and GG was a twenty-four-year-old brilliant grad student who had won an award for best teaching assistant in the English department at my Midwestern university. Even more prestigious, he'd recently received a handwritten rejection letter from *The New Yorker*, asking him to revise and resubmit a poem about killing and eating a squirrel. This made him the most famous writer I'd ever met. So I smiled, put out my hand, and said, "Nice to meet you, Miriam. Please come eat with us!"

Miriam removed her hand from GG's shoulder, but instead of shaking mine, she reached into the pocket of her cape and pulled out a crushed package wrapped in tin foil. "I wouldn't intrude on your Valentine's dinner, but I almost ran a clown over on Green Street," she said.

"A real clown?" I asked.

GG said, "As opposed to what? A fake clown?"

Miriam said, "Yes. A real clown. She terrified me. She had green cotton candy hair, giant purple shoes, and a red rubber nose. She flung herself in front of my car as if she wanted me to run her over. I think she was suicidal."

GG said, "Maybe she was just clowning around."

I'd been playing Joni Mitchell's album *Court and Spark* over and over and had stopped hearing the lyrics when Miriam's voice joined in with my record player. I loved how she sang:

Everything comes and goes
Marked by lovers and styles of clothes
Things that you held high
And told yourself were true
Lost or changing as the days come down to you

"Cubette doesn't like Joni Mitchell," GG said, walking through my tiny living room, where I'd hung red construction paper hearts on ribbons and attached them with Scotch tape so they dangled from the ceiling. It was all supposed to be arty and romantic, but it looked like a first grader's Valentine project. GG brushed through the hearts as he walked to my stereo, and then lifted the needle off the record. He called out to my bedroom door, "What do you want me to put on, Cubette? As if we all don't know."

I'd fallen in love with GG one humid summer night when he entered a coffee shop where I was studying Microbiology, eating popcorn, and drinking water. He'd raced into Treno's carrying a copy of James Joyce's *Finnegans Wake* in one hand and a two foot high toy teddy bear in his other and called out, "Who the fuck left this young bear in a hot car with the windows closed?"

When he'd grabbed my glass of water and held it up to the bear's red velvet mouth, I'd been intrigued by his seriousness of purpose as he asked the bear her name. There was something so tender in his regard for the teddy bear. He'd turned to me and said, "She wants to come home with you. She says her name is Cubette and she's all alone in the world and that you appear to be all alone in the world too."

Miriam pulled me out of my memory. "Who's Cubette?" she asked.

"Claudia's only true friend," GG said. And then he called out loudly, "No Cubette. I'm not putting on that song. I'm sick of that damn song."

"Am I supposed to be able to hear Cubette talk?" Miriam asked.

"Don't you dare tell me to fuck myself," GG shouted as he ran into the bedroom.

"Cubette's not real. Cubette's a toy... a stuffed animal," I said, embarrassed to explain Cubette and yet ashamed that I'd betrayed her by denying her reality, the way as a kid I'd felt sad when I'd stuck all my dolls in a dark box after a friend said I was too old to play with them.

GG walked out of the bedroom looking exasperated. "Cubette won't come out and meet Miriam until I put her song on. I told her fine. Be that way. Sit there on the bed and pout. Go ahead and ruin Valentine's Day."

I heard my living room windows rattle with wind and looked out them. The snow was blowing hard from the north and it looked as if many houses had lost power in the winter storm, but I could see far in the distance the flashing red neon lights of Mr. Donut. It was one of the only places on campus open late into the night. Once, a friend of mine had run into Tennessee Williams sitting in Mr. Donut crying. The playwright had told my friend he thought Mr. Donut's warmly iced cinnamon rolls were the best thing to eat when a person is heartbroken but determined to go on living.

Miriam picked up my *Court and Spark* album and said, "I love the way David Crosby and Susan Webb join in on that line 'love is gone.' Do you know her?"

"Me? Know Joni Mitchell?" I asked. "No. I mean I know her music. I own all her albums."

GG said, "Miriam's a singer. She opened for Joni Mitchell once."

"Joni was afraid she had nodes on her vocal cords. She consulted with my mom," Miriam said. "I think she let me open for her so if she needed surgery my mom would try extra hard."

GG said, "Her mom is this world-class throat surgeon."

"Mainly, my mom's a world-class bitch," Miriam said. "Guess what she's going to say when she hears her precious Cadillac got totaled tonight."

"The car's totaled?" I asked. "I thought you said you only hit a snowbank."

"I hit the snowbank eventually. First I hit another car. It was icy and the car was tiny—a white Volkswagen Beetle. People shouldn't be allowed to drive those in snow. Anyhow, my mother's not going to give a shit that I saved a clown's life. In fact, she's probably going to say I'm making up the clown and that GG and I were driving too fast and were probably strung out on LSD."

"Imagine that," GG said. And then he began to giggle and she began to giggle. They laughed and laughed as if this was the funniest thing ever.

So GG had been in the car. I didn't want to think about that, so instead I tried to laugh too. But my laugh was fake. Miriam's laugh was real and beautiful. She had a great singer's laugh, throaty, full, lush. But I felt there was something sad in her laugh. She laughed in some minor chord.

Miriam handed me the tin foil package she'd removed from her pocket. I noticed the tin foil had the name **LORRAINE** written on it in black Magic Marker. Miriam said, "I brought alfalfa sprouts for our meal. I want to share them with you—so long as you love them as passionately as I do."

"Oh I do. Thanks." I opened the package carefully, because I'd grown up in a family that treated tin foil as if it were platinum, and headed from my living room toward the kitchen. I wanted to check on the food. I'd made a steak, roasted potatoes, and green beans, and then had put everything back in the oven to stay warm. I hoped things wouldn't be too dry after two hours. "The sprouts look delicious," I said over my shoulder.

"I'll help you prepare the sprouts," Miriam said, following me into the kitchen. "My mom makes them for herself all the time with this great recipe. Do you have saffron?"

"No," I said. I didn't even know what saffron was other than the name of a girl in Donovan's song *Mellow Yellow*.

Miriam stared at the table I'd set with pink carnations, a used gold tablecloth I'd found at the Salvation Army that day, and settings for three—two normal sized plates, two sets of regular forks, spoons, and knives, and then one tiny china doll dish and a miniature sterling silver baby spoon. Everything that had looked whimsical to me earlier when alone now looked not only pathetic, but perhaps even slightly insane. Quickly, I gathered up the phone books I'd put on Cubette's chair as a kind of booster seat, and tossed them on my Formica countertop along with her doll dish and baby spoon. I could feel my skin turning red with mortification.

I wished GG would join us in the kitchen, but instead I heard him shout out, "All right already! Stop blubbering! I'm putting it on!" And soon the country singer Tom T. Hall's twangy voice filled the air with Cubette's favorite song:

I love little baby ducks, old pick-up trucks,
slow moving trains…and rain.

I asked Miriam, "Do you think I should put the sprouts on the steak or serve them on top of the green beans or maybe on some lettuce?"

Miriam removed her red cape and tossed it on Cubette's chair. "Here. Let me check your refrigerator." She opened the door of the fridge, making it impossible for me to get to the oven. She was wearing a gypsy skirt, an unbleached muslin kind of peasant blouse, and at least 5 fabulous silk scarves. I was dazzled by how chic, long and thin she was. Even her wrists and neck were chic, long and thin. She crouched down to examine the entire contents of the refrigerator—milk, half and half, orange juice, Kraft American cheese, iceberg lettuce, Wishbone Italian salad dressing, eggs, Heinz catsup, and Jell-O Pudding Pops for Cubette.

"I have some wheat germ in a cabinet if that would help," I told Miriam.

She looked up at me. "Help with what?" she asked. I saw she was starting to cry.

"Miriam, is something wrong?"

"Your refrigerator moves me to the core of my being," she said. "Nothing is labeled. It's an unselfish refrigerator. My mother was in a concentration camp when she was a girl and has this strange thing about food. She has our family's food labeled on one shelf and all her own food wrapped in tin foil and labeled on another shelf. We are never, ever to touch her food but she can touch ours. Isn't that weird? Everything fell apart for me in LA; I couldn't pay my rent. The only singing job I got was as a clown for a birthday party and the kids hated me. I didn't know how to get an agent. I didn't know…anything. I hitchhiked home. Started out blind drunk three weeks ago. Got home last night sober and told my mom how I've decided I'm going to stop imbibing and get my degree teaching music. My mom rolled her eyes. *You wouldn't survive a month in the camp* she told me. I wanted to say *You think I haven't thought that every single minute of my life Mom?*"

I looked over at the tin foil wrapping with the name **Lorraine** printed on it and said, "Is your mother's name Lorraine?"

"Yes," Miriam said, amazed. "Are you psychic?"

Suddenly, I heard the needle of the stereo screech across the record. GG shouted from the living room, "God damn it Cubette! Now you've ruined your record and you're in big, big trouble. Mr. GG's going to pour himself a scotch and listen to Bob Dylan's *Blood on the Tracks* and you are going to bed without supper."

Miriam wiped her beautiful eyes, and took the bottle of Wishbone Italian dressing out of the fridge. "I think if I put a touch of this on the alfalfa sprouts, it will enhance their natural flavor. Do you have a bowl?"

I found a bowl and said, "It must have been so awful for your mom in the concentration camp. Did she lose any family members?"

Miriam said, "All of them. She says she has no family, as if my dad and I are these people who don't exist because we weren't in Poland in 1944. All I wanted was some orange juice and she told me to get in the car and go buy some when it was already starting to snow and the orange juice was sitting right there on her shelf. Why couldn't she give the orange juice to me as a Valentine's gift?"

GG entered the kitchen and poured himself a Scotch as he said, "Cubette won't be joining us this evening but she sends her regards to you, Miriam, and says she too once almost ran over a clown while she was driving." Then he added *sotto voce*, "She doesn't actually drive. Cubette's a bit of an L-I-A-R."

"How're you doing with your doctoral thesis, GG?" Miriam asked as I squeezed past her and peeked in the oven.

"It's in about as good of shape as your mom's Cadillac," GG said.

"Oh God," Miriam said. "I don't want to talk about that car."

"Well, I don't want to talk about my dissertation," GG said.

"Miriam was telling me about her mother being in the concentration camp," I said.

"There," GG said, raising his glass of Scotch. "Claudia found a more cheerful subject to discuss: The Holocaust. Happy Valentine's Day everyone! L'chaim!"

I reached with potholders into the oven and pulled out the steak, potatoes, and green beans on the wobbly cookie tin where they were warming. The steak looked dried out, the green beans were a sad yellowish green, and the potatoes had blackened, but everything looked much better than it would a few moments later when Miriam turned with her bowl of alfalfa sprouts and collided against the cookie sheet. Suddenly, the steak, beans, and potatoes were flying through the kitchen with Miriam's alfalfa sprouts, and Miriam was screaming that I'd burnt her on purpose.

GG rushed to attend to Miriam's burns in my bathroom, while I crawled around the floor picking up food. Could I rinse anything in the sink and save it? Maybe boil things to sterilize them?

"Is your girlfriend a witch?" I heard Miriam ask from the bathroom. "She knew my mother's name."

"Cubette's the witch, not Claudia," GG said. "Claudia's this chick without anything to say. I have Cubette talk so I don't get bored. God, you're beautiful."

"I'm not beautiful. Ali MacGraw is so much more beautiful than I am."

"Ali MacGraw is shit compared to you."

"Really?" Miriam asked. "So why did you and I break up? I know I cut you that one time giving you a blowjob, but I'd just had Novocaine at the dentist."

"Today in the car was the most incredible sex I've ever had," GG said. And they began to giggle again.

I could dimly hear moans and panting as I finished piling up the steak, beans, sprouts and potatoes from the floor and flung them in the garbage.

Then I walked into my bedroom. There was Cubette, lying face down on my bed. I picked her up and looked at her. She was wearing a little red corduroy dress with pink hearts on it that I'd sewn. I thought how I was finished with GG and that this meant being finished with Cubette, too. A chick with nothing to say? Was that who I was? I put on my boots and jacket, grabbed Cubette and headed to the kitchen. But just as I was about to toss Cubette in the garbage can with the food, I looked at her black button eyes and realized she wasn't a witch. She was a young bear cub who, like me, had not found her own voice. But one thing was certain. Neither of us would ever let GG talk for us again.

So I tucked Cubette inside my jacket, reached for the orange juice carton in my refrigerator, got a roll of Reynold's Wrap out of a drawer and a black Magic Marker. I wrapped up the orange juice carton with the tin foil. Then I took the Magic Marker and printed **MIRIAM** on it and placed my gift on the kitchen table.

I looked at Cubette, and her eyes seemed pleased. We headed out the door into the night and hurried along the icy streets of Champaign-Urbana, Illinois. At first it was difficult to walk, and I didn't know where we were going, but soon I was running, sliding and slipping along the streets with joy. I put Cubette up on my shoulders so she could watch the white snow falling from the black sky, and realized we were on our way to find out who we were to become, and that our first stop on this journey would be Mr. Donut and its warmly iced cinnamon rolls for the broken-hearted.

WARM CINNAMON ROLLS FOR THE BROKEN-HEARTED

DOUGH

INGREDIENTS

3 cups all-purpose flour
3 tablespoons granulated sugar
1 package instant yeast
3/4 cup milk
2 tablespoons butter
1 egg
1 tablespoon ground cinnamon

TO PREPARE

1. In a large bowl, mix flour, sugar, cinnamon. Set aside.
2. Put milk and butter in a microwave for 30 seconds then add yeast. Let sit until yeast bubbles up then add to flour mixture.
3. Add the egg and knead with hand or mixer for 3-4 minutes or until the dough is no longer sticky.
4. Place in a lightly greased bowl and let rest for about 5 minutes.

FILLING

INGREDIENTS

¼ cup (1/2 stick) melted butter
2 tablespoons ground cinnamon
¼ cup brown sugar

TO PREPARE

1. Row dough into a rectangle on a floured surface until it's about ¼ inch high (or less).
2. Spread the 2 T of melted butter on top.
3. Mix together the cinnamon and brown sugar and sprinkle it all over the dough.
4. Roll up the dough tightly and cut into 9–12 pieces.
5. Place in a lightly buttered 9 x 13 dish, then let rise for half an hour in a warm place.

Bake: Turn on the oven to 375F. Bake the cinnamon rolls for 20 minutes or until golden. Remove from oven and top with glaze.

GLAZE

INGREDIENTS

½ stick butter
1 cup powdered sugar
1 tsp vanilla
I T butter

TO PREPARE

1. Mix the powdered sugar, vanilla, 1 Tablespoon of butter and 2 Tablespoons of milk in sauce pan at low heat.
2. Stir until smooth and lump free. Drizzle over warm rolls.

The important thing: Make yourself a cup of coffee. Enjoy your warm cinnamon rolls while pining over someone who is unworthy of your love. Despair until you have finished at least two rolls. Wipe your mouth. Sigh. Worry about your weight and lack of self-control. Know the future will be better.

Breakfast at Morenci Lane

by Cathy Ladman

My doctor just told me that I have to put on weight. The scale said I'm down six pounds, and I'm not surprised. My pants have been falling down—not to my ankles, but enough to make a point. I've had to tighten my belt to a notch I haven't seen in a long time. So, I get it.

But, it's not that simple for a recovering anorexic to put on weight. Even though I know, intellectually, that I have to do it, the buzz I feel when I'm skinny is intoxicating. And this is after more than thirty years of recovery. It's a powerful disease.

Even in recovery, I am careful about my food choices. I don't eat with abandon. There's always a calculator in my head, keeping track.

But now, it's time to stop fucking around. Anxiety has likely been the cause of this weight loss—anxiety over career, money, marriage, parenting. The whole damn thing. And anxiety is not an appetite's best friend.

On this recent Saturday morning, I slept pretty late, and I woke up hungry. Really hungry. Well, *that's* good. And I thought, "I want French Toast. Cooked in butter. With maple syrup."

Without hesitation, I went into the kitchen and got everything out—bread, egg, milk, butter, maple syrup, frying pan, spatula—and I began doing what I'd seen my mom do so many times, so many years ago.

"I have to call my mommy," I said out loud to myself. (I talk to myself a lot. I spend a lot of time alone, or with my dog, or with my husband and daughter, who are always so absorbed in what they're doing that I've long since expected them to be listening. And forget about getting a response. Ugh.)

At that moment I thought of her as "Mommy," because that's who she was in those French Toast Days. Mommy. She was not a particularly fantastic cook, but she made the best French toast.

I called her and left her a message, telling her what I was doing, and that I was making it just like she did, soaking the bread in the egg until it could not possibly absorb any more. The bread was so very egg-soaked that she, and now I, would have to very gingerly move it from the soaking bowl to the frying pan, very carefully, so that it wouldn't break before it hit the sizzling butter.

The smell of the butter and the sound it was making were incredibly evocative of those cold winter mornings on Morenci Lane in Little Neck, Queens. My mom would cook the French toast until it was a darker shade of brown on both sides, so that when I cut into it with the side of my fork, it would crunch, the perfect foil to the creamy interior.

When I was very little, my mom would cut it into a house. There was the front door, windows, and a chimney. It was sort of Cubist, since it remained a square. I so clearly remember this that I'm almost time-traveling.

I poured lots of syrup on it back then. Log Cabin Syrup. We called it "maple syrup," but there was nothing maple in it. It was just "syrup." And I poured it the fuck on.

I can remember the shape of the bottle. And sometimes we could get it in an actual log cabin-shaped tin. Now *that* was practical. Try opening that metal screw cap, on the slanted roof, when it's caked with built-up syrup residue.

My mom knew how to do breakfast. Weekdays were more hurried, but still, always comforting. Every morning, my mom made us hot cocoa. Well, what I *thought* was hot cocoa. First step was milk, heated in a small saucepan. (No microwave!) She had to keep an eye on it because, if it was on too long, it would form a skin, which my mom would carefully remove with a spoon and rinse down the sink. Yuck! Nobody wants hot cocoa with skin on it!

Then, she poured the hot milk into a mug on top of—brace yourself—some powdered Nestle's Quik. Yes!! That was our "hot chocolate!" And we loved it! What did we know? It tasted good. We didn't know what horrors existed in Nestle's Quik. (I looked up the ingredients of Nestle's Quik. Chocolate is not even mentioned!)

Remember: We didn't know what real maple syrup was. Log Cabin and Nestle's Quik. They were home to me. They were cozy and safe.

Every morning, before school, I would have the Ladman Hot Cocoa and "cat cereal." We called it "cat cereal" because, on the box, there was a picture of a cat, riding a scooter. I'm sure it also had some sort of human outfit on, like a hat or a scarf. It was baby cereal, Beechnut or Gerber, which we continued to eat, several years into elementary school. I loved it. I would put sugar on it, and the sugar would get dark, and I would stir it in and watch it swirl into the cereal. I liked it sweet.

I ate it with my baby spoon. I used my baby spoons for almost everything, whenever possible. They were tiny metal spoons, which were tarnished. I had a couple of them.

When I was an adult and moved away, I took them with me. I still have them, somewhere. In fact, last year, I happened to turn one of them over and look at the handle, and I saw something written there. I squinted to make out what it said. "Waldorf Astoria." My baby spoons were stolen from the Waldorf Astoria! Jesus! My baby spoons were loot!

Hot "cocoa" and cat cereal were weekday breakfasts, as were soft-boiled eggs with toast. My mom would soft-boil an egg perfectly, slip it into a Pyrex custard cup, and then break toast pieces into it. Then she'd mash it all up with a spoon, and the yoke would break and ooze, and the toast would absorb it. A little salt, a baby spoon. So perfect.

Weekends were reserved for more complicated, time-consuming breakfasts. Eggs and onions was one of my favorites. My mom would yell upstairs, "I'm making eggs and onions!" which was met with, "Yay!!"

These were no crunchy, lightly cooked onions. They were slowly and painstakingly caramelized for almost 30 minutes, until they were soft and a beautiful dark, sweet brown. It took patience and being near the stove.

When the onions were ready, my mom would yell upstairs, "How many eggs?" and we would each yell out a number. Mine was always, "Three!"

Three! Three eggs! I probably ate seven eggs a week, or more. I was eating three scrambled eggs at a time when I was a young kid, about eight years old. I loved my mom's scrambled eggs. They were creamy. Never runny, never dry. Just perfect.

So my mom added up the number of eggs that we all called out, and in they went into the pan with the onions. When she taught me how to make scrambled eggs, she showed me to wait until the eggs began to set at the outer edge and then to bring them in, to the center. I would keep doing this, not allowing them to set too hard—just the right amount of finesse. Mmm. I can smell the caramelized onions now. (I hope that doesn't mean I'm having a stroke.)

There were often fresh bagels at the table on weekends, so easy to come by in New York. No one would ever describe a bagel in New York as being "pretty decent," the way they're described in Los Angeles, where the bar for bagels has been substantially lowered by at least 50%, right there with the bar for pizza.

Bagels, lox, cream cheese, and whitefish were another great breakfast. We'd get these little fish, called, "chubs." They were whole whitefish, and I loved them. I'm telling you, I had oddly sophisticated culinary tastes for a young kid. I could make my way around the bones, too. I was pretty fearless.

Those fish were kind of creepy, though, the way one eye would be staring at me from my plate. I am not interested in eating any staring fish these days, but they were a delicacy to me then.

My father was only around for breakfasts on the weekends. When we were having bagels, sometimes I'd drive to the bagel store with him. He'd halve all the bagels when we got home. That was a daddy job. I loved pumpernickel bagels. Or bialys. I loved the onions. Sometimes we'd get onion board at the bagel store: it was like a bialy in a giant, rectangular form. It would have been delicious with butter, but I wouldn't have known that because we ate margarine then. And onion board was so good that it even was tasty with margarine.

Uch. Margarine. The bastard food of the '60s. It was thought to be healthier than butter. Yeah, guess what? It wasn't. It had no taste. It was awful. Flavorless oil, with salt. When I grew up and lived on my own, margarine was the first thing to go.

Back then, when we'd go out to restaurants and there was delicious, warm bread and butter served, my dad would say, "There's nothing like real butter." Then he'd discover that the wrapped pats of butter were ice hard.

"I hate that," he'd say. "How're you supposed to spread it when it's like this? It's like a rock!"

Then he'd do something that I still do today, when I encounter hard, individually wrapped pats of butter. He'd put one between his palms and he would rub his hands back and forth, as if he were trying to warm himself up while waiting for a city bus in the deep of winter. And then he'd have soft butter to spread on the warm Italian bread. And it was so good.

Dad was in charge of pancakes and waffles. The waffle iron was something that only Daddy touched. When the waffle iron finally broke, my dad wouldn't replace it, no matter how much we pleaded. I think it was his only way out of having to clean the fucking thing after using it. What a mess. Remember, this was pre-nonstick cookware. I can only imagine what a pain in the ass that must have been. Of course, the waffle iron remained downstairs, broken, until the house was sold in 2005. It stayed with the other broken appliances in the closet in the basement: The Appliance Cemetery.

But Dad kept making pancakes, although not every time we asked, because he was no pushover. When he did make them, it was a lovely time, hanging out in the kitchen with him. He showed me how long to wait before I flipped the pancake. "Wait until there are a lot of dimples and the edges start to look a little cooked." He would let me spoon some batter onto the griddle, by myself, and watch it cook. Then, we'd flip over a pancake together. And he'd ruffle my hair with his hand.

I love breakfast. It's at the beginning of a brand new day. There's hope in breakfast. And it also brings me back to a time when there was not much anxiety. It was a small window of years, but they stay with me. When I see a picture of me back then, with my beautiful, young mom, or my handsome dad, or my funny sister, Leslie, my heart swells, I close my eyes, and I'm back there, on Morenci Lane, in the only house of my parents that I knew, and I remember the beautiful part of it.

Cathy Ladman and her mother, May.

MAY LADMAN'S FRENCH TOAST

INGREDIENTS

Bread—whatever you have in the house. Doesn't need to be fresh. But, if you want THE BEST French Toast, use challah. (Please ask a Jewish friend what this is.)
Eggs—1 per slice of bread
Butter
Syrup (optional)

TO PREPARE

1. Beat an egg in a bowl that will accommodate a slice of bread. Soak it well. Press down gently with flat of fork.
2. Heat pan on low-medium, add some butter.

3. Gently flip the soaking bread to do the other side in the same way.
4. When butter is sizzling—but not burning!—carefully lift the soaked bread into the pan. (I suggest having the pan and bowl as close to each other as possible so that the transfer is a quick one. The egg-soaked bread can fall apart easily.)
5. Let cook until as well-done as you like it, and flip to the other side.
6. Add more butter to the pan, as necessary.
7. Repeat the process for as many pieces of French Toast that you and everyone desires.
8. Serve with REAL maple syrup. (Or Log Cabin, if you absolutely must.)

Mustard's Last Stand

by Davis Alexander

I knew there were advantages to postponing marriage until I was thirty-eight, but now I was trying to convince myself there was also an upside to having my first child at age forty. The one thing I knew is that I'd grown up over the prior two decades; I told myself my baby would benefit from my maturity and I could apply the same focus and thoroughness I'd used furthering my career to my new position as mother-to-be. Starting from that first positive pee test, I dove into research, study and planning. I took notes and made myself promises. I'd be the mother of my dreams. And I would start by rockin' this pregnancy.

Pre-natal vitamins and organic food were a given. Mommy yoga a must. I would treat my body in a manner that would only benefit the little one growing inside. The first trimester went pretty well. I managed nausea with ginger tea and an occasional salt-free whole-wheat cracker. I made a habit of salads with dressing-on-the-side for lunch and lean protein and veggies for dinner. The scale remained my friend.

Second trimester was even easier. It seemed I gained only energy and stamina. And when other mothers knowingly asked what I was craving, I shrugged—I had no cravings! "The only thing I crave is a healthy child," I'd beam. I must have been intolerable—healthy inside and out and acting as pleased with myself as sugar-free punch. I should have known I'd get my comeuppance. What I didn't expect was that it would hit without warning and take no prisoners.

One morning, while I was scrambling my daily breakfast of egg whites, shallots, spinach and Spike salt-free seasoning, I was suddenly overwhelmed by the aroma of Jewish deli-style corned beef. So strong was the smell, I looked around the kitchen for the evil-doer who'd snuck in my house to tempt me. But there was no one. I turned back to my nonstick skillet, but the unmistakable scent of pickled meat remained, and with it bloomed a mental image of thinly-sliced, brined brisket stacked impossibly high between two slices of warm, crusty rye bread. I shuddered, and retrained my focus on egg whites, but as I ate my diminutive meal, gazing out at the hills I would hike afterward, I once again flashed on that behemoth sandwich—cut in half, sitting open-jawed on a restaurant plate, the kind with the thin burgundy stripe around the rim, which in my vision, complemented the pink beef seductively. Then it dawned on me—why was I planning a hike when I had errands to do?

In no time, I was sitting at a red light, working on a to-do list.

1. Check out the cribs at Bellini. (I scrawled Solly's in the margin.)
2. Drive into town to try out some rocking chairs. (I scribbled Nate 'n Al's underneath.)
3. Pick up low-VOC paint in Culver City—

A horn blast reprimanded me from behind. As I accelerated through the intersection, I snapped out of it. What the hell was I thinking? This crazy delusion had to stop. I. Must. Resist. I took 3 deep cleansing breaths, in through the nose and out through the mouth, and repeated to myself, *Healthy-body-healthy-baby-healthy-body-healthy-baby-healthy-body-healthy-baby.* Within less than a mile, my mixed-up thoughts had rearranged themselves, and I had arrived at a self-rescuing revelation. I pulled over to the curb, took out my pen and next to low VOC paint jotted, HALF SANDWICH ONLY! Factor's Deli in parentheses.

Like others who've been held in the grip of obsession, I lived in denial. At Solly's, I contemptuously tore the fat from the edges of their juicy slices and left those greasy bad boys on the plate next to the offensive pickle. I daintily removed the frilly, cellophane toothpick and bit into my diet sandwich, telling myself I probably wouldn't even eat the other half already wrapped in butcher paper and sitting in my purse.

Another day, I decided that Nate 'n Al's version was way too dry. It wasn't worth the calories. I would not be back. I squirted on more mustard and took a bigger bite.

But there were other times, those days of unashamed bliss, at Junior's and Cantor's and Brent's, when the crunch of a caraway seed, the perfume of yeasty bread, the ooze of meat juice in my mouth were just what I needed—all right, what I *craved*—and those irrepressible flavors and fragrances mingled to form the perfect, the *indispensible* antidote to night-after-night of smiling at my husband while picking at the flounder on my plate.

By my third trimester, my body was unrecognizable. I was a VW Bug. I looked like I was carrying one child under the hood and another in the trunk—pregnant from the front and behind. My fingers swelled, my ankles expanded and the soles of my feet throbbed from carrying weight far in excess of what they could handle. I'd grown bigger than I'd imagined possible and at only 5'2, looked as wide as I was tall. The giddy anticipation of being a mother, of holding my baby and gazing deeply into his eyes, was now compounded by the urgency to get this thing out of me.

Despite my bad behavior, I was nonetheless rewarded with a beautiful, healthy son. Every time I gazed at his sweet face, I renewed my commitment to my mothering goals. I played him CDs of Amadeus Mozart, went to La Leche League meetings and wore my wondrous boy in a sling. And told myself that, given time, I'd lose the weight, make up for my lapse in will power (*maturity?*), and forgive myself.

Then, one night, my husband put the baby in his car seat and suggested we go to Jerry's Deli. *What?!* Afraid any objection would betray my shame, I went along, and as my slim hubby indulged in a plate of potato pancakes with sour cream, I watched the server place a plain turkey sandwich in front of me. As she turned away, I tried to ask for the side of Russian dressing I'd planned to dab on with the lightest touch, but she was gone. I resignedly reached for the mustard. And, then, something bizarre happened. When I bit into my sandwich, I was unexpectedly flooded with what I can only call—

Happiness! Endorphins! Serotonin! Oxytocin!! All of them flowing at once and holding me in their loving caress. My eyes rolled back, my chest heaved and my husband looked up and asked, "Are you moaning?" "Dear Lord!" I gasped out loud. "I hadn't been craving corned beef at all! I'd been craving mustard!" My better half, his mouth full of potatoes, mumbled, "Wha id oo ay?" I slumped back in my seat in shock and disbelief. "Nothing, Sweetie. Nothing," was all I could manage. What he didn't know wouldn't hurt him.

For months, I'd been desperate for the sharp, vinegar tang of yellow mustard and mistaken that longing for the one food I associated it with—corned beef. If I had only realized, I could have stowed a French's squeeze bottle in the glove compartment and squirted it directly in my mouth, as needed. I'd have saved sixty pounds and an equal amount of hurt pride. I'd have eaten more egg whites and spinach. I'd have fulfilled my well-laid plans.

Which brings me to the lesson this painful episode taught me:
1. Pride and comeuppance go hand-in-hand.
2. Demand perfection of myself and I'll always be disappointed. And
3. What I think I know is nothing compared to what I don't know.

When in doubt, I need to stop and tune in to my intuition, to my natural instincts, to what my body and soul are *really* telling me. That happens to work best for all life's challenges, especially with my now twenty-something son and nineteen-year-old daughter. Mommy only knows best when she truly listens to her *gut*.

MOM'S SECRET (MUSTARD) SCRAMBLED EGGS

Even those who don't like mustard will love these scrambled eggs. I know because my kids hate mustard and eat up these eggs. Everyone does. Just don't tell them the secret ingredient.

INGREDIENTS

Eggs
Butter
Yellow mustard
Yellow onion
Cheese – Gruyere, Swiss, Monterey Jack or Parmesan
Salt
Chopped parsley (for garnish)

TO PREPARE

1. In a bowl, lightly beat 2 to 3 large, organic, free-range eggs for each person.
2. Add one small squirt of yellow mustard for each egg and lightly beat to blend. If you can just smell the mustard when you hold the bowl to your nose, you've used the right amount.
3. Set aside the eggs so they can come to room temperature.
4. Next, cut up a yellow onion in a small dice, (about 1 tablespoon diced onion per person,) and set aside.
5. Grate some Gruyere, Swiss, Monterey Jack or Parmesan cheese (about 2 tablespoons cheese per person).
6. Place a skillet on medium heat. When hot, toss in a pat of butter and, when melted, swirl the butter around the pan.
7. Add the diced onion and a dash of kosher or sea salt. Sauté the onions until soft and golden.
8. Turn down the heat to medium-low, wait a minute for the temperature of the pan to decrease, and pour the eggs in the skillet. As the eggs cook, push them gently from the edge of the pan to the center using a heatproof spatula or wooden spoon. You want large, soft curds with no browning.
9. When nearly done but still slightly wet, sprinkle in the grated cheese and fold gently until just combined.

   Serve garnished with finely chopped parsley.

No One Begs Me to Cook Chicken and Vegetables

by Kim Allen-Niesen

When I think of my mother's cooking, I remember creamy white food in cozy sepia tones. Just picturing it gives me solace.

I grew up on stroganoff created with Campbell's Cream of Mushroom soup; beans and ham hocks simmered in a crockpot for hours then mixed with a full bottle of Heinz ketchup (always a crowd pleaser); and 'homemade' baked beans created from large cans of B&M beans, with added bacon, barbecue sauce, mustard and brown sugar (a cherished family favorite).

A white sauce made of milk (full fat), flour (white and processed) and Imperial Margarine (never butter) was the root of many recipes. If you added creamed chip beef, then ladled it over buttered (well, margarined) white toast and dinner, you had 'shit on a shingle.' Toss in Minute White Rice, a can of tuna, and frozen peas, cover with bread crumbs (freshly made from white bread), and voila, tuna casserole.

Every holiday meal still includes ambrosia made from a variety of canned fruit, sour cream, a bag of coconut flakes, and fresh bananas if we remember to add them in right before serving. It wasn't Fourth of July without my mother's famous macaroni salad— pasta, canned pimento, canned olives, canned pickles, an onion, and lots of mayonnaise.

I grew up on meals colored fifty shades of beige, the quintessential comfort food.

My mother learned to cook during the post-WWII era of convenience foods, and canned food laid the foundation of dinner. Every week I unloaded grocery bags heavy with cans. These days, I can count the number of cans in my own pantry on one hand. There isn't a designated shelf for them, and no need to arrange them in the neat rows of my childhood. When I ventured into the kitchen in the 1990s, the Silver Palate chefs and the Berkeley Wellness newsletter were my inspiration. I learned, and had the resources, to cook from the outside edges of the grocery store where the fresh food is displayed and walk right past the inner aisles of processed food. I raised my kids largely on a dinner diet of protein and vegetables.

Of course, inevitably, over the years we've each grown to detest certain vegetables. I agree with George H.W. Bush that broccoli is awful. The last time my husband bought asparagus for dinner, my son looked at him and said, 'You've betrayed me.' My kids won't eat any white root vegetables in a dish if there's a chance one of them is a parsnip. Neither of them likes corn. (What's wrong with them? Who doesn't like corn?) My favorite meal is chicken, sweet potato, and green beans, in part because I can eat my kids' servings of sweet potato and my husband's share of the green beans.

Thirty-five years after leaving home, I still craved my mother's cream of mushroom stroganoff and requested it when I visited her. Which made me wonder: when my kids went to college, would they crave the foods of home if they weren't creamy or bready? I was afraid they might not, but consoled myself with the thought that kids crave the *idea* of home cooking, not specific recipes.

Wrong. Never has one of my children called home and said, "Mom, will you make chicken and veggies tonight for dinner?" Never.

Okay, sort of once. When he was thirteen, my son repeatedly complained of too many dinners of chicken and vegetables. (I stir-fried them, sautéed them, baked them, roasted them! I experimented with seasonings!) So I bought one of those 'a different dinner every night' cookbooks. Three weeks in, I asked him how he liked the variety of meals. He said, "I never thought I'd miss chicken and veggies, but I didn't know how bad it could get." Apparently, my healthy cooking was his first lesson in life's harshest reality: things can always be worse.

What do they request as adults? What are their comfort foods from childhood?

In sorrow and celebration, my daughter wants the banana chocolate muffins I make from an old Betty Crocker Cookbook recipe—and since she's at college now, it's "please ship them overnight." What's the first breakfast they request after returning home? The chocolate chip pancakes my husband will only make from Aunt Jemima's box mix. At Thanksgiving? They have to eat their father's yams (canned yams simmered with a bucket of brown sugar, then baked with a huge bag of marshmallows on top). This yam 'recipe' is the only one my son has bothered to learn and has cooked for his friends. Interesting that their favorites are the foods that slipped past my wall of healthy eating.

I don't regret how I raised my kids—they're foodies, they'll try anything, and I believe they're healthier for it. What is it about white flour, sugar, and butter that we love? Why isn't roasted red pepper a comfort food? I'm sure there's a long scientific explanation in some healthy eating magazine, but my experience shows that it goes beyond what you're raised eating. And yet, it's more than the food. My daughter could walk to the local Starbucks and buy a banana chocolate muffin, and every diner across the nation serves pancakes with some chocolate chips on top, but that isn't what my kids want, and not what they order. Those foods provide comfort because they're from home and soothing in some way, for some reason, that sautéed fresh vegetables will never be.

BANANA CHOCOLATE MUFFINS

(with healthy variations)

INGREDIENTS

2/3 cup sugar
1/3 cup of margarine (NO!) or butter (YES!—go organic)
2 eggs (cage free)
3 to 4 bananas
1/3 cup water
1 2/3 cups whole wheat pastry flour
1 teaspoon baking soda
½ teaspoon salt
¼ teaspoon baking powder
1 cup chocolate morsels (I think this is too much; my family thinks it's too little; add as much as you want)

TO PREPARE

1. Heat oven to 350 degrees.
2. Mix sugar and butter.
3. Stir in eggs until blended.
4. Add bananas and water; beat 30 seconds.
5. Stir in remaining ingredients except chocolate until moistened; stir in chocolate.
6. Spoon into 18 muffin cups.
7. Cook for 20 minutes, then check to see if wooden pick comes out clean, continue baking until it does.

Thursday's Child is Full of Crepes

by Nell Scovell

In *The Book of Genesis*, God created the heavens and earth, oceans and continents, creatures in the water and on land, and humans, all in only six days. This seems like a lot to accomplish until you remember that God began his work in a "void," and had *zero distraction*s. I can't even tell you how much I could get done under those conditions. It's still impressive but he had advantages. For example, on the third day, while creating vegetation, God didn't have to stop to watch a video about an unexpected friendship between a dog and a bunny. He didn't even get around to creating the dog and bunny until day six. And then what happened as soon as baby penguins and hedgehogs started roaming the earth? God's focus was shot. He kept it together for one more day and created humans and then He quit. God rested on the seventh day. . . and presumably did nothing but watch kittens doing the *most adorable* things.

Those who buy into Genesis follow God's lead, carving out a seventh day for rest and contemplation. For some, the Sabbath begins Friday at sundown with rituals like candle-lighting and tearing off pieces of dry challah bread. For others, the Sabbath falls on Sunday and is devoted to the Holy Trinity of church, football and Yorkshire pudding. My four-person family has its own sacred day which falls in the middle of the week. God invented the Sabbath, but we invented Crepes Thursday.

We are not subtle people so Crepes Thursday is exactly what you think it is: I make crepes for the family on Thursday. We usually have them sweet at breakfast although occasionally we will opt for savory at dinner.

I use a standard recipe: eggs, milk, sugar, flour, vanilla, butter and guilt. The guilt comes from being a mom who worked outside the home. As a TV writer, I worked late hours but didn't need to be at the office before 10 am, so I shifted the concept of family dinner to suit my schedule. Breakfast became my time to sit with my kids over food and talk.

To entice my sons out of their beds required more than instant oatmeal, so I made buttermilk pancakes from scratch…popovers and bacon…eggs-in-a-frame…waffles (until our waffle maker broke.) When my eldest son was in second grade, they had a cooking presentation and he told me of this wondrous concoction he had tasted: a crepe. I had never made crepes before, so I ordered a book (*Crepes*) and bought a pan (copper) and the next morning, at around 6:30 am, I started making the batter. Today, I can recite the recipe for "Dessert Crepes" by heart, but that first time, after pouring in the melted butter, I consulted the recipe again and read this: "Cover and refrigerate for at least 1 hour (2 hours is preferable) or up to 24 hours."

Okay, to any recipe writers who might be reading this, it's kind of a dick move not to note a time requirement like this right at the top of a recipe. Sticking it in the middle is like making out with someone and having this conversation:

Him: *You know what I want to do to you?*
Me*: Ooh, what?*
Him*: I'll tell you in an hour—two is preferable.*

I didn't have time to let the batter stand so my first batch of crepes was not stellar. But here's the thing about crepes: you put enough Nutella on them and nobody cares whether or not they're perfect. And the next time I made them, I started the night before.

Just as the Jewish Sabbath begins at sundown the night before, Crepes Thursday begins on Wednesday night right before bedtime. I prepare the batter, then place the bowl in the refrigerator so the liquid absorbs the flour. Thursday morning, I remove the bowl, heat the pan, melt the butter, pour the batter, swirl the pan, flip the crepe… and throw it out.

The first crepe is known as the "Chef's Crêpe" and after ten years, I can attest that it is a little unevenly cooked, a little greasy. . . and absolutely delicious. I've always assumed it's the "chef's crepe" because the chef gets to cut off a chunk and sample the butter-y, eggy warmth.

With the pan now heated, I call out: "Who wants first crepe?" Three voices usually respond, "Me!" and we're off. My younger child Dexter sets the plates and silverware at the kitchen island. My older child Rudy fills the water glasses. And my husband grabs the napkins. I stand in front of the stove and customize for each. Colin's crepe is filled with Nutella, bananas and freshly-toasted pecans. Rudy's is filled with Nutella and pecans. Dexter likes Nutella and marshmallows and prefers his crepes to be folded not in quarters, but in half like an omelet.

The batter works out almost exactly right for two crepes per person, plus the discarded one. Friends were always welcomed which meant slightly thinner crepes for all, but again, with enough Nutella nobody cares.

As I stand over the pan, conversation flows. We talk about practical things like science and weekend plans. We talk about impractical things like comic books and magic tricks. For a while, I tried reading a poem each week. That tradition didn't catch on.

And so it was week after week for years and years. Crepes became something we looked forward to as well as a way to measure our lives. When Rudy went off to college, we continued the tradition although, with one person fewer at the counter, I sadly poured the extra batter down the disposal. Two years later, Dexter headed off to college, too. The point of the meal was to spend time with the kids, and once they were gone, our taste for crepes dimmed. Hot breakfasts became a reminder of what was no longer there. There's an old saying: "Parents go to church for the kids and the kids go to church for the parents." It was like that with us and crepes. The tradition had served its purpose and now had come to an end.

And yet…

The first college winter break where the kids returned, Rudy arrived home on a Wednesday night and Dexter arrived late the next afternoon. I said I'd make crepes on Friday morning, but Rudy was adamant. "No, mom," he said. "It's Thursday. We should have them tonight." And so we did.

As it was in the beginning, is now and ever shall be… Crepes Thursday.

DESSERT CREPES

INGREDIENTS

1 cup flour
2 Tbs sugar
1 cup milk
1/3 cup water
1 tsp vanilla
2 Tbls melted butter

TO PREPARE

1. Mix the dry ingredients and add the liquids.
2. Cover and refrigerate from one to twenty-four hours.
3. Take batter out of refrigerator.

DESSERT CREPES (CONT.)

4. Heat a small pan and melt a small chunk of butter in it.
5. Once the butter's hot, pour enough batter in to cover the bottom of the pan. Swirl.
6. Cook until bottom is golden brown then flip and cook other side.
7. Throw out the first one. (Or quietly eat it.)
8. Repeat with more butter and more batter.

Serve with nutella and bananas. Or whatever sounds good to you.

A Friend Indeed

by Kathy Bidus

I like food. Food and I have a good relationship. We're friends.

We all need food to live. Food sustains us and gives us strength. It's essential to our health, and to life itself. It can cure our ills, keep us active, make our skin glow and our hair soft and shiny. Food doesn't have to be so damn good. We'd have to eat it anyway. That's what I love about food. It goes the extra mile.

I've often wondered how early man figured out that cooking the food he found made it taste even better—that the fire he'd just discovered could be used to heat and enhance his food. Maybe he just accidentally dropped his piece of meat in the flames and liked the result, and now there are $1,000.00-a-plate restaurants at the top of tall buildings in Manhattan.

I moved to New York City in 1979, with no money and no plan, which didn't seem like such a dumb idea, because I was so young. It was the first time in my life I'd experienced hunger day to day, as an ongoing condition. It's not that I felt sorry for myself at the time, since everyone I knew seemed to be just scraping by. ("Hey, Howard let me sleep in his tub last night." "Cool. Good for you.") The city was abundant with food. It was the place to go to eat. I once stood on a side street in midtown and noted that only two storefronts on the entire block were not establishments dealing in food.

People passed in and out of the doors freely. But I didn't seem to have the key.

One day, I wandered around the Village trying to expel the images forming like clouds from the fragrance of the outdoor cafes. I wondered if strangers could see that a person was hungry, or if it was just a shameful secret.

Then I saw it. A long, narrow white bag lay on the sidewalk in front of me. I recognized the red script logo from the Italian bakery on Bleeker Street. Instantly, I

Portrait of K. Bidus by Drew Friedman

understood how it came to be there: some hurried shopper whose bags were so full of food, so packed beyond capacity, had let it get away. The loaf had toppled out unnoticed, as he struggled to bring it all home with him in the cab.

I lifted the bag and inhaled. The scent of the fresh bread took me back to the time and the street and the incomparable safety of banging through the front door on chilly twilit days after school, smelling hearing my mother in the kitchen. Sometimes there'd be a cake there, something she'd managed to create as simply and swiftly as slipping down to tie my shoes. Just a few extra minutes in her afternoon might yield a pie, or cookies cut into the shape of little birds, their plumage brightly dyed sugar. And on these special afternoons, all rules against spoiling your appetite were suddenly suspended, like the declaration of an unexpected holiday. "Of course you can have some, little one, if you sit down and eat it at the table."

I slid the white paper down, held my palm against the crusty heel and tore off my first bite.

It was still warm.

CRUMB CAKE

INGREDIENTS

1 ¾ cups sifted flour
1 cup sugar
½ tsp. salt
¼ tsp. soda
½ cup shortening
2 tsp. baking powder
1 egg, beaten
2/3 cup buttermilk
½ tsp. almond extract
½ tsp. cinnamon

TO PREPARE

1. Sift together flour, sugar, salt, soda; cut in shortening.
2. Reserve ½ cup of this mixture.
3. Blend remainder with baking powder.
4. Combine egg, buttermilk, almond extract.
5. Add to dry ingredients, beat thoroughly.
6. Pour into greased 8 x 8 inch pan.
7. Blend cinnamon into the reserved mixture, sprinkle over top of the cake.

Bake at 350 degrees for 45 minutes.

THE SANDWICH GENERATION

Robyn's Tuna Guacamole Melt

Butter Sandwich

Melting, a poem

The Best Tuna Sandwich Ever

Hello, Sexy Gorgeous!

by Marcie Smolin

I come from a long line of dieters. Truth be told, I went on my first diet in vitro—my mother has shared that while pregnant with me she lived on a steady diet of Tab and Metri-Cal cookies. She only gained nine pounds with me, and I came flying out at about 7 pounds 4 ounces. I'm pretty sure that, as I left the birth canal, I gave her a little tiny air high-five…and as we locked eyes for the first time, we silently congratulated each other on a dieting job well done!

Dieting was a way of life for the ladies in my family—for all but my sister Robyn. Robyn got a diet reprieve, a free pass, a food restriction *Get Out Of Jail Free* Card! You see, Robyn was born with Down Syndrome…and she was the most hilarious, glorious, unfiltered, non-judgmental and deeply wise human being I have ever known. And oh how she loved to eat. I think we all lived a little vicariously through Robyn—her joy for food became ours too. While we all publically extolled the virtues of carrot sticks, calorie counting, Weight Watchers, diet soda, cabbage soup, fasting, mail-order tapeworms (okay I never did that one…but it was tempting), or whatever the trend of the minute was, secretly we all kind of wished we had Robyn's freedom. Robyn, who could eat whatever she wanted with no guilt, no shame, and no fear!!! Robyn, who relished every messy delicious morsel of whatever it was she ate…because she could!

Oh Robyn was not thin. Quite the contrary—there's no such thing as a Jewish girl who has no caloric consequences. But the difference with Robyn was the girl she saw in the mirror. As opposed to us serial dieters who would look in the mirror and see every calorie consumed, what Robyn saw when she looked in the mirror was a girl who was just simply gorgeous!

So all bets were off when it came to food in Robyn's world. Around the time my brother and I started college, my parents started the tradition of the Friday night restaurant dinner. We are a close and loving family and this was our way of holding us together gently—meeting every Friday night, no matter what. It is a tradition that we carry on to this day. Oh sure we may not be big food consuming Jews…but we still have our gatherings around food!

It was at one of those Friday night gatherings that I first encountered "Robyn's Tuna Guacamole Melt." It was truly the most disgusting thing I'd ever seen. The first time Robyn ordered it and it was delivered to the table, you could just hear the whir of mental calorie counters, BMI tables, and fat ratio abacuses going off in the minds of all the calorically-challenged ladies at the table. We watched in horror as this greasy, cheesy, carbohydrate-y, cholesterol-y sandwich with two whole pieces of bread and lots of avocado (this was back in the day when avocados were considered bad… unlike now, when they are "good fats,". . . although by the time this story is published, they could be bad again…hard to keep up).

This sandwich contained all that we had been trained to believe was bad. We believed that one bite of it would suddenly undo all the careful work we had done on our bodies…and send our asses unraveling into the streets. It was evil to all!

Except Robyn!

Robyn cherished every messy, fattening, caloric, cholesterol-y, carb-y, evil bite. She loved it. And watching her consume that sandwich was a secret joy to us all. As we dipped our forks into our tiny cups of dressing to get just a taste of flavor as we gingerly consumed our "breast of chicken salad, no cheese, no croutons, dressing on the side," we secretly dreamed. We dreamed of a world where, like Robyn, we could openly enjoy such a messy wrong dish…Consequences be damned!

As I mentioned previously, in Robyn's eyes there were no consequences from that sandwich, because, as opposed to the serial dieters that I am descended from, who likely know where every calorie consumed lives on their body and see those areas when they look in the mirror, Robyn only saw the most ravishing gorgeous creature in the mirror. She would look at her reflection and say…

"Hello, Sexy Gorgeous!"

I think we all lived a little vicariously through that as well.

Though we all knew deep down that our time with Robyn was likely going to be more brief than we would have liked, I think we were in denial about it. How could one so funny, so warm, so full of life at all times leave us? It was unfathomable.

But she got sick…so sick…and there came a time when she needed a wheelchair to get around. But still we had Friday night dinners…and she had that sandwich…and still she would look in the mirror…and though her lips were blue from lack of oxygen and her skin was gray and her hair was falling out…still she looked in the mirror and said…

"Hello Sexy Gorgeous."

Because that is who she saw.

Early one rainy morning in June, she was failing. My mother and I rushed her to the hospital, but we lost her in the car. My beautiful Robyn, whom I lived vicariously through. I held her hand and we sang a song from our childhood…and that is how she went. In the car with the people she loved… As far as choosing a way to go…I think she did pretty well.

I have never seen a funeral like hers. Packed to the gills. So many people loved her. It was a sad and happy day as people shared wonderful Robyn stories.

And then, of course, we ate…at the restaurant where the Tuna Guacamole Melt lived. When we got there, a menu was presented to my mother, who began to cry and then held out the menu to show us that the restaurant had changed the name of the sandwich to:

"Robyn's Tuna Guacamole Melt"

So in that moment we decided to order that messy, fattening, caloric, cholesterol-y, carb-y sandwich. Every serial dieter in my family. And you know what?

Robyn's Tuna Guacamole Melt was friggin' delicious!!!!!

We savored, we moaned, we cried, and we made a pact that for that day we would enjoy that sandwich, consequences be damned. And when I finished, I walked to the mirror, I looked at myself, and I said,

"Hello Sexy Gorgeous!"

As Robyn would have wanted me to!

ROBYN'S TUNA GUACAMOLE MELT

INGREDIENTS

2 pieces of rye bread
Really messy tuna with tons of mayo
The cheesiest of cheese…more than you should have
Tons of guacamole
Tons of butter for grilling

TO PREPARE

1. Combine the tuna, cheese and guacamole
2. Make a sandwich with the rye bread
3. Spread the outside with butter, and slap it on the grill.
4. It must be consumed with love, abandon, and tons of self-esteem. You must savor every morsel…consequences be damned… and when you are done, go to a mirror and take a good look at yourself and say…"Hello Sexy Gorgeous!"

Butter Sandwiches

by Liane Kupferberg Carter

"No eating in my car!" my father said, even as Aunt Jeanette was spreading slabs of salty butter on slices of bread.

He always said that, and we always ignored him, though not without a little *frisson* of fear. What if this time he confiscated our going-home snack?

Every time we visited my Great Aunt Jeanette at her Manhattan apartment on East 36th Street, my brother and I clamored for food for the long car ride home. It was an arduous twenty minute trek through the Midtown Tunnel and beneath the East River back to our house in Queens, and we couldn't make it without provisions. Aunt Jeanette always obliged. She sliced apples and wrapped up butter sandwiches in large, quilted paper napkins—treats that wouldn't leave crumbs. She knew Dad was meticulous; his car maintained its new car smell far longer than most people's. Clutching those delightful butter sandwiches to our chests, my brother and I swore to eat very, very carefully.

Aunt Jeanette was my mother's aunt. My mother's mother had died before I was born, so Jeanette served as honorary grandparent. She had two grown sons, but no daughter. She was slim and elegant and tall, although I know now that she wasn't more than 5'2." Aunt Jeanette had a warm laugh that felt like a hug.

Her cozy living room contained welcoming down-filled sofas and chairs slipcovered in cream-colored silk. The bathroom was filled with perfume flasks on glass shelves and dainty finger towels. The hall table, artfully covered with millefleurs paperweights and silver boxes, was so highly polished you could see your reflection. Aunt Jeanette and her husband, Uncle Charlie, didn't have a great deal of money, yet their home radiated comfort and elegance.

My brother and I would squabble over who got to push the elevator button.

Jeanette and Charlie lived on the seventh floor, and even before the grilled gate of the elevator slid open, you could smell the mingled odors of simmering soup stock, savory pot roast, and something else deliciously indefinable.

After a brunch of bagels and smoked fish for the grownups, and tuna fish with mayonnaise and apples for my brother and me, I would retrieve several large books of *New Yorker* cartoons, and hunker down on the down sofa to read, while the grownups lingered and laughed over coffee and rugelach.

When Mom was first dating Dad, she brought him to meet Jeanette and Charlie. Dad brought them a batch of his mother's famous challah rolls. After dinner, Aunt Jeannette pulled my mother aside and said, "Marry him and get that recipe!" Food is *mamaloshen*, the mother tongue of Jewish families, and Aunt Jeanette and my mother both spoke it fluently. Mom wasn't a baker, nor was Jeanette, but she showed Mom how to doctor up a Duncan Hines yellow cake mix. She'd add a can of apricot nectar, and boil sugar with bourbon to make a delicious icing that also shellacked the cake and preserved it for days. She filled deep glass saucers with butterscotch pudding and kept it in the fridge till it developed a deliciously silky skin. From Jeanette, Mom also learned the alchemy of turning ladyfingers and whipped cream into something called an icebox cake that required no baking at all.

Though nothing rivaled those butter sandwiches, anything from Aunt Jeanette's hand was delectable. She cooked special baby-sized burgers for my brother and me. She made us creamy chocolate milk, and served it in tall chilled glasses with long silver straws. The straws had hearts at the tips, perfect for spooning up the last delicious syrupy bits. She never insisted—as my mother did—that we eat vegetables, which in those less enlightened times always came out of a can.

Jeanette was my favorite aunt in the world. That is saying a lot, because in addition to having three great-aunts, I also had seven regular ones. Jeanette was one of four sisters, which I romanticized as being like my favorite book, *Little Women*. My grandmother died tragically young, so she was the "Beth" of the family. Jeanette was "Meg," the responsible, motherly one. But Jeanette's sisters Mae and Rose were nothing like "Jo" or "Amy," or like Jeanette either. Jeanette was the only one who cooked. Rose made a few dishes, all of them badly. She'd proudly serve a platter of hamburgers she'd pounded to death and revived with onion powder.

Once a month, my mother took me to see the special eye doctor on Madison Avenue in Manhattan. After each appointment, we would meet Aunt Jeanette at Schrafft's, a ladies' lunch place. My mother always ordered the same thing for me: a white meat turkey sandwich on crusty white bread, slathered with mayonnaise. It was nearly as delicious as Aunt Jeanette's butter sandwiches.

I loved Scrafft's—the enticing display of heart-shaped boxes filled with chocolates;

the pink and white stuffed animals lined up against the mirrored wall; the uniformed woman who smiled at me before she unhooked one end of the burgundy red velvet rope and allowed us to enter.

Sometimes, afterwards, we'd walk to the department store B. Altman's. Once they bought me a coloring & activity book as thick as the New York City phone book. Back at Jeanette's apartment, I perched on the kitchen stepstool, balancing on the lowest rung and using the large "seat" above as my desk. Some of the activity book pages were magic—they looked like ordinary coloring book pages, until you dipped a water color brush in a Dixie cup of water, swirled it over the page and made pastel colors bloom.

Sometimes I'd stay overnight. When I couldn't fall asleep on the guest room sofa because I was homesick, Uncle Charlie swooped me up and deposited me next to Jeanette on their bed. Then, heroically, he folded himself in two to fit on the couch. In the years before they had grandchildren of their own, I filled that role. They both doted on me.

Saturday afternoons, we'd cross the wondrously wide 42nd Street to the Automat, a glass and chrome Art Deco marvel of marquetry, marble and gleaming vending machines. Every food item I could imagine was on dazzling display behind glass-doored dispensers, each item nestled behind its own sleek window. Salisbury steak smothered in gravy. Flaky-crusted chicken potpie. Brown pots of baked beans. Tapioca pudding. Slices of huckleberry pie. Cinnamon-dusted donuts. Dishes of quivering Jell-O.

"First we need change," Jeanette explained the first time, and handed several dollars to a woman in a glass booth who wore rubber tips on her fingers. The woman pushed nickels under her window into a shallow depression in the counter. Clutching my fistful of nickels, I made my lunch selection and fed coins into the slot. "Abracadabra!" Aunt Jeanette said, and lifted the glass door to retrieve my dish of elbow macaroni covered in creamy, custardy cheese and buttered breadcrumbs. "Does my mom know about this place?" I asked, incredulous. Aunt Jeanette laughed.

After I'd eaten, she bought me a cup of cocoa and a cruller, then filled a mug for herself from a gleaming silver spigot in the wall. She took a sip and sighed. "They just make the *best* coffee."

Of course the Automat wasn't *really* automated. Once as I pulled out a wax-paper wrapped egg salad sandwich, I glimpsed a worker behind the machine rapidly slipping another sandwich in place. But it still felt like magic.

Mom often told me that Jeanette was the aunt who was most similar in personality to her own mother. Perhaps that was why they were so close. Jeanette and Mom were

Jeanette and Charlie.

more like sisters than aunt and niece. They even looked alike to me, with their high cheekbones, slim figures, and the same anxious look that evaporated in the healing warmth of their laughter.

I didn't know then that their furrowed brows indicated more than concern for me. Like most children, I thought the world revolved around me. It was only years later that Mom confided that while Jeanette was making me butter sandwiches and taking me to see the Rockettes at Radio City and the Christmas windows on Fifth Avenue, she had also been undergoing treatment for breast cancer. My grandmother had died of the same disease at the age of forty-eight, and all the women feared they wouldn't live past that age either. Mom and Jeanette kept this secret from me.

After Uncle Charlie died, Aunt Jeanette's cancer returned. Mom and I flew down to Florida to stay with her for a week. My mother shared a bedroom with her; I slept on the den sofa. "Now don't be frightened, girls," Jeanette said our first night, and pulled off her wig. I felt splayed open. She'd lost her beautiful silver hair to chemo.

For days we tried to tempt her invalid appetite. Mom braised a brisket. We made endless pots of Earl Grey tea and served it in Jeanette's beautiful Wedgwood tea service that was decorated with green Chinese dragons. We made cinnamon toast and butter sandwiches.

I'd given my mother a beautiful sky blue silk robe that she loved, and she'd brought it with her. Aunt Jeanette's aide Geraldine admired the robe. When it was time for us to leave, Mom gave the robe to Geraldine. I asked why she had done that. She said, "Because I hope she'll take extra good care of Jeanette."

They were both skilled at taking extra good care of everybody.

Jeanette died thirty-five years ago. I named my first child after her. It's been longer than that since I've had a butter sandwich, or chocolate milk. But I have Jeanette's silver straws, the long slim silver ones with the heart-shaped spoons at the tips. I keep them wrapped in Pacific cloth to keep the tarnish away. I treasure them. In my memory, they still gleam.

BUTTER SANDWICH

INGREDIENTS

Bread
Butter
Salt (optional)

TO PREPARE

Take two slices of bread. Spread thickly with butter. Salt is optional, but sprinkle liberally with love. Cut into triangles. Savor.

Melting

by Annie LaZebnik

pancreatic cancer they said
just a few more days they said
a sandwich would be nice she said

my face began to burn
there was pressure to perform
it had to be perfect
it just had to be

the bread didn't toast well
the cheese didn't melt
the turkey was lumpy and cold
tears started running down my face
i had failed her
i had failed her, and she would remember me this way

i asked my uncle to help and
he showed me how to toast the bread
and melt the cheese
and cut the turkey

i brought it to her bed and
she lay there skin and bones
as carefully as tightrope walking
i placed the sandwich next to her

my face burned again as she took a bite
she smiled
"best sandwich i've ever had" she said
"what do you want for dessert?" I said

Sex, Lies and Tuna Sandwiches

by Ann Brown

I used to fantasize about sex. Getting all naked and crazy with a man. Or two. My sexual fantasies were hot. Now it's a tuna sandwich with capers and lemon that gives me a warm fuzzy in my innards. A big tuna sandwich. Or two. Which I eat alone. Fully clothed. Layers, even.

Oh, sex is great and all, but frankly, after sex I just want to eat a sandwich. Whereas after eating a sandwich, I rarely want to have sex. Furthermore, I have often forgotten to have sex—for weeks!—whereas, barring virulent Norovirus, I cannot recall even one meal I have missed in all my sixty-two years.

Plus—and this was a huge factor back in my pre-menopausal days—one does not need to insert a diaphragm into any part of herself in order to have a nice meal. I mean, one *can*, I suppose, but to what benefit when a napkin on the lap will suffice?

Sex is a lot of work. When Robin and I were first together, I used to sneak out of bed before he woke up so I could brush my teeth, put some blush on my cheeks, tweeze anything that had emerged during the night, adjust my boobs so they weren't all cattywampus from sleeping on them weird, and then get back into bed so he could see what a natural beauty I was during morning sex. We were blanket-toting, weed-smoking hippies, living a Birkenstocks and granola life, and vanity—especially accompanied by Revlon Barely-There Blush—was my secret shame.

It's good thing I was young, because it's exhausting to keep up the charade in the beginning of a relationship. There was a lot of holding in my stomach during those first months. (I just tried to hold in my stomach while I wrote that last sentence and now I have to lie down. And eat something. I feel woozy.)

Eating in front of Robin in those early years was also a charade. For one thing, I told him I was a vegetarian. It was Santa Cruz, 1974, and we were subverting the dominant paradigm—I really had no option. Well, I suppose I did have the option of actually *being* a vegetarian, but, frankly, I needed protein to keep up my strength for all the jumping out of bed early and all the holding in of my stomach.

Once, after making us a hippie-regulation meal of tofu, tamari and assorted birdseed, I saw that one of my roommates' friends had put leftover chicken in the refrigerator. And not just any chicken: Kentucky Fried Chicken. The naughtiest of all chicken. It was chicken. And it was *fried*. And worst of all, it was sold by that right-wing reactionary, Colonel Sanders. It was everything I stood against.

It was delicious.

Oh my GAWD. I scarfed down that bad boy while crouching behind the refrigerator door. I told Robin I was making herbal tea. After about ten minutes, he asked if I needed help. I told him I was meditating.

I ate four pieces before slinking back to the living room. That night, for the first time, I did some *extra special* things in bed. You know, the thing that's all about him. And a few other things. Mostly to distract him from asking me any questions about my chicken breath. It's not the worst reason in the world to go that extra mile in sex but it wasn't a strategy I could keep up forever. I'm just not that good in bed. Or that motivated.

Time passed. Robin and I moved in together. We moved to LA. I got cocky. Then I got careless. A wrapper from a chicken burrito left in the trashcan where Robin could see it. A punch card from a burger joint in my pocket. A greasy stain on my Indian bedspread. Maybe I wanted to get caught. I am by nature an anxious, hand-wringing Jewish girl with a nervous stomach. Lying was giving me diarrhea. I was going through the Pepto Bismol like it was patchouli oil. Something had to give.

My salvation came when I got bronchitis that winter.

Robin asked if I would mind if he made me chicken soup.

"I'm really pretty good at it," he said apologetically. "It's my grandmother's recipe."

I feigned a moral dilemma.

"I could leave out the chicken," he offered, "but it really wouldn't be the same."

I sighed the bogus sigh of a fake vegetarian who was pretending to choose between her health and her made-up beliefs, and who wasn't up to distraction sex that night.

"Maybe just a tiny bit of chicken," I said feebly. "To keep up my strength. I feel so weak."

And so it began.

Robin and I have now been married for thirty-six years. Or maybe thirty-five. I cannot do math, which is another thing I tried to hide from him for a while. There are very few secrets left between us at this point. He has seen me count on my fingers.

He has seen me eat meat. He has seen me when I'm not holding in my stomach. He has seen me naked, with no makeup. Once, he saw me naked, out of the shower, slowly bending over to pick up a Q-tip I had dropped. I muttered "oy oy oy oy" all the way down to the floor. I muttered "oy oy oy oy" all the way back up. And still he loves me.

Thank God his eyesight is failing. We have agreed that this—presbyopia—is the key to a long happy marriage. We both look all gauzy and cataracty and lovely to each other. And our sense of smell is fading, too.

Which is great. Because I am about to make myself a tuna sandwich. And get naked. And then get into bed with him.

THE BEST TUNA SANDWICH EVER

INGREDIENTS

Canned tuna. I like packed in water because it seems healthier, but it's actually not.
Lemons
Capers in brine
Scallions
Carrots
Fresh dill
Mayonnaise (optional)
Romaine lettuce
Bread
Potato chips (optional)

TO PREPARE

1. Mash up the tuna.
2. Add more lemon juice than you'd ever think you should.
3. Then add capers, chopped green onion, chopped carrots and fresh dill.
4. If your mother never told you that mayonnaise is "feh" poison, go ahead and put some in. Who am I to judge?
5. Make an open-faced sandwich with the tuna mixture, add Romaine lettuce.

Because it was open-faced, you deserve to have another sandwich. And maybe some potato chips on top. And also, a little bit more tuna on the heel of the bread because the heel of the bread doesn't count as eating bread. Especially if you eat it standing up. Eating while standing up cancels out all the calories.

RX: SOUP

Pork "Turnip" Soup

Christmas Eve Potato Soup

Chicken Soup à la Bachelor

Gram's Vegetable Soup

Inheritance

by Amy Wang Manning

When my mother opened the front door and welcomed us in, I knew immediately that something was wrong. There was no smell of cooking.

As soon as she and my father had finished greeting my two friends, I went into the kitchen. Maybe she'd prepared our lunch earlier and planned to reheat it, though that would have been unlike her. But everything looked clean and neat. There was no sign of any meal.

"I thought you were making lunch," I whispered to her.

She stared. "I thought you were taking us out to lunch." She didn't bother to lower her voice.

I could have shaken myself. I'd carelessly assumed that my mother would be delighted to play personal chef for me—because that was how I'd grown used to thinking of her. For most of my life she'd stayed home, a choice that baffled me when I thought of the education she'd fought to obtain. And she'd only grown more reclusive as I spent less time at home, where she held sway, and more time in the outside world, where she was just an immigrant housewife. Often it seemed she was happiest and most confident in the kitchen, a place too small to contain the goals and ambitions we'd agreed upon for me.

But I didn't have the guts to back down in front of my friends. "Can't you just make lunch?" I pleaded. We were already here, I argued. She didn't like most of the restaurants in town anyway (the menus were too unfamiliar, the etiquette too intimidating). And my friends had never had Taiwanese food.

She finally agreed to cook, but she didn't yield gracefully. My father silently slipped away, leaving my friends and me to sit stiffly in the living room and make awkward small talk while my mother clanged pots and pans and slammed her cleaver into the chopping board.

But soon the sounds softened and became more regular, and I knew she was getting into her groove. The familiar aromas of her cooking—garlic, ginger, scallions, pork, chicken stock—wafted toward us. I began to relax.

Perhaps an hour later, my mother emerged from the kitchen into the dining room with a steaming dish. I jumped up to help and discovered that she'd outdone herself: For a casual family-style lunch, she'd prepared six courses. One of them, I realized as I filled my plate, I'd never seen before. I waited for her to mention it, but she merely began eating.

"What's this?" I asked, pointing my chopsticks. The dish held what looked like miniature sausages that had been wrapped in swatches of nori seaweed and then deep-fried.

She shrugged. "Seafood roll," she said. "It has shrimp in it." She turned to one of my friends. "Try one," she urged.

He grinned sheepishly. "I've had three," he said.

She laughed then for the first time since we'd arrived, her dark brown eyes crinkling with pride and pleasure. And I knew I would be forgiven, again.

My mother once told me that she had been assigned the job of preparing the family dinners when she was twelve, that her mother had refused her requests for instruction, and that she had simply had to teach herself how to cook on a coal stove. I wasn't close enough to my grandmother to confirm all this with her, but my mother was not one to make up stories—and there was no question that she could cook.

Such was her cooking, in fact, that it imprinted food memories onto each of our homes as we followed my father from job to job and state to state.

In my earliest such memory, my father and I sit at the kitchen table in the first house my parents bought, in Pittsburgh, while my mother deep-fries strips of dough to make *youtiao*, a traditional Chinese snack that she serves with a bowl of warm soy milk for dipping. Another night, as we eat in the dining room, I lift a half-moon of turnip from amid the pieces of pork in a bowl of soup: I take a tentative nibble, announce that I like turnip, and am rewarded with a smile from my mother. In between meals, I sometimes play in the basement, where I must remember to dodge the containers of bean sprouts my mother grows to make tofu. I also have to be careful coming back up the stairs, or I'll walk into the homemade sausages she hangs from the basement rafters to cure.

When I'm nearing the end of fourth grade, we move to central Connecticut, to a house with a half-acre lot. My mother buys seeds, then writes to a sister in Taiwan; more seeds arrive by mail. Soon my mother is watering and weeding two vegetable gardens, one American, one Taiwanese, every growing season. I sometimes join her along with my best friend, Heidi, from up the street, Heidi ostentatiously admiring everything until my mother invites her to stay for our next meal. Heidi's family is white, of German descent; she has no idea most of the time what she's eating. But she always cleans her plate. When we briefly reunite two decades later over the Internet, she writes that she still thinks fondly of my mother's cooking.

We move again when I'm twelve, this time to central New York. My mother discovers U-pick apple orchards and teaches herself how to make juice, filling the kitchen with the scent of apple mash. The resulting jugs of cloudy brown liquid are our family fall treasure, the gleaning of an afternoon amid the trees. She scouts the local lake and we all learn how to fish with a single rod that we take turns using, my mother crowing over each sunfish bass we reel in. While other anglers throw back the green-yellow fish, which are barely more than bones and fins, we grill them on the spot and pick out all the meat. Then there is the day she packs us all into the car and drives a long way to a river she's learned is home to something called smelt. Back at home, she dips the little fish in batter and deep-fries them; they are unexpectedly, and memorably, delicious.

It's in this kitchen that I remember listening to her stories. She'll be rolling out dumpling wrappers atop her favorite table, an Ethan Allen cherry wood model she plucked from an estate sale, and I'll sit down to help by pinching off balls of the dough. As we work, she'll recite the memories I've grown to know as well as my own: How cooking the family dinner and doing other chores consumed so much of her evening that she rarely started her homework before ten. How my grandmother initially objected to my mother's going to college because higher education was wasted on girls, until my mother met my father, a fellow student whom my grandmother considered enough of a catch to be served chicken for dinner. How when my mother and father arrived at the University of Oregon, where he enrolled as a graduate student, she took a job washing dishes in a Chinese restaurant to pay their bills. How when my father decided to transfer to the University of Pittsburgh, my mother's boss gave her a parting gift of barbecued pork and rice, which kept my parents alive as they rode a Greyhound bus across the country for four days with no money left over from the fare.

I'll still be trying to wrap my mind around a life so different from mine when she'll suddenly excuse me from the kitchen, saying, "Don't you have homework?" Or she'll comment that she hasn't heard me practice piano yet that day. The message is clear: Your path does not go through here.

When I leave that house to start my adult life, I cannot cook.

Oh, I knew the basics. I could make a sandwich, fry an egg, boil noodles, use the rice cooker, bake simple cookies. Once, in a rare moment of inspiration during high school, I poached salmon in store-bought gravy, a dish that made my father pause and blink, then ask if there were seconds. But the dishes my mother assembled so effortlessly were beyond my reach—and my interest. Whenever I looked ahead to my future, it never included time in the kitchen. Besides, if I ever did have to produce a meal, I knew how to read a cookbook. How hard could cooking be?

Shortly after turning twenty-one, I got my first solo apartment, and my first solo kitchen, courtesy of my first real job, at a small daily newspaper two hours from home. By the time I left that job, nearly two years later, I'd become the assistant news editor. I'd had to explain to my mother what that meant, and she wasn't impressed by any title that had to be explained to her. During that same time span, my most memorable culinary achievement was a pot of chili that I burned so badly, it was practically charred. I had to scour the pot for days before it was usable again, and it was months before I could even think about eating chili. Naturally, I didn't tell my mother about the fiasco. I couldn't remember her ever burning a dish in my life.

My next stop was graduate school, in New York City. My mother was so thrilled about my new life as a master's candidate at a world-famous university that she agreed to pay my rent, as long as I repaid her after I graduated. At first, mindful of this debt, I practiced fiscal responsibility, buying modest amounts of meat and vegetables at the neighborhood market and cooking them simply. But, surrounded by cockroaches and convenient cheap food, I soon abandoned the kitchen and ate out or got takeout like everyone else. Except when the classmate I had a crush on finally agreed to come over for dinner. I promised to cook for him. And I did: I boiled spaghetti, then poured jarred sauce on top. My mother, I later realized, would have been aghast. That wasn't at all how any child of hers should have fed a guest.

Then there was the time a rookie mistake should have gotten me evicted from the ritzy Philadelphia apartment tower where I'd lucked into a cheap studio. On a day off from my job at a newspaper my mother could finally brag about because everyone had heard of it, I'd started baking chicken wings, then forgotten about them and gone out. I had to call the building staff to advise them that someone should probably get into my apartment and turn off the gas oven before the entire block was blown to kingdom come. When I got home, a tray of blackened bits was sitting on my range top in silent rebuke. How could I, my mother's daughter, have messed up so spectacularly?

I wanted to do better. I was ready to do better. But when I finally started to investigate how my mother cooked, I was confounded by her speed and her blithe disregard for measurements.

"Wait," I'd say, trying to take notes and watch her hands at the same time (it would be years before I'd own any sort of video recording device). "What's that white stuff?"

"Cornstarch."

"How much do you use?"

She'd show me a small mound in her palm.

"But how much is that? A tablespoon? A couple of teaspoons?"

She'd twitch impatiently. "It's the amount I use!" While I tried to assign a measurement to what I'd seen, she'd dispense of the cornstarch—and then turn immediately to another dish in progress, or dig another unidentifiable ingredient out of the refrigerator, or yank out of the oven something whose initial steps I'd missed.

It took a bona fide food journalist to get my mother to finally give me a recipe—and then she did so only indirectly. I had joined the staff of *The Philadelphia Inquirer*'s Sunday magazine, a job that introduced me to Rick Nichols, one of the city's most respected food writers. One morning he arrived in the office to find me fuming over a *New York Times* column by Russell Baker, in which the humorist had taken a potshot at tofu. Clearly he had never had tofu as prepared by my mother, I ranted, because he didn't know what he was missing. Rick was intrigued. Perhaps he, too, needed enlightenment. Would it be possible for him to get my mother's phone number?

A few Sundays later, Rick's weekly magazine column featured his conversation with my mother, in which she extolled tofu as a healthier substitute for meat. She described to him one of her recipes, which he put into a format the rest of us could understand, christening it Tofu-Tomato Egg-Drop Soup. He wrote that he liked the soup so much, he'd made it as Sunday breakfast. I clipped out the column, sent a copy to my mother, and put the original in the binder that held my most prized writing and editing clips.

Then my path took a turn that surprised both my mother and me. Thirty years and two months after she had arrived in Oregon with her new husband, I moved there to start over myself with the man who would become my husband. My mother was at first perplexed, then indignant. She and my father had lit out for the east in search of civilization as soon as they could. Why was I now taking the family backward?

It took some time and coaxing, but my mother finally consented to visit me in Portland. As I planned for my parents' arrival, the one thing I didn't think about was their meals. I was busy eating my way through Portland's bounty of restaurants, and I carelessly assumed that my mother would be delighted to play foodie along with me.

When I opened my apartment door and welcomed her in, she must have suspected right away that something was wrong. There was no smell of cooking, nor did I bustle into the kitchen to start pulling out dishes to refresh my parents after their long trip. As their visit stretched from hours into days, she waited in vain for me to cook for her. Finally, the night before my parents were to fly out, she confronted me with my failure—then announced she would not spend another night with such an inhospitable person, and stormed out. I followed, pleading, but she would not even look at me until I promised to take her and my father to a hotel by the airport. When my anger had subsided, I felt ashamed, and vowed to redeem myself as soon as possible.

But although my mother and I reconciled, and although I did eventually learn to cook for guests, she never trusted me to feed her again, even after she and my father joined me in Portland years later. We had lunch together every Tuesday, but the only place we ever went was back to our original roles: She cooked, I ate. I was always welcome in her kitchen; she never came to mine.

She seemed content with the peace between us. I was desperate to keep the peace, for by then she was battling a recurrence of lung cancer—she and my father had come to Portland so she could see a lung cancer specialist I'd chosen to replace her general oncologist. The specialist did well by my mother, who seemed hardly sick at all, even going back to golfing and traveling. But the specialist warned that the treatments could do only so much. We'd be lucky to have her for another year and a half.

A year ticked by. I pulled aside my brother, then my father. Time is running out, I told them. We have to be prepared. But I was the one completely caught off guard on the spring day my mother told me she was no longer cooking.

"Why?" I didn't understand what could possibly make her stop.

"The pots and pans are too heavy," she said, simply.

That August, her time ran out.

I took only a few of my mother's things, mostly kitchen items. When I'm rushing to get dinner on the table or seizing s spare afternoon to use up what's in the refrigerator, it grounds me to see flashes of her: her soup ladle, her knife, her bowl. It's al the inheritance I have from her. It's all I need.

PORK "TURNIP" SOUP

When my mother first served me this soup I was six and deeply suspicious of the daikon. My mother probably told me it was "turnip" because that was a more familiar word. (To this day I can't help calling it turnip.) I've tweaked her recipe over the years, but only in ways I think she'd approve.

Note: Daikon is sometimes labeled in supermarkets as "Asian radish," "Chinese radish" or "Japanese radish."

INGREDIENTS

5 to 6 cups chicken stock or broth
1 pound thin boneless pork loin, cut into 1-inch pieces and patted dry with a paper towel
2 cups of sliced daikon, cut into half-moon shapes
1/2 cup cornstarch
1 tablespoon light soy sauce
2 teaspoons toasted sesame oil
1 teaspoon minced or shaved fresh ginger
1/4 to 1/2 cup chopped green onions (optional)

TO PREPARE

In a medium pot, heat stock or broth to boiling, then lower heat to a simmer.

1. Add daikon slices to pot and cook until almost tender, about 10 to 15 minutes.

2. Meanwhile, put cornstarch in a shallow dish. Coat pork pieces thoroughly with cornstarch. Let sit until daikon is done.

3. Add pork pieces and ginger to pot and cook until pork is done, about 5 minutes. Add soy sauce and sesame oil; stir.

4. Remove from heat and serve.

If using green onions, sprinkle on top of soup as garnish.

Frankincense and Leeks

by Lunaea Weatherstone

As a child, I was obsessed with Christmas. Not the religious aspect—I was a little heathen—or even the prospect of getting presents. Christmas morning didn't matter much to me. It was all about Christmas Eve, and the nights leading up to it. I was bewitched by the lights, the sparkles, the sense of ancient mystery, though I didn't know to call it by that name. The essential mystery of a holiday that comes into its full glory at night called to something deep within me. It required a solemn pilgrimage to the mall, where Raj of India was a treasure cave filled with gold, frankincense, and myrrh. (Brass and cheap incense, but still, I was transported away from mundane San Bernardino, and that's all that mattered.) I had my own little tree in my bedroom, and I carefully chose ornaments one at a time from the gorgeous displays at the Broadway and May Company department stores.

Back then, I preferred to do things on my own, or at least, without my family. For weeks ahead of time, once my family was safely asleep, I rehearsed for my secret nighttime mission that took place on Christmas Eve. Edging out of bed in slow motion to avoid any squeaks or creaks, I made my way down the hall to the dark living room as stealthily as any slinky Sixties spy. My mental soundtrack: the sneaky-tiptoe music of the Sugarplum Fairy. My goal: to see the glorious piles of presents for the first time all alone, without my three maddening little sisters and their screams of delight. Many years later, when I told my mother about these nocturnal maneuvers, she was a bit put out that I had been faking my surprised delight, having already seen all the goods on my own.

But that was my tradition, and tradition was something I craved much more than the rest of my family. Mom was already overwhelmed and wanted to keep things as simple as possible, and Dad expected her to take care of everything domestic—with one exception. Christmas Eve was the only time my dad ever cooked. On that night, and only that night, he made his special potato soup, a very specific soup with a recipe so arcane that I regret I never asked him where he got it. Was it ancestral, brought from the old country? Or maybe he learned how to make it in the Navy? In any case, the assembly went like this: Find the big white tureen that only gets used once a year. In the bottom of the tureen put chopped raw onions, crisp crumbled bacon, and a blob of butter. Boil cubed potatoes in water, and when they are almost ready, drop in weird little dumplings made of flour and egg. Pour all this into the tureen, add milk, celery salt, and lots of black pepper.

I adored this soup. It was the taste of Christmas Eve, which was the emotional highlight of my year. Potato soup triggered the feelings of winter mystery and magic, like Proust's madeleine.

I tried hard to hang on to that magic as I got older. I left home when I was 18, moving northward as fast as my four wheels could carry me. My sisters grew up, got married, had children, and made them the potato soup every Christmas Eve. In time, Dad died, and then Mom. As an orphan alone on Christmas, family tradition felt particularly precious. I wasn't a child anymore, but I needed that innocent goodness and warmth. It was comforting to know that we were all eating the same soup at the same time. I called my sister Diana every Christmas Eve and asked her, "Hey, what's for dinner?" "Potato soup!" Though we were hundreds of miles apart, the soup tradition made me felt closer to my kin, my clan, linked by the starchy bonds of potatoes.

But then, a few years ago:

"Hey, what's for dinner?"

"Tamales!"

"Say what, now?"

"We're making homemade tamales."

"But it's Christmas Eve! Potato soup!"

"The kids don't like it."

"Too bad!"

"I made it every year, and every year I ended up throwing most of it away. Now everyone's happy—isn't that the most important thing?"

"No, of course not!"

She laughed. "It's like that oyster dressing only Dad liked, which Mom kept making even after he died. Nobody else would even taste it. It went straight from oven to table to garbage disposal."

"Well, it wouldn't be a family holiday dinner without someone having a hissy fit and throwing something down the sink."

"Ha!"

"I don't make potato soup like Dad's anymore, by the way. Mine has cream and chicken broth. And chives. I got rid of the dumplings."

"Sounds good. I'm sure you'll enjoy it."

And so it came to pass that a new tradition was born. I call Diana every Christmas

Eve and try to guilt trip her into eating soup she doesn't like.

"Hey, what's for dinner?"

"I'm having French toast. Hunter and Augustina just went to Jack-in-the-Box. Everyone else is coming over tomorrow."

"It breaks my heart that no one has Christmas Eve potato soup anymore. My childhood memories are dying before my eyes."

"Get over it."

"Gee, thanks, DAD."

"See? We don't need his soup, he's here in spirit."

She can always make me laugh. Whatever loneliness I feel starts melting away.

She asks, "So, what are *you* having for dinner?"

"Nothing. I'm much too sad to eat now."

"Oh, shut up."

"*You* shut up."

"Merry Christmas. I love you."

"Love you too, pinhead."

We hang up, and I go back to the stove to stir my soup. I take a sip from the old wooden spoon. Sisterly love is the perfect seasoning. I fill my bowl with comfort and joy.

Lunaea in 1957, the last time she looked
good in a hat.

CHRISTMAS EVE POTATO SOUP

(Serves one)

INGREDIENTS

One bunch leeks, washed well and dried.
Two Yukon gold potatoes
Chicken stock
Lean bacon
Half-and-half, or cream
Fresh chives
Salt and pepper

TO PREPARE

1. Sauté a thinly sliced leek in butter until soft.

2. Peel and slice two Yukon gold potatoes and add to the leeks. Barely cover with chicken stock and cook gently until the potatoes are soft.

3. Meanwhile, cook some lean bacon until crisp.

4. Smash some of the potatoes in the soup pot, add the bacon, pour in some half-and-half or cream until it's the consistency you like.

5. Add fresh chopped chives, salt and pepper to taste.

6. Heat through again, pour into your most charming bowl, and eat it with your favorite spoon while watching *A Charlie Brown Christmas*.

Bachelors

by Ellen Twaddell

"This is the first time I've lived by myself!" My mother Kristie was 69 when she found a small apartment above a sea of trees by a park in Washington DC. She had had two husbands, two children, and almost fifty years of cohabitation after going straight from a college dormitory into her first marriage.

This was the beginning of a one-year window in which we were both bachelors.

"How do you like it?" I asked. I was calling from my own new apartment, also living by myself. Three hundred miles and four hours of Megabus separated us, but I knew our two tiny spaces reflected many of our similarities. Kristie had turned her master bedroom into an office, her bed wedged between two towering bookshelves. My cup of tea tottered on my own stack of tomes as I kicked back to chat. She had chosen her new home partly for the view of Rock Creek park and proximity to the Washington D.C. zoo. I was in a leafy, sleepy neighborhood in southern Brooklyn, a short jog to Prospect Park, where I still got lost regularly. Kristie had moved into her own place after accompanying my stepfather to an assisted living residence during his last long illness. Several years of romances and roommates had left me with a craving for solitude matched only by my craving for cheese. I popped a morsel of cheddar and cracker in my mouth and covered the mouthpiece as Kristie answered.

"It's wonderful!"

I was relieved but not surprised that she liked it. Kristie is one of the most self-sufficient people I know. She's warm and kind, with a wide circle of friends, but would sometimes slip out of a crowded room to make a cup of tea or crack a book. Her own space after nearly seventy years of sharing must have felt like a sunbeam to a chilly cat.

"But…" she said.

Uh oh, I thought.

"But I don't know what to eat! How do you cook for just one person? I had cereal for dinner last night!"

I laughed. My long years of eating and cooking in New York were finally paying off. Here was one arena where I had the chance to show something to my mother, who had taught me everything from riding a bike to revising a manuscript. She had handily if not passionately cooked a repertoire of thirty-minute, high-health, low-controversy dinners for two picky children and a long-suffering husband who livened up our mostly beige foodstuffs with shelves of hot sauce and jam. She had accommodated the insane brown-bag lunch requests my brother and I made, packing peanut butter and bacon bit sandwiches or ham and pickle. She made a cake that one time. She was a perfectly able cook, but not a passionate one. She had never had to listen to her own appetite and cook for just one.

Since I'd moved to New York in my late twenties, I'd been absorbing lessons in cooking and eating along with the dead-eyed subway stare and the correct jaywalking protocols for each neighborhood from Greenpoint to Lincoln Center. Tim introduced me to raw oysters and studio kitchen risotto; Elizabeth took me to chocolatiers who displayed their wares like jewels in immaculate glass cases; the whole gang went for Turkish rotisserie and lemony chicken soup after frosty February dips at Coney Island.

I honed my own recipes, with a few fancy company dishes like skillet chicken with apples and onions fried in the drippings and plum buckle cakes. Being a bachelor came with a lot of freedom. I could have anything I wanted, any time. Peanut butter and Cheerio sandwiches for dinner at eleven at night? Don't mind if I do!

But living alone had its obstacles. In my new tiny space, I didn't have much company, since I had exactly one chair. I dined at my desk. Sometimes I was good about making a proper meal for myself, something hot, something that required both knife and fork, something with more than one food group. But there were plenty of times I just wanted a stack of toast. I would think of what Kristie would say about my skimpy, lazy eating habits. I remembered what it felt like to sit across from someone as I ate and talked about my day.

So Kristie asking for some advice made me think of what I wanted for my mother and what I owed myself. I could boil my lessons down into a few philosophies, or at least a few habits that kept me from despair and scurvy. A bachelor needs to make friends with her future self. Pre-cooked vegetables, like sweet roasted beets or garlic sauteed greens, can sit in wait and jump into a salad or omelette at a moment's notice. Garnishes can make a meal for one more exciting and celebratory—a bag of walnuts or sprigs of cilantro can be stashed at the front of the fridge so a bachelor can chop and sprinkle and admire and devour. But most of all, a bachelor needs to take care of herself. Of the recipes I passed along during this period, Kristie's favorite was a simple one for the chicken soup I made for myself every time I started coming down with a cold. Without a spouse or roommate to run out to fetch Jell-O and NyQuil, a bachelor needs a soup like this to restore and nourish. I fill mine with every kind of onion and a last-minute grating of raw garlic and ginger, making it as funky as it is comforting.

At the end of our year of solidarity, Kristie had new routines of cooking and eating, and I was ready to dip into dating again, with my usual high hopes and low expectations. I met Daniel at an H.P. Lovecraft-themed bar in Alphabet City. We went from tepid beer to hot chocolate over the course of a six-hour date, and I fell in love as we kissed in a cloud of fragrant smoke from the halal cart in Union Square.

The rest of that winter, we holed up in my suddenly cozy apartment in Brooklyn, and he made me grilled cheese sandwiches as I studied, and I added the raw red peppers he loves to eat like apples to my grocery cart. He called me Clementine for the dozens we ate, sharing them section by section.

One year later, I proposed on a gray day in Prospect Park and we celebrated at a fancy pizza place that served their slices with hot chili honey. We moved into an apartment in Hell's Kitchen, and Kristie came to visit three days later to see our new neighborhood. We stood on the snow-dusted sidewalk on Ninth Avenue debating where to eat.

"We should go to the diner across the street," I said. "We don't have anywhere to sit!" This wasn't how I had imagined inviting her into our new home. I wanted to give her tea and toast across a table so we could see each other's faces. I wanted to show her that although bachelorhood has its benefits, I was continuing her work of building a family with people we loved. I wanted her to belong in this new kitchen as much as I did.

I should have known a complete lack of furniture wouldn't stop her.

"I want to see it. I want to imagine you there," said Kristie firmly.

I gave her my desk chair, parked Daniel on the storage ottoman, and put a pillow on a cardboard box for myself.

"I don't have anything to eat," I said.

"How about a drink?" said Daniel. He got up and I watched, bemused. We didn't have anything but a mostly-empty box of peppermint tea. He rummaged around in a drawer and emerged with an imaginary corkscrew. He opened an invisible bottle of wine for my mother and poured her a generous glass of nothing. She accepted graciously and the family raised our glasses in a toast.

CHICKEN SOUP À LA BACHELOR

INGREDIENTS

Olive oil
3-4 bone in, skin-on organic chicken thighs
One onion
Two or three carrots
One leek
One shallot
3-4 cloves garlic
Thumb-sized knob of ginger
Salt
Pepper
Greens (spinach is the easiest!)
Herbs (thyme and rosemary are nice!)
Noodles or toast

TO PREPARE:

1. Put a big, heavy pot on the burner on medium heat and put in the oil.

2. Chop leeks, onion and carrots into bite-sized chunks and start sautéing.

3. Before they brown, nestle the chicken in skin-side down. They should sizzle a little so the fat renders.

4. When the skin is golden, flip, and when there's color on both sides, add quite a lot of water, and at least a teaspoon of salt, and a few grinds of black pepper.

5. Put a big ball of fresh herbs into a tea strainer and let it dangle in the water, along with a tea ball with minced ginger.

6. Bring to a boil, then turn down to a simmer. Let simmer about half an hour. Taste it—has the broth reduced a little and does it taste fantastic? If so, you can fish out the chicken, shred it off the bone when it's cool enough, and start prepping the finishing elements. If not, add some salt and let it cook another 15 minutes.

7. Prep the greens and starch—I usually just boil some noodles and throw in baby spinach in the last minute. If I use a stronger green, I sauté in a non-stick pan with oil and a ton of garlic. Nice to have some greens in the fridge anyway for eggs or toast!

8. Put some shredded chicken, the noodles and greens, and a clove of grated garlic and a knob of grated raw ginger into a big bowl. Spoon veg and broth over everything. Add hot pepper or sauce if you like. Eat!

Song of Soup

by Alice Scovell

Sing to me, oh Muse, of that divine stuff that warms mortals' bodies and souls, that heals the sick and enlivens the healthy, that scents the air with its rich perfume and delights the eye with its golden hue, that fills the belly but does not bloat, that serves the multitudes without kingly expense, that is both nectar and ambrosia with its combination of liquid and solids, that is savored by the powerful and meek alike, that has elicited delight since the distant past to the immediate present although it contains neither kale nor chia. Yes, oh Muse, sing to me of that great elixir that is the crowning glory in the repertoire of any Jewish cook worth her (kosher) salt.

* * *

From a young age, I had partaken of the platonic ideal of chicken soup, served by my paternal grandmother, "Gram," steaming hot in handsome china soup bowls, large and shallow with wide rims. The soup spoon, too big for my small mouth and heavy in my hand, delivered dark yellow—I'd say "goldenrod" but just thinking of the weed makes me sneeze—broth teeming with chunks of chicken, glistening translucent onions, rounds of softened carrots, crescents of celery hinting at their former crunchiness but boiled into submission, and sweet-as-candy parsnips. A sprig of parsley or dill would float on the surface, like exotic flora. And, of course, in the bowl sat a matzoh ball, emerging high above the surface, with form following function, as the lofty height declared, "I am queen of all I survey." Although the adults ate their matzoh balls along with the soup, I saved mine for last, savoring each bite that—defying the laws of physics—managed to be simultaneously substantial and airy.

Gram deservedly prided herself on her cooking. Like the matzoh ball in her soup, she stood tall as queen of her realm. Surprisingly, her culinary talents hadn't always been recognized. As a young bride, she had toiled to prepare meals for my grandfather Louis that would meet with only limited approbation. In his heavy Russian accent, he'd say with a pat on her arm, "That's a very good chicken, Ruchel, but not like my mother makes it." And then came the time—now an-oft told family tale—that Gram was roasting a chicken and got called away from the kitchen right before the crucial moment of removal. When she finally got back to the oven, she pulled out a desiccated, inedible bird. She left it on the counter to cool before consigning the ruins to the trash bin, then hurried out to buy a replacement. Upon her return, she discovered my grandfather standing at the counter, a drumstick in his hand and a look of bliss on his face, "Now THIS is like my mother makes chicken!"

Learning how to cook from one's elders was crucial in the days before the Internet. Nowadays, if you have a hankering for Szechuan Deer with Gingerroot or Cherry Duck Flambe, not only can you find a recipe, you can find a dizzying number of them. In my grandmother's day there were cookbooks—grease-spattered, pencil-annotated, corners-of-the-pages-bent, broken-spined warriors—but the best guidance came through hands-on training.

Sometimes information passed on from mother to daughter got distorted, like an intergenerational game of telephone. As the old joke goes, an ambitious young woman decides to make chicken soup for a friend with a cold. She calls her mother for great-grandma's recipe. "Take a chicken, cut off the legs, cut off the wings, cut the body into eighths, put it in a pot, fill with water to cover…" The young woman asks, "Why do I have to do all that cutting?" "Huh, " says her mother, "I'm not sure. I'll ask grandma." Grandma is consulted, "Hmm," she says, "I never thought about it, I'll ask great-grandma." Great-grandma is called and asked, "When making chicken soup, why do you cut the bird into lots of pieces?" In her gravelly voice she answers, "The pot's too small."

The right way to make chicken soup might be disputed, but no one would dare to question its magical medicinal powers. Research suggests that its curative properties were recognized as early as the 12th century, when chickens were more of a luxury item, leading to the profound medieval serf question, "Do I want a new Rolex or a bowl of life-restoring chicken soup?" As the proverb goes, "If a poor man eats a chicken, one of them is sick."

An authority of no less standing than *The New York Times* has tried to establish scientifically that chicken soup is a helluva healer. Although the results of various studies were not entirely conclusive, there are theories on why it works to alleviate wheezes and sneezes. First, steam rising from the bowl opens up nasal passages. Second, fluids help replace lost ones. And, third, salt is a natural fighter of infection.

On the surface, you'd think you could ingest a bowl of steaming salted water and get the same Lazarus effect, but you'd be wrong. Experts say that with chicken soup, the whole is greater than the sum of its parts. It contains a compound called carnosine that helps to boost the body's immune system. In other words, Bubbe knows best.

So what ills can this super-potion combat? My grandmother thought it was a cure-all, like the snake oil offered by a mountebank, for everything from flu to sore throat to depression. She was like the little old lady in the joke who attends a funeral and sits in the back row. She listens as the rabbi begins his talk about the deceased man's virtues. After a few of his intoned sentences, she calls out, "Give him some chicken soup!" The rabbi ignores the disruption and soldiers on. A few sentences later, she barks her refrain again. The rabbi carries on. This pattern continues, until finally the rabbi explodes, saying, "Madame, death is final. Chicken soup will not help. " And she responds with a shrug, "Well, it couldn't hurt."

For my grandmother, chicken soup was viewed as having semi-religious qualities, akin to the wine and wafer. In JD Salinger's *Franny and Zooey*, the soul-sick Franny is told by her older brother that she should eat their mother's offering of the dish: "You don't even have sense enough to drink when somebody brings you a cup of consecrated chicken soup—which is the only kind of chicken soup Bessie ever brings to anybody around this madhouse." Why is Bessie's chicken soup sacred? Because it is prepared and served with love.

So what's a grandmother—who has mastered the art of chicken souping—to do when her *meshugina* college-aged granddaughter becomes a vegetarian? I bet you didn't see that plot twist coming. Gram rallied. It turns out you *can* teach an old cook new recipes.

Gram came up with a vegetable soup that rivaled her long-standing culinary achievement. The new soup had a compelling, but not cloying, sweetness, was thick and chunky, hearty and filling. Upon sampling it, I felt like I was being wrapped in a downy comforter, from the inside out. I immediately requested the recipe.

And then Gram did something unexpected: she balked. She put me off, evaded the request, "forgot" to write out the recipe. She, who had always generously shared her kitchen secrets—unlike many of her contemporaries—suddenly guarded her recipe as tightly as the Coca Cola Corporation. I figured that she wanted to keep me coming back for more, and I stopped asking. But when I graduated from college and was moving from Boston to New York for law school, I knew the soup-well would run dry. I made another bid for the indulgence of divulgence.

In my final visit with Gram before heading south, she ushered me to the dining room table and served me a bowl of soup. She sat down, holding in her hand a sheet of paper bearing her distinctive scrawl. She couldn't look me in the eye as she told me that "this wasn't much of a recipe." I protested that I loved her vegetable soup and couldn't wait to start making it.

She sighed and unburdened her guilty soul: Tabatchnick's frozen soup served as the base. She used the commercial soup and doctored it with steamed fresh vegetables. What to her seemed sacrilege, to me was liberation. I could make the soup quickly and easily, a godsend to a first year law school student.

As I ate a spoonful from the bowl she had set before me, I tasted the ingredient that made it—even if partially store bought—consecrated. I tasted love.

GRAM'S VEGETABLE SOUP
(now made without Tabatchnick as its base)

INGREDIENTS (AMOUNTS ARE EASILY DOUBLED):

½ pound of carrots, peeled and diced into rounds (if you're lazy like me, use the organic pre-peeled baby carrots)
½ pound of parsnips, peeled and diced into rounds (be careful; don't cut yourself)
2 potatoes, peeled and diced (skip the potatoes if you're spud phobic)
½ pound of celery stalks (wash them well, looking out for hidden dirt), diced
A large onion (or two medium ones, silly), peeled and diced (think about something sad so you don't waste your tears)
A little olive oil for sautéing
Water (I use filtered) or vegetable stock (you can buy this or make it)
A dried bay leaf (Gram's favorite) OR dill (fresh or dried)
Salt to taste (but not enough to raise blood pressure)

Optional vegetables (steamed/microwaved to add at the end); amount of each at the cook's discretion (Do I have to do everything? Make up your own mind!)
green beans, ends cut off, cut into pieces about an inch or so long
peas (fresh or frozen)
corn (fresh or frozen)
cauliflower and/or broccoli florets
canned beans like garbanzo, kidney, or cannellini (no need to cook)

TO PREPARE:

1. In a medium-large saucepan, add a little olive oil and sauté the onions over low-medium heat to light brown.

2.   Throw in the carrots and parsnips for a bit of sautéing.

3.   Add the potatoes and celery, then barely cover with water or broth; add either a bay leaf or a bit of dill (fresh or dried).

4.   Cover and bring to a boil, then lower flame and cook until the vegetables are softened, but not mushy. Stir occasionally.

5.   While the soup cooks, prepare any of the additional optional vegetables that appeal to you. Steam and/or microwave them. Set them aside.

6.   When the vegetables in the saucepan are ready (meaning soft but not mushy), remove about half of the vegetables and half the broth and pulverize it (in a blender, food processor, etc) to create a thick, smooth texture. Add the smooth soup back into the saucepan and stir for a thick base with chunky veggies in it. Add a little water if too thick. Pulverize more veggies if too thin.

7.   Add the additional vegetables at the end to make the soup chunkier. Remember to remove the bay leaf if used. Add salt to taste; start light (a scant tsp).

8.   Serve hot.

9.   Enjoy! (Gram's sign off on all her recipes.)

CARBS, SHMARBS
(SO LONG AS YOU'RE HAPPY)

Jörg's Pasta with Potatoes

Ravioli, a poem

Savory Bitch Ramen

Insanely Good Stuffing

Spinach Pie Roll-Up

Sabudana Khicidi

Spaghetti Carbonara

You Are What You Eat

by Anna Winger

My German husband, Jörg, makes breakfast for our children every morning. We live in Berlin, where carbohydrates never developed a bad reputation. The more thick slices of *Vollkornbrot* (whole grain bread) smeared with real butter and strawberry jam he manages to pack into them before they go off to school, the happier he starts his day. He has been eating more or less this exact breakfast himself, plus or minus Nutella, for almost half a century. His belief in its nutritional value is nearly religious.

So when our friends in New York told us that they try to make sure that their own kids never eat bread at all, Jörg looked at them like they were lunatics who were starving their children.

Germans eat their hot meal at lunch. Both breakfast and dinner are served cold and are organized entirely around bread. Breakfast is sweet (jam on bread) and dinner is savory (cold cuts on bread) but you could argue that they are basically the same meal because if you were to remove the bread from the equation, there wouldn't be much left besides butter.

Potatoes are the only other food that Jörg considers close to bread, in terms of nutritional value. On the weekends, he likes to make the kids his favorite hot lunch: an all-white, all-carbs pasta with potatoes. It also involves butter. That's it. American friends shiver with delight at the sheer taboo of it. But no one else around here blinks an eye. My German mother-in-law, raised during post-war rationing, likes to say that "children only really need to eat potatoes" to survive. My German father-in-law, once a refugee from Bohemia, has never willingly consumed a green vegetable in his entire life. Both are fit as a fiddle.

That's the weird thing. Germans eat bread and butter and cake on Sundays (every Sunday), and they basically mainline whole milk. Apparently, the average German consumes 67 lbs. of pork sausage a year. In other words, their children are growing up on foods that have come to terrify American parents. But you almost never see a fat child in Germany, or even a fat adult. Superior genes? (I'm kidding!) Obviously, there is some objective truth to the sway of nutritional fads, but these things are also cultural. As a friend of mine likes to say, one man's yuck is another man's yummy.

When I was growing up we lived in many different places around the world. But no matter where we were, like good Americans, we ate Kellogg's cereal for breakfast every day. So on an off-day, when I'm the one making breakfast, I default to the same old cereal I grew up with. It's quick and it's easy. I mean, those hard loaves of *Volkornbrot* are tough to cut if you haven't been doing it all your life.

But if Jörg catches me with corn flakes, he invariably launches into a rant worthy of any neurotic New York parent. Quoting Michael Pollen (yes, *Das Omnivoren-Dilemma* was huge here, too), he suggests that I'm slowly poisoning our children. "Right," I retort defensively. "Just like my own parents poisoned me!"

He just shakes his head, resigned to the naked truth of it. "That's why I must be in charge of breakfast," he says, getting out the big brown loaf, the butter and the milk.

And I go back to sleep.

JÖRG'S PASTA WITH POTATOES

INGREDIENTS

Three big potatoes
Package of pasta
Broccoli (optional)
Butter
Salt
Parmesan cheese

TO PREPARE

1. Peel three big potatoes and slice very thin.
2. Boil a pot of water. Add a package of pasta. When almost done, add potatoes. (Sometimes at this stage he actually adds broccoli.)
3. Before you strain it all, take out a cup of starchy water.
4. Strain.
5. Melt butter in same pot, add the starchy water back in to make a sauce.
6. Add pasta and potatoes to cook for a moment and absorb.
7. Salt to taste. Parmesan cheese on top.

Ravioli

by Annie LaZebnik

My favorite food is ravioli
My favorite food is ravioli, although I've never tried it
My favorite food is ravioli because when I was young
My grandpa would look me in the eyes
And take my hands in his
And sing
raaaaviollli I love raaaaaviooolliiii
And I would laugh
And laugh
And in that moment, we were the same
The seventy years between us didn't matter
The wars and heartbreaks and moon landings disappeared
The veins and freckles on his skin vanished
All that mattered was
Ravioli
Ravioli
I love ravioli

Savory Bitch

by Sarah Thyre

Ask most people what they eat when no one's watching—"shame-eating," I like to call it—and they'll usually say something sweet. Cake, pie, candy, sugary cereal like Cap'n Crunch and Cocoa Puffs: these are things that we as adults aren't supposed to crave, or at the very least, shouldn't admit we do. Yet these are the things we quite literally cut our teeth on, as children. As such, they possess magical powers of sense-memory. Who doesn't remember the first time you ate something you'd hoarded, hidden under your pillow, in the dark, after you'd brushed your teeth? Most likely it was a primo piece of Halloween candy like a fun-sized Three Musketeers, but maybe—just maybe, if you were anything like me—it was a can of Chef Boyardee Ravioli.

I don't have a sweet tooth. I'm a savory bitch. I like salty food, always have. Why mess with sugar when you can have salt? I grew up in a house that rarely had sweets. It makes sense, then, that I would crave the sodium-based foods that form my own childhood sense memories: cottage cheese, Campbell's Cream of Mushroom soup, Lawry's Seasoned Salt. My favorite first grade snack was dill pickle slices blanketed with Lawry's and soy sauce. If we were out of pickles, I would put Lawry's on slices of raw potato. I'd eat the dust leftover in the bottom of the dry-roasted peanut jar. I was basically dying for salt. Or rather: living for it.

As a female, you learn pretty early on that you're not supposed to admit you eat, perhaps because then you would be admitting that you shit—also a no-no. I was always a scrawny kid, so I could eat whatever I wanted. In high school, other girls would sigh, "I'm so FAT," and pass me their fries and rolls, cheering me on while I gorged on their food. It was okay to be seen eating as long as I was thin.

I remained skinny until my mid-twenties, when I finally grew breasts and hips. I went so long without them, part of me doesn't believe they ever came. I suffer from a sort of reverse body dysmorphia: I think I'm thinner than I actually am. Sometimes I see a photo of myself and don't recognize me. Skinny 16-year-old Sarah was allowed to wolf down piles of carbs in public, but grown women are expected to approach eating from the oblique angles of deprivation and guilt.

Well, fuck that. I eat. I eat a lot. And I eat some pretty gross stuff. Life is more than laughing forkfuls of salad and colon cleansing. I hereby declare that I eat, I shit, and I don't care whether you like it. I'm a savory bitch.

On this leap from the salt-cellar of shame-eating, I need to drag my friends out with me. An informal poll yielded two primary categories of shame-eating: sugar, and McDonalds. The Quarter Pounder with Cheese and the Filet-O-Fish were cited as especially disgraceful: always eaten alone, usually in one's car, often ducking low to take furtive bites because god forbid Jessica from your spin class happens to drive by and see you.

Sugary confessions came mainly by the spoonful: peanut butter, Nutella, whipped cream, vanilla frosting, or just plain granulated white sugar, easily ingested behind a cabinet or fridge door. My friend Grey admits that after she makes brownies, she pours milk into the crusty pan and mixes up a chocolate slurry that she slurps down in her "eating robe." (Yes, some of us have special garments for shame-eating, and they're invariably ratty, stained robes.)

But it ain't just women who shame-eat. My friend Jack and his husband Chris remodeled their bathroom at the same time they decided to banish sugar from their household. Jack admits he made several unnecessary trips to Home Depot because it was located next to a drive-thru donut shop.

"I'd put the donut bag in the trash down the street so Chris wouldn't see it," Jack confided. "To this day, *he has no idea.*"

Being a savory bitch, I found myself teasing out, shall we say, *saltier* responses. Upon further prodding, some friends coughed up the goods: Pickle juice for Ben. Chicken drippings for Claudia. Bologna sandwiches for Emily and Cynthia. Shredded cheddar cheese out of the bag for Alison, eaten over the sink, or on the floor if she's tired. Cary chugs ranch dressing, and it's Totino's Party Pizza for Jonathan, who admits, "It's pretty much the exact opposite of a party." Mark told me he got the sourdough bread bowl of gumbo at Disneyland, ate most of the gumbo, then made a sandwich out of smoked turkey leg on the gumbo-soaked bread. Kelly copped to eating onion bagels dipped in SpaghettiOs—"the kind with hot dogs."

"Cottage cheese," my friend Ele said. "But don't tell anybody, it's embarrassing." No shame, Ele. No shame.

While my culinary skillset includes an uncanny ability to nacho-fy any cuisine— I've made fried rice nachos, hummus nachos, vindaloo nachos, Korean BBQ sriracha nachos, sushi nachos—what do I eat when I'm home alone, with enough time for a sad sodium coma afterwards?

Ramen.

These days ramen is socially acceptable—gourmet, even. Chefs seek it out and sing its praises. I ain't talking about *that* ramen. I'm talking about that dirty, nasty ramen we've all got history with, that last resort of sustenance ramen: something eaten at 2 AM in your college dorm, when you're drunk and penniless because you spent all your Pell Grant money getting drunk in the first place.

When I was in college, Top Ramen was literally 8 packages for a dollar. That was a whole week's worth of food, at a time in my life when I saved my cash for necessities like cigarettes, beer, and drugs.

Since college, I've traveled. I've lived in diverse cities. My tastes have broadened and my palate has gone global. Like the old fable about soup from a stone, I take a humble package of instant ramen and gussie it up with exotic ingredients like imported sardines and Calabrian chili. Then, just to make sure it doesn't get too big for its britches, I bring it down a notch with that mainstay of every 1950s American housewife's reducing regimen: cottage cheese.

I eat it alone, so no one can judge me.

I'm a Savory Bitch, motherfuckers, and this is my ramen.

SAVORY BITCH RAMEN

INGREDIENTS

1 package chicken-flavor Top Ramen
1 tin sardines (or tuna, if you're a wuss)
Small curd cottage cheese
Calabrian pepperoncini piccante in olive oil, or crushed red pepper flakes
Freshly ground black pepper

Optional: hot sauce, salsa, grated cheese, bonito flakes, yuzu kosho, edamame, sliced tomatoes, arugula, chopped cilantro, anything <u>not sweet</u>

TO PREPARE

1. Boil ramen noodles as directed on package (they say 3 minutes but I find half that suffices for an al dente texture).
2. Drain noodles, dump back into pan, add half the sauce packet, Calabrian pepperoncini piccante, and black pepper to taste.

SAVORY BITCH RAMEN (CONT.)

3. Add drained sardines to ramen and stir.
4. Place ramen in a large shallow bowl with a generous dollop of cottage cheese next to it. Top everything with more freshly ground black pepper.
5. Eat with a fork, scooping first the ramen then dipping into cottage cheese.
6. Brush your teeth before kissing or breathing on anyone.
7. Sleep.
8. Wake up and brush your teeth again, it lingers.

It was Jelly!

by Carolyn Omine

I always go a little overboard on Thanksgiving. Having grown up in a family splintered by divorce, addiction and a multitude of other bummers, I compensate by going full-Martha-Stewart at holidays. I don't consider myself a "cook," but there are six dishes I make that are insanely good. Four of them are Thanksgiving dishes. Superstar comfort foods served on tableware and decorations I've perfected over the years. I invite only my sanest family and dearest friends. Toss in a makeshift "karaoke" set-up, and a board game or three. It is an afternoon and night of eating, laughter and marathon conversation. A time to fall deeper in love with my extended family. An hours-long, wine-warmed hug.

There was one Thanksgiving, however…

A Thanksgiving that was epic in its terribleness.

It was ten years ago. Samantha was ten and Kai was three. I decided to spend Thanksgiving in New York City—just the three of us. Catch the Macy's Thanksgiving Day Parade, The Rockettes' Christmas Spectacular…I hoped it might even snow.

It was an exciting idea. It made me feel like a jetsetter. Not a common feeling for a single mom. In my twenties, when I planned a trip to New York, I imagined myself a slightly overweight Audrey Hepburn. But once I had kids, my fantasies became more like Angelina Jolie: holding gloved hands with my eclectic children in chic winter get-ups as we bustled along to wildly original, age-appropriate off-Broadway shows.

New York does not disappoint. New York lives up to its hype. The kids loved the fast-paced, urine-tinged grittiness. The giant toy stores and Mars-themed restaurants. Being Southern Californians, we enjoyed the novelty of scarves and hats. Most of our trip was a blur of candy-colored fun.

I was concerned, though, about Thanksgiving itself. I'm an "older" parent. The older you get, the faster time seems to fly by. I'm hyper-aware that I have a limited number of Thanksgivings before the kids grow up.

So maybe I put too much pressure on the day. I certainly overthought my New York Thanksgiving options. I Googled and Googled before deciding on a restaurant that was accessed from Manhattan by "water taxi." I imagined the water taxis I'd seen in movies set in Venice. Sleek, swift boats of glossy wood, whisking us to the restaurant's private dock. The website showed the lights of the Manhattan Skyline reflected in the water, sparkling through a wall of windows. It seemed like a wonderful way to spend an evening.

We arrived at the hotel cabstand all dressed up. One of the rare, post-motherhood times I wore heels. Wedges, really. Not super-sexy but sexier than my usual extra-wide running shoes avec orthotics. These shoes made me taller and had black grosgrain ribbon that wrapped and tied around my ankles, ballerina style. I felt pretty wearing them.

When we got to the front of the taxi line, I told the cab stand fellow, "We're going to Pier 3!" (Pier number changed to protect the innocent and because I don't remember the pier number.)

Cab Stand Fellow: "Which Pier 3? Jersey or Brooklyn?"

I probably should have known this information—but I never dreamed there would be two Pier 3's! (New York friends assure me this pier-numbering system has since been made less confusing.) I stammered and said, "Um…it's a restaurant? With a water taxi?" I sounded annoyingly Californian. The Cab Stand guy asked, "What's the name of the restaurant?" I told him. He nodded his head confidently and motioned us into the cab as he told the driver, "Pier 3, Jersey side."

The cab pulled up to a deserted looking dock. I saw a "Pier 3" sign, but it was a bit of a walk from the road where we were dropped off. As the car drove away, I realized how eerily still it was. It was getting dark and there were very few cars on the road. I guess not many other families decided to spend Thanksgiving at an abandoned shipyard. The kind of place Tony Soprano would bring you when he wanted to "have a little chat."

It was bitingly cold; our scarves and hats were becoming both a bother and not enough. Even before we reached it, I could see that Pier 3 was a darkened shack next to a ship-less slip in an empty harbor.

Oops.

Most of the time, I take "single parenthood" in stride. I have a fun job. A network of close friends. Most of the time, I don't think of myself as "alone." But as I struggled to carry a trembling, parka-wrapped Kai while Sammi clutched my waist in fear, I felt, very acutely, my singleness. I tried to appear calm.

There were no cabs and no people. With no other plan, I started to walk, feeling foolish and vain for wearing such stupid shoes—why had I strapped three-inch ramps to my feet with ribbon? The ballerina wraps had collapsed into artless coils on the tops of my feet.

We tottered along for just a few minutes when suddenly, a burgundy Montecarlo crossed two lanes to pull up beside us, the passenger window gliding down. An elderly driver, with a Middle Eastern accent, leaned across his passenger seat and said, "Do you need a ride?"

I felt simultaneously relieved and terrified. I asked, "Are you… a taxi?" A silly question. Of course he wasn't a taxi. Taxis have taxi thingies on them. (This was in the days before Uber.) The man shrugged casually, as if to say "Sure, I'm a taxi. Let's go with that."

I gazed down the empty street at my no-other options. I said, "How much would you charge to take us to the dock on the Brooklyn side?"

Another shrug, then: "Twenty dollars." That seemed reasonable. Maybe he *wasn't* a gypsy cab bent on taking advantage of our obvious tourist-ness.

That's when the rain began.

I decided that even with two kids in tow, I could probably take this old guy if the shit went down. I bundled my darlings into the back seat and slipped into the front, because, I kid you not, I figured if he tried anything, I would knock him out and take control of the vehicle. Years earlier, I had taken a self-defense class. Now, as I answered his chatty questions, I mentally rehearsed the choreography I'd learned: heel of hand to the nose, knee to the groin, knee to the groin, knee to the groin. He was about eighty years old.

As we drove, the rain got heavier. When we pulled up on the Brooklyn side, we could see Pier 3 in the distance, lit up with people milling about. Still, I must have looked unsure when I gave our "Cabby" his twenty, because he said, "See if this is the right place. I won't leave until you wave." It was so considerate I felt guilty that I'd imagined punching his kindly face and going to town on his balls with my knee.

When we were sure it was the right place, we waved and he pulled away, the beams of his headlights cutting through the rain, which was really starting to come down.

We were herded onto our "water taxi" with ten other people. It wasn't a glossy wooden boat so much as a run-down barge covered with AstroTurf and a couple of inches of water. Did I mention the roof? No, because there wasn't one.

As we bounced across the Hudson River, Kai shivered and whined, and Sam looked miserable. Kai pulled his arms out of his sleeves and hugged himself beneath his coat. The puffy sleeves of his jacket bounced at his side like lifeless wings. This made him giggle. He twisted his body to wiggle his empty sleeves again and laughed that throaty baby laugh, which was so welcome on this grim night. Sammi's rain-flecked face smiled fondly at Kai's silliness. Then a wave bumped the barge and Kai crashed to the deck on his face like a fallen tree.

I picked him up quickly. He was screaming in pain. Thankfully it was just a bumped lip. A little blood, a teeny bit of swelling—but it added up to a miserable little boy.

I have since learned that a restaurant on Thanksgiving is not a happy place. Serving a bigger-than-usual meal to bigger-than-usual crowds pretty much guarantees they will be in the weeds. This particular restaurant on this particular night seemed particularly fucked. It's probably not the best business plan to have boat-fulls of wet customers arrive at your restaurant at the same time.

After a tense and drippy wait, we were finally seated—far from the wall of windows and the skyline view. We were tucked away near a kiosk where busboys scraped plates and grabbed pitchers of water, which gave us front row seats to the hushed arguments among the stressed-out waitstaff. A busboy used tongs to put one muffin on each of our bread plates. Mine was completely black, as if it had recently been on fire. I asked a passing waiter for another muffin. "No!" he snapped. "Everyone gets one muffin!" I showed him my burnt muffin. I have never felt more certain I was about to be slapped. Restraining himself with a vicious sigh, he snatched the muffin from my plate. He stormed to the kitchen, chucking the muffin loudly into a bucket at the busboy station. I never got a replacement.

The kids ordered the turkey dinner. It looked like it had been plated the night before. The gravy, which covered most of the plate, had a shiny thick skin. Sam complained that the thin slices of turkey were stuck together and as she put it, "looked wrinkled."

I had ordered pasta. One of my mom tricks—always have a pasta back-up in case the kids hate their entrees. But this pasta had a cheese that—well, I hope it was the cheese, because something on this pasta smelled like human feces. I'm no cheese expert. I know fine cheeses can be pretty… aromatic. But from our tableside view, I could see that tempers were running high in the kitchen. Someone shitting in the pasta seemed entirely in the realm of the possible. I couldn't bring myself to take a single bite.

By the time they cleared our barely-touched plates, the kids were… sullen. So much so they didn't want dessert. This concerned me for my son, because he hadn't had dinner. Anyone who's dealt with a three-year-old knows — don't let 'em get too hungry. So I suggested a safe favorite: a scoop of vanilla ice cream. Kai nodded. "Okay. Yes! I'll eat that." They brought Spumoni to the table, took it back, then brought it to the table *again*, before finally saying that they didn't have vanilla ice cream. At that point, we asked for the check.

As we were about to leave, the man at the door held up a small giftbag decorated with ribbon and holly. "A present…" he said as he handed the beautiful gift bag to

Kai. "For you, young man!" Kai's face lit up. He thanked the man with a hushed, hopeful voice, and I prayed that this present would be a bright spot and make up for the disastrous meal. But I had my doubts—so I told Kai not to look in the bag until we got out of the restaurant.

We settled on the bench where we were to wait for the horrible barge to bounce us back across the Hudson in the rain.

I told Kai he could open his present. He reached in and pulled out a small jar of brownish-red goo. In fancy calligraphy, the label said: "*Chocolate, Strawberry and Balsamic Vinegar Jelly.*" The most horrible jelly flavor I could imagine—were they *trying* to recreate the taste of vomit?

Kai's face contorted in disappointment. "It's jelly?!" he screeched, in toddler fury. "That's not a good present! That's a terrible present!"

Samantha scolded him, "Kai, you shouldn't cry about a present!" Which is something I usually said to Kai.

But, in a moment of sudden clarity, I said, "You know what, Sam? Kai is right: jelly is a terrible present. We should ALL cry because this has been a terrible night and this…" I shouted to the raging river in the rain. "Is. The. Worst. Present. EVER!" There was no one on the dock with us, so we all threw back our heads and wailed dramatically, Charlton Heston-like, "It… Was… Jelly!" "The present was JELLY!" And then laughed very hard.

It felt good. Like we'd broken a spell. It dawned on me that we didn't *have* to take the boat back. We tossed the jelly in the trash and headed to the front of the restaurant to see if there were any non-water taxis available. Seeing none, I said, "That's fine, we'll call a cab." But before we took another step, I heard, "I can drive you."

We turned to see a uniformed limo driver standing in the eaves of the restaurant, trying to stay dry. He motioned to a black stretch limo parked a few feet away. "Where do you need to go?" I told him the name of our hotel. He shrugged, "I can take you. The guys who hired me just walked in to dinner. They'll be a couple hours at least." I didn't know what else to say except, "How much?" He waved me away, like, fuhgedaboutit! I insisted and he said, "I dunno, thirty bucks, then." Deal. The kids climbed giddily into the gorgeous car. The driver slid open the partition, happy that the kids were so happy. "You want the lights?" Before we could answer, the ceiling lit up with multi-colored, LED fireworks. I'd seen them before, and it always seemed cheesy. But here, in this limo that appeared out of nowhere like Cinderella's pumpkin, the light show seemed magical.

Our fortunes had changed. We were warm and sprawled out in a stretch-limo, as the Christmas-decorated buildings of Manhattan flew by. I felt very Angelina.

Back at the hotel, we changed into pajamas and ordered a movie and three entrees.

We shared everything on a room-service table rolled between the two beds. Then we giggled and pillow fought and fell asleep in one bed.

And though it was the only difficult part of our New York trip, it was the story we recounted the most—laughing every time we got to the part where we yelled in the rain, "It was jelly!" It still makes us laugh.

It's fitting that this all happened on Thanksgiving, because remembering it makes me grateful for the old man in the Monte Carlo and for the limo driver. Twice that night, a stranger saw we needed help and gave it to us. It's reassuring to know people like that exist.

I am so thankful for the awesome adventures I've had with my kids, and I'm comforted to know that the worst times can quickly turn into stories that make us laugh.

INSANELY GOOD STUFFING

INGREDIENTS

Neck and organ meat from turkey
6 oz. Portuguese sausage (also called linguiça) *
Salt and Pepper
1 stick (1/2 cup) butter
2 cups diced onion (approx. 2 medium onions)
2 cups diced celery
2 boxes Mrs. Cubbison's Traditional Stuffing – Seasoned
Milk

TO PREPARE

1. In a large (3-4 quart) saucepan, place organ meat, neck and plenty of water. Bring to a boil, then lower to simmer. Cook for at least half an hour. I like to cook it for a couple of hours, adding water if needed.

2. Melt butter in a sauté pan, then add onions and celery and generously season with salt and pepper. Sauté until vegetables are translucent. Pour into a very large mixing bowl.

3. Dice Portuguese sausage and lightly brown with any remaining butter in the sauté pan. Pour sausage and pan drippings into the bowl with the onions and celery.

4. Remove organ meats and neck from saucepan, saving the water. Dice organ meats (if you've cooked it long, it may fall apart). Pull meat from neck and dice. Add meats to bowl with vegetables and sausage.

5. Gradually add Mrs. Cubbison's Herb Seasoned Stuffing. I prefer to do this with gloved hands (Be careful that the meat and sausage are cool enough to touch!) Each box of Mrs. Cubbison's has two bags of bread crumbs. I add a bag at a time, tossing the mixture with my hands until it looks like a good ratio of breadcrumbs to the other stuff. Usually, I end up using a box and a half (three bags) It's good to have some breadcrumbs left over.

6. The mixture will be dry at this point. Add one cup of the water used to boil the organ meats and mix. Add splashes of milk (each splash approx. 2 tablespoons), mixing well between splashes until mixture is the consistency of uncooked bread pudding. I usually do two splashes of milk total. If mixture is too wet, add more breadcrumbs.

*(NOTE: Portuguese sausage or linguiça can be found in stores that carry Hawaiian or Brazilian foods. I've found linguica in regular grocery stores, but it's not common. It can also be ordered online. I have substituted spicy Italian sausage, and it's still pretty good—but the secret of this stuffing is the Portuguese sausage.)

TWO WAYS TO BAKE

BAKING DISH

Butter a casserole dish. Pour stuffing into dish and cover with foil. Bake at 350 degrees until thermometer at center reads 160 degrees F (approx. 20 minutes), uncover and bake an additional 10 minutes until the top is toasted and the center temp reads 165 degrees.

INSIDE THE TURKEY

I prefer to stuff my turkey. With this recipe, after stuffing a 20 lb. turkey, I still have a good bit left over that I cook in a casserole dish. Overwhelmingly, people prefer the stuffing from the turkey—but they finish the casserole dish when the other kind runs out.

Stuffing a turkey is not particularly hard, but it's a visual thing best learned from a YouTube video.

If you do stuff your turkey, be sure to follow safe stuffing guidelines, which include:

1. Use only cooked ingredients in your stuffing.
2. Stuff turkey just before roasting. Stuffing the night before is an absolute no-no.
3. Make sure the turkey cavities are fully-thawed.
4. Don't pack stuffing too tightly.
5. Stuffing should be 165 degrees at the center when done.

Strong to the Finich (Thanksgiving 2016)

by Ann Brown

Still reeling from the election, I had no desire to think about holiday recipes last fall.

When I am upset, I eat. But when I am devastated, I lose my appetite. I hadn't eaten a normal meal since the election. I had been stuffing my face, however, with eating-my-feelings kind of foods: huge jars of chocolate chip granola, bags of yam chips, fistfuls of Xanax.

For the first time ever in my life, Thanksgiving was not going to be about the food. I had no desire for it. I just wanted to sit out the holidays, drinking Cranberritinis (vodka, a splash of cranberry juice for urinary tract health, lime wedge) and blocking FB friends with whom I disagree politically. But my niece was hosting our family get-together and I adore my niece, I adore our family, and even if I was miserable, the election results weren't going to change just because I was living on junk food and booze.

Plus, people gotta eat. Strength for the years ahead. I planned to do a lot of marching.

My daughter-in-law is a vegetarian, as are a handful of others in our family, so I offered to make a vegetarian entrée. I had, in the past, relied on various expressions of tofu, which I placed defiantly right next to the turkey to shame the animal-eaters because I am competitive and self-righteous that way even though I eat meat. I am what you—and my shrink—might call a *self-loathing carnivore*.

There is nothing more satisfyingly self-righteous than placing a platter of tofu on the Thanksgiving table. Except, maybe, refusing to celebrate because, you know, genocide. There is that.

I have a long history with tofu, coming from my hippie days on a commune in Santa Cruz, California. Tofu was our everything. Well, that and henna. Those two things were emblematic of the times. We pretty much spent our days eating tofu and putting henna on our hair. Sometimes we got high and ate henna and put tofu in our hair.

Man, I really miss the old days. Now when I get high, I just watch PBS and do a collagen facial.

One autumn afternoon on the commune, we all went to this wellness guy in Big Sur who charged us a hundred dollars and told us to drink a half-cup of pure virgin olive oil every morning.

Unquestioningly, we paid up and went directly to the co-op to buy, like, fourteen gallons of pure virgin olive oil.

We began our wellness diet the next morning.

After a week, we were sitting around the kitchen table eating spinach pie, and Dan asked if any of us felt better since drinking the oil.

Nope.

Bummer.

I really *wanted* to feel different because we paid that guy a shitload of money for the consultation, and because how awesome would it be to simply drink oil every morning and have all your ailments disappear? Although, come to think of it, we were *twenty-somethings*, what the hell kind of ailments could we have had?

Oh. Right. Crabs. There's another story and another recipe for another time.

So we went around the kitchen table that night, admitting that none of us felt any different after eight days of drinking the oil. It was like a really sad version of the Chanukah story. That would be a perfect holiday for us Jewish melancholics, right? "We drank the oil for eight days. Nothing good happened. Okay, kids, presents! Ha ha. Just kidding. No presents. Brush your teeth and go to bed. You have school in the morning. Happy Chanukah."

The beautiful traditions of my people.

Just as Dan was putting the oil back up on the shelf, Lassie said, "You know, actually, I've been feeling pretty great."

She told us that before she started drinking the oil she had been sluggish and a little bit constipated. But now she had to say she was in tip-top shape.

"Okay," said Dan, putting the oil back on the table. "We'll keep it out, then."

"What's that?" Lassie asked.

"The *oil*. What do you think it is?"

Lassie shook her head. "That's not the oil I've been drinking."

She got up from the table, walked over to the cupboard over the stove and took

The Main Street gang. Soquel, California, 1974.

out a bottle of murky yellow oil.

"This is the oil," she said. "See? You wrote 'DON'T THROW THIS OIL AWAY' on the label."

Dan turned the bottle around. "It says 'USED TORTILLA OIL' on the other side," he said.

And oh how we laughed. We laughed and laughed until the landlord banged on our door because we were waking up the cows. Which, even if you aren't high, is funny enough to make you start laughing all over again.

I took a good look at Lassie. She did look good. Her hair was amazing, come to think of it. Thick and shiny. And her skin? Gorgeous. Her boobs even were perkier.

Dan was checking her out, too. They got married about a year after that night. I'm not saying it was the oil, but I'm not saying it wasn't.

Remembering that story, I made a mental note to call Dan and Lassie and see how they were doing. Also, I finally knew what I was going to make for the first post-election Thanksgiving:

Kale and spinach pie roll-ups. That's what we were eating the night we discovered that Lassie had been drinking old tortilla oil. We ate a ton of them. And, by God, we felt great the next morning. The world seemed brighter.

I'd been feeling a little bit constipated and sluggish, anticipating Inauguration Day. Maybe I needed some spinach and kale. Sprinkled with old tortilla oil. It couldn't hurt. My hair was pretty lackluster, truth be told. It had been a tough few weeks since November 8. I was so down. Even my boobs were low. So low.

I made the roll-ups and brought them to my niece's house for Thanksgiving. They were delicious.

The next morning, the world did not seem brighter. The election results were still the same. My skin was sallow. My hair was still the post-menopausal pubic hair transplant I've had to contend with for the past few years.

I called Lassie and asked her if she remembered the tortilla oil story. Dan got on the phone, too, and the three of us laughed and laughed, reminiscing about the old commune, remembering the old days, laughing and laughing until we woke up the cows.

SPINACH PIE ROLL-UPS

INGREDIENTS

Pie crust. You can make your own or you can buy the ready-made refrigerated kind and hide the box under your bed until recycling day.
For the Filling:
Three bags/boxes of frozen chopped spinach, thawed and drained
Three bags/boxes of frozen chopped kale
One container of ricotta cheese
Grated Parmesan cheese
Salt, pepper, nutmeg

TO PREPARE

1. After you have recovered from the physical demand of draining the frozen veggies and taken an Advil for your aching, frostbitten hands, mix it all with the container of ricotta cheese. Mix well until your arms ache and you cannot sing the first verse of Wilson Pickett's "In The Midnight Hour" without needing a hit of oxygen and a long nap.

SPINACH PIE ROLL-UPS (CONT.)

2. Rest. Hydrate. Sign online petitions to protect our Constitutional rights. Return to the kitchen.

3. Add Parmesan, salt, pepper, nutmeg to the mixture. Keep tasting until you get it right. You might have to add more spinach, kale and ricotta if you eat the whole thing while tasting. Not that it ever happened to me. You can also shake in some dried chili pepper flakes.

4. When the mixture is really tasty, spread it out over the rolled-out pie dough. The mixture should be about ¼ to ½ inch thick on the dough.

5. Carefully roll up the dough like a cigar, a sushi roll, a fatty, whatever your reference might be.

6. Brush egg wash over the top of the roll, and place on a lightly greased baking pan. You can sprinkle some herbs on the top. Or not. Whatev.

7. Bake at 350 degrees for around 25–30 minutes.

8. Go back to bed and turn on the TV. Watch a Hallmark Channel Christmas movie. Admit that you—a hardass liberal Jewish activist—love those movies more than anything. You just want to get into a pair of flannel jammies, have a cup of cocoa and imagine you lived in Christmasville and everyone was nice and the man who you picked up hitchhiking was actually Santa and he made all your wishes come true. You only need to watch around 25–30 minutes of the movie to get the benefits.

9. Take the roll-ups out of the oven. Let them rest for at least a half hour. You rest, too. Baking is hard.

10. To serve, slice the rolls into larger-than-bite-sized pieces. You can eat it warm, room temp, cold or frozen, depending on your hunger level.

Bloat Sweet Bloat

by Asmita Paranjape

Golden sands. Vibrantly blue waters. Gently tousled hair.

Why is everyone but me at a beach?

My ass freezes outside Logan Airport, at 6 am, in my Forever21 leggings, while I scroll past beach after beach on Instagram as I wait for my dad to pick me up. After moving to LA, I no longer have the wardrobe for an east coast winter. To my left, stand unfazed passengers, sipping iced coffees with a Bostonian grit I'd lost the moment I Ubered to a barre class. To combat the cold, I list all the great things I can do at home in Massachusetts that I can't do anywhere else, like writing all day in a quiet house, never leaving said quiet house, or buying very reasonably-priced sneakers on clearance at the New Balance Factory Store.

My dad and I drive home, the car ride filled with every detail of our new family cell phone plan. I greet my mother and finally accept her fourth offer of tea. She flaunts all of the WhatsApp group chats she's joined, and shows me what feels like every Indian man on the planet. I try not to yawn. My parents always insist on red-eye flights from Pacific to Eastern, so that I can uncomfortably nod off for six hours while experiencing the privilege of losing nine.

Before submitting to the magnetic pull of my bed, I tell my mom that I've washed my clothes before packing them—a statement artfully crafted with the subtext of both "Look how much I've matured at college!" and "Please don't wash my clothes, there are almost definitely headphones in the pockets and I have absolutely no other pairs." After a few hours, I groggily blink awake to my dad standing over me. "I scheduled you a dentist appointment for tomorrow at 8:00 AM." My dad wastes no time. I begin to unpack as my mother hovers. "Do you have enough underwear?" she asks with a curious blend of affection and accusation. She extends a handful of beige, high-waisted, plastic-value-pack granny panties. "You know, I have a few pairs that wouldn't fit me now."

I've read that as you grow older, your relationship with your parents evolves. Though I have only evidence to the contrary, I will myself into viewing her blatant disregard for personal boundaries as a DIY recycling effort. "Thanks, Mom. I think I'm all set on the underwear front," I respond.

This interaction is thankfully cut short once the scent of sabudana kichidi makes its way through the house. Sabudana is essentially spongy tapioca, and kichidi is a hash-like preparation of rice and legumes. As Wikipedia condescendingly puts it, "For infants and sick persons or during fasts, Sabudana is considered an acceptable form of nutrition." Naturally, it is my and my brother's favorite dish. My brother, however, was not home with us at the time, which did not stop my dad from preparing enough to feed a pack of lions—assuming those lions just fuckin' loved carbs. After becoming empty nesters, my parents lost the gauge on how much one additional human being, no taller than five feet, might add to their portion sizes.

Every time I try to eat anything that wouldn't put a dent in the heap of sabudana kichidi, my dad asks, "Why are you eating that when we have real food?" So I stuff spoonful after spoonful of my former favorite food, the memory of pizza, hummus, or any other flavor palate merely an elusive fantasy.

The week goes by, and I avoid the items on my to-do list. On the last day, the adrenaline kicks in. I cross off to-dos left and right. Any semblance of a balanced or fun vacation has gone out the window in favor of desperate productivity. The last item: buy some very reasonably-priced sneakers at the New Balance Factory Outlet Store. Shit. It's 4pm. The store closes at 5pm.

I race to change out of the athletic shorts with built-in underwear that I'd worn as purported "motivation" to burn off the mounds of little starchy balls I've eaten in the past week. In actuality, the shorts were just the only bottoms that didn't squeeze my bloated belly. I soon stop short...*Where are my clothes?*

They're gone.I rush to the basement to confirm my fears: everything is mid-wash-cycle.I return to my room to find only two articles of clothing: the skin-tight jeans from junior year of high school...and my mother's beige, high-waisted, plastic-value-pack granny panties. Time slows. *Did she...plan this?* It's 4:15. There is no time. I quell my swelling rage as I suck in my tapioca tummy, pulling the tightest pair of jeans I've ever owned over the loosest underwear I've ever been duped into wearing. I only remember there's a hole in the crotch of the pants after I step out into the thirty degree weather. And again while I try on sneakers in front of parents and their children at the goddamn New Balance Factory Outlet Store.In the car, my head shakes involuntarily with familiar feelings of frustration and rage. Why did my mother feel such a specific need to micromanage the most personal aspects of my life? When would this "relationship evolution" I've been hearing so much about occur? What did slight hunger use to feel like?

I return home, ready to take a stand, when I see my clothes, miraculously returned, immaculately laundered, and crisply folded, like the closing statement of a case she's already won. The next day we leave for the airport. I've been commuting between coasts for years, but my parents still run through a frantic checklist as if I'm traveling for the first time. I hug them goodbye and promise to call them when I land. Alone again, I wait in the TSA line, scrolling past beach after beach on my Instagram feed. "Miss, I think you're overweight." "Excuse me?" "Your bag, miss. Either take something out, or check it as baggage." Confused but relieved, I leaf through my bag. Neatly buried under my clothing are Tupperwares of sabudana khichidi, and my mother's goddamn underwear.

For a moment I stare at the trashcan next to me, and then I make a decision. I take out a sweatshirt and a pair of baggy sweatpants, and put them on over my clothes, out of the eye line of the TSA agent. Sweating, I waddle through security, embarrassingly bloated and overdressed compared to the other Los Angeles passengers—but with my parents still in my backpack.

SABUDANA KHICIDI

INGREDIENTS

*1 cup Sabudana **
1 cup Peanuts
Salt
Sugar
Tumeric
*Hing (also known as Asafetida) ***
Chilli Pepper

Optional:
Lemon Juice
Cilantro, Coconut
Yogurt
*Sweet Lime Pickle ***
*Found at any Indian grocery store

SABUDANA KHICIDI (CONT.)

TO PREPARE

1. Wash the grains a few times until the water you're soaking the grains in is clear.
2. Let them soak for four hours. In order to make sure the grains don't clump together, stir them occasionally, or drain the water and fill with fresh water about half way through those four hours (since they are so starchy).
3. Drain and keep them in the strainer for at least 10 minutes, at which point you should be able to mash one grain easily between your fingers.
4. Roughly blend 1 cup of peanuts.
5. Add blended peanuts, a pinch of salt, a tsp of sugar and mix with a spoon or paddle.
6. Heat 1 tbsp oil and add 1 tsp mustard seeds.
7. When the seeds pop, add 1/2 tsp hing (asafetida), 1/2 tsp turmeric, and 1 cut up chili pepper.
8. When chili pepper curls up, add the Sabudana mix and lower heat to medium.
9. Cover. Stir every few minutes. It will steam up with the contained moisture.
10. If it starts browning at the bottom, add a tsp of water and let it steam for ~ 20 minutes.
11. (Optional) Add 1 tsp lemon juice to taste.
12. (Optional) Dress with cilantro, grated coconut or grated raw mango.
13. (Optional) Serve with a dollop of yogurt and sweet lime pickle.

While Cooking Spaghetti

by Liza Donnelly

When I was little, I had trouble saying the word "spaghetti." This fact really has little to do with my story. Except the word—which finally became accessible to me, as did the cooking of the dish itself—is part of my story.

In second grade (back when, or whenever that was, I couldn't say "spaghetti"), little did I know that, years later, I would live in Rome—the Capital of Spaghetti. My father had decided that we would live in Italy for a year, and that it would be good for the whole family. I didn't agree. Not one to easily cry, I cried; after all, I had just made the gut-wrenching decision to try out for cheerleading (it was going to be my brave attempt to become "popular").

So off we went. I attended the American School in Rome, my older sister studied in Perugia, and my parents played. My father was on sabbatical, and planned to write; my mother took Italian cooking classes, which I found very brave of her. She took notes in a little green Italian notebook. I still have the notebook.

All my life in our suburban Washington, DC home, my mother did the cooking. My father was a doctor, and I never ever saw him cook anything. It was the traditional split of that time—housewife cooks, husband and kids eat.

The trip to Italy shook things up. I immediately loved being in Rome; it was of course radically different from the safe and predictable life I hadn't wanted to part with. I felt like an adventurer, part of a generation of young people who were discovering Europe, escaping a status quo in the US that we didn't trust. I became an independent teenager and the time in Rome helped me to continue to grow into the artist I was to become. I fell in love with Jimmy Hendrix and flea markets. I drew all the time and drew cartoons of Italians; as an "outsider" it was easier to draw cartoons of others.

My desire to be popular disappeared completely; in fact I felt like a rebel in my own quiet way. I was evolving, and apparently so was my father.

He started cooking. I don't remember what he cooked; it was that he cooked at all that I noticed. My father had been a chemist, a high school science teacher, a principal, and now an internist, so it's not that he was a rigid person. But the move to cooking reflected a side of him that only in retrospect I really understood.

By the age of sixteen, I was used to going to baseball games and golf driving ranges with my father; we also went fishing together and sometimes played lacrosse and badminton. This may not seem unusual for a father to do with his daughter today, but it sort of was unusual in the 1960's. Since I have a sister, there was a running joke in our family that my father had wanted a son. But that wasn't it—these things we did together were coming from a different sensibility.

When my father took up cooking at the age of forty, it was something husbands and breadwinners rarely did at that time, but he didn't care about perceptions. And this is a key approach to life that I got from him. First from example—exploring what work he really cared about, living in Italy for a year, taking up cooking—all things that show a person open to new experiences. And secondly, from his taking me to do things as a kid that fathers normally would not do with their daughters. In essence, he was saying to me, you can be whoever you want; you do not have to follow socially accepted norms or gender stereotypes. Be who you are, not what the world expects of you. Particularly as a woman.

I became a good cook mostly through osmosis from my mother. She had ease with food and a degree of creativity, which I inherited; she never "taught" me. Although I still have her Italian notebook of recipes and notations from her Italian cooking

classes, I have never used it. My father was not a natural cook, but he grew to love it while we were in Rome, and taught me the two recipes he picked up there: spaghetti carbonara and spaghetti alio olio.

Since then, I have cooked these two dishes often. My father was not a demonstratively affectionate person; in that way, he fit the male stereotype of his generation. But by cooking, by bucking the male stereotype in a small way, he showed me how to become my own person. Every time I make those spaghetti dishes, I think of him and what he and I shared until he died two years ago. Every time I make them, I feel the joy he shared by creating food.

The year in Italy opened me up to possibilities, to learning how to explore and be open to change. I never again wanted to be a cheerleader; I didn't want to be anything that others expected of me. I could be my own person and follow my dreams. All while cooking spaghetti carbonara.

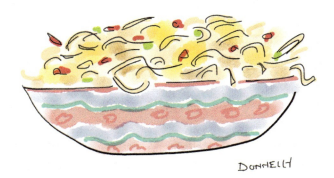

DONNELLY

SPAGHETTI CARBONARA

INGREDIENTS

1 box of long pasta of your choice
1-2 cloves of garlic
2 T of olive oil
4 eggs
2-3 slices of prosciutto or bacon (can be vegetarian bacon)
¾ c parsley
ground pepper
salt

TO PREPARE

I have never written this down, so bear with me.

1. Put a large pot of salted water on to boil.

2. Crack four eggs into a bowl and whisk until blended. Set aside.

3. Chop about ¾ cup of parsley. Set aside.

4. In a rather large skillet, heat a few tablespoons of olive oil and add one large clove (or two, if you like garlic) of smashed garlic. Sauté for a few minutes before it gets brown.

5. Meanwhile, if you are not vegetarian, you can slice up the prosciutto (or you can use bacon: pork, turkey or otherwise) into small pieces and throw in the pan with the garlic. Use however much you want—the equivalent of 3 strips of bacon, I guess. Don't overcook the meat. Turn off the heat.

6. When your pasta water is boiling, throw in the pasta—a whole box is fine. You can use regular pasta, linguine, or angel hair. Totally up to you.

7. When pasta is al dente, strain it and reserve a cup of the water from the pot off to the side.

8. Immediately (you want the pasta to be very hot) pour the strained pasta into the large skillet with the garlic and prosciutto. Stir to mix and add the beaten eggs.

9. In small amounts, pour a little of the reserved pasta water to add a little moisture to the mixture. Don't dump it all in, dribble it to see how much you need, if any.

Technically, there should be on NO heat on this skillet at all (ideally it will still be warm from when you cooked the prosciutto) —the hot pasta should cook the egg. But often I turn the heat on low to slightly cook the egg. You don't want to overcook the egg—it shouldn't be clumps of scrambled eggs, should just coat the pasta nicely. But also you don't want raw egg either. It's tricky, but you can do it.

10. Add fresh ground pepper and the parsley as garnish on top.

I like to bring the large skillet to the table and serve the pasta there!

FISH, FOWL, AND MEAT
(THE OTHER VEGETABLES)

Kimberly's Famous Santa Monica Salmon

Steve's Salmon

Gefilte Fish à la Grandma Esther

Chicken and Shells

Chicken Pot Pie

Turkey Blues, a poem

Mom's Tacos

Roasted Opossum

Jiaozi

Funeral Casserole

Sales at Loehmann's

By Kimberly Brooks

I learned how to cook from my mother. And my mother loves to save. It doesn't matter what, whether it's photographs or time or money, but nothing drives her more crazy than wasting any of it. An ardent sifter of the racks at the now defunct Loehmann's Department store, she once arrived with a 50% off coupon, went to the 70% discount rack which was an additional 25% off and they practically paid her to leave with bags of clothes from which she assembled inspiringly fashionable outfits.

The same zany frugality extends to her cooking. She constantly strives for the most fabulous dish with the fewest ingredients. As I was learning to cook, she would call me up and announce, "I just made the best easiest salad: garbanzo beans, toasted pine nuts, avocados and cherry tomatoes, balsamic vinaigrette. That's it." Or try this one: "Cherry tomatoes, toasted sesame seed oil, lemon pepper, that's it." Or, for Passover, "You must make my brisket -- one brisket, two red onions, 1 bag of carrots, potatoes, one jar of heinz chili sauce, put it in the oven at 300 for six hours—that's it." When I was in college, I told her I absolutely loved a cream sauce she made for a salmon. "Sour cream, one stick of butter and dried tarragon, in a saute pan—that's it." The next time she went to Costco she bought me a an entire quart of tarragon in case I wanted to make it myself. I had that quart for the next four years.

One day, when my husband and I were dating, I thought i would surprise him with my mother's famous poppy seed cake.

"It only has four ingredients!" I proudly exclaimed. I whipped it up, threw it in a bundt pan and voila, behold the creamiest, most fabulous cake he had ever had.

"This is unbelievable," he said. "What are the four ingredients?"

"Easy!" I replied. "One tub of sour cream, one cup of poppy seeds, four eggs, and one box of Betty Crocker Yellow Cake Mix. That's it!"

He picked up the box of Betty Crocker Yellow Cake Mix and slowly read all forty two ingredients, something he once did on Johnny Carson with a tub of whipped cream.

I love fresh ingredients and still make all my mother's simple healthy snacks for my kids: slices of Granny Smith apples with sharp cheddar cheese, celery and peanut butter, a halved avocado with a dollop of mayonnaise in the pit. I invented this dish because I love both poached and crispy skinned salmon and figured out a way to create both at once, with vegetables, all in the same baking dish! There are never leftovers!

KIMBERLY'S FAMOUS
SANTA MONICA SALMON

Serves 4

INGREDIENTS

2 lbs farm-raised salmon with skin
1 bunch of dill
1 carton of cherry tomatoes
1 lb green beans
1 cup of white wine, any kind
3 lemons
A few pinches of black lava salt (any salt will do)
That's it!

TO PREPARE

Preheat the oven to 350 degrees.

1. In a glass baking dish, create layers in order: green beans, cherry tomatoes and salmon on top, skin side up. Rearrange the cherry tomatoes to prop up the lower parts of the filet so that the surface of the skin is as even as it can be. Cluster a few sprigs of dill at one side only for flavor. Add 2 cups of white wine and fill the rest with water so it reaches just below the skin. Quarter and squeeze a lemon in the water and tuck it amongst the crevices of the salmon. Cover with tin foil. Put in the fridge for as long as 24 hours or as little as thirty minutes.

2. Bake on the top tray of your oven for 30 minutes.

3. Remove baking dish from oven, remove tin foil and pour off a majority of the poaching liquid in the sink.

4. Put back in the oven and put it on broil for five minutes. Watch the skin bubble and get crispy.

5. Remove the baking dish from the oven.

6. Spread the remaining bushel of dill on a large serving platter. Place the salmon on the dill and surround with deliciously poached cherry tomatoes and green beans. Quarter another lemon and squeeze all over the salmon. Sprinkle lava salt (although any salt will do) and cut crispy skin with a serrated steak knife into the desired portions. Add lemon wedges for garnish.

*I can prepare this dish in the morning or night before as the longer the salmon lives in the poaching liquid the tastier the fish. If the fish is not coming from the refrigerator, deduct ten minutes from the baking/poaching time. Pair it my version of the world's best easiest salad: Arugula, watermelon chunks, feta cheese, candied pecans, balsamic vinaigrette, that's it!

Steve's Salmon

by Jeb Sharp

Recently a friend arrived from Sitka, Alaska with a bag of frozen shrimp wrapped in a towel inside her suitcase. Shrimp that I knew, long before I tasted them, would be sweet and succulent, uncontaminated by either pollution or slave labor. Shrimp from the relatively pristine waters of Southeast Alaska. Their taste would take me back, however fleetingly, to my own time in Sitka, a small town with a rich Native history and a surprising Russian one, nestled on the edge of Baranof Island in the northern Alexander Archipelago.

I was just starting out in public radio, learning news reporting at the local station. It was a time and place of unlocked doors and deep friendships; many of us were far away from our loved ones in the Lower 48. My first Christmas there, I encountered a potluck feast the likes of which I haven't seen before or since—white king salmon, Dungeness crab, venison backstrap, all harvested by people seated at the table. I was new to Alaska and the bounties of subsistence hunting and fishing. But I was taken with it, and with my new life in rubber boots in a temperate rainforest.

In the end, I stayed just two years. I was restless in those days, never satisfied, grass-is-always-greener. I was twenty-something after all. Looking back, I can't believe how little I bothered to learn.

Don't get me wrong—I earned my journalism stripes. I learned how to pull all-nighters writing stories after city council and school board meetings on alternate Tuesdays; I learned the craft of radio, cutting and splicing quarter-inch audio tape on an old analog reel-to-reel machine. I learned how to report, and hold city officials accountable when they trucked our carefully rinsed cans and bottles to the municipal incinerator rather than explain to their constituents that the bottom had fallen out of the recyclables market, and it no longer made sense to ship them south.

But there was a lot I didn't learn. Useful life skills like hunting, fishing, gathering, even cooking. I have a feeling that if I had known how to pay attention I could have learned more in two years there than I could learn in a whole lifetime of public radio listening.

I was reminded of this when I had to text my friend a few weeks after her visit to ask for her favorite shrimp recipes. That in turn reminded me of another cooking experience, 23 years before.

I had just left Sitka for good, giving notice at my radio job and driving my car onto the ferry for the trip south, once again entranced by the land and seascapes of the Inside Passage on the way down to Washington State, and then driving with my ancient dog through Oregon and northern California to San Francisco, where I would move back in with the person I was in love with two years before I left for Alaska, as if that could ever work. And indeed it didn't.

Here's where the memory is fuzzy. Somehow I acquired a beautiful wild king salmon. Did I bring it on ice from Sitka? Did I buy it at Pike's Place in Seattle? At any rate, I was back in San Francisco and ready to present a party of friends with beautiful fillets of fish. And I suddenly realized I had no idea how to cook it. None. Post-Alaska shame, as if the whole big adventure north had never happened. What had I been thinking? So I called Steve, the man who had hired me for that first radio gig. The first person I met when I touched down on Alaskan soil for my job interview. The guy who trained and mentored me. Whose family had me over for countless meals. Who collected fine wine and grilled a tender steak, and knew his way around a fillet of salmon.

"It's easy," he told me. "Chop tons of garlic and ginger. Add equal amounts of olive oil and soy sauce. Lay the piece of fish down into the marinade, flesh side down, skin side up. Let it soak a while. Take the fish out and lay it skin side down, flesh side up on a big piece of aluminum foil. Wrap the fish up and put the whole package on the grill or simply bake it in the oven. Take a peek once in a while. Until white milk seeps out of the flesh and translucent turns to opaque. Then it's done."

I'm paraphrasing—I don't remember the actual words he used. I remember his voice almost perfectly. He was a radio guy. But somehow the cadence is gone. I'm no longer sure exactly how he would have phrased his instructions. What I remember is probably just the way my own brain has interpreted and distilled those original directions. In any case that's how they translate years later, years of passing on the recipe to other people who oohh and aahh over it. The moistness, the taste, the simplicity. My mother passes on the recipe too, but she calls it "Jeb's salmon." I, of course, call it "Steve's salmon." Who knows where he got the recipe. Maybe its teriyaki flavor is anathema to real Sitka salmon cooks; I don't know. But I treasure it, and it has never failed me.

The recipe took on new meaning when Steve died far too young in a bike accident a few years ago. I still make it and I still pass it on. But what once tasted of youthful adventure now reminds me of everything that eludes us as we age. He was always supposed to be there when I went back.

STEVE'S SALMON

INGREDIENTS

Fillet of wild salmon
Fresh ginger, finely chopped
Garlic cloves, finely chopped
Olive Oil
Soy Sauce

TO PREPARE

Preheat oven to 350 degrees

1. Chop enough garlic and ginger to cover the bottom of a Pyrex baking dish or other convenient container.
2. Lay the fillet flesh down, skin up, on top of the ginger and garlic pieces.
3. Add equal amounts of olive oil and soy sauce until bottom of pan is just covered and fish is slightly submerged.
4. When oven is hot and fillet has had a good soak, remove fish from marinade and place skin side down on big piece of aluminum foil.
5. Spoon some of the extra garlic and ginger back on top of the fish.
6. Fold extra tin foil over the fish to make a package.
7. Place the whole thing in a roasting dish or on a thick baking sheet (I like to have dish or sheet already in the oven so the bottom of the fish gets slightly seared when you place it on the hot surface). Or even better, cook on an outdoor grill.

Check in 20 minutes and keep checking until you see what looks like milk seeping out of the fish or the flesh is opaque all the way through. (But only just—don't overcook as it will keep cooking after you take it out.)

The fish will separate easily from the skin once it's cooked. Just lift gently with a spatula and serve.

I'm My Own Grandma

by Susan Senator

I don't believe in reincarnation, exactly, but I do believe in something like it. The renewal, or recycling of people. Especially when it comes to my paternal grandmother, Esther Senator Gross. I think Grandma is still here, though not as some unhappy waif-like ghost. She may have been reincarnated as a hawk. A carnivorous, formidable, voracious, watchful big bird with a gigantic breast. An animal that will fight to the death for what it loves.

It makes perfect sense to me that she comes by every once in a while, staring me down with that terrible hawk eye or circling overhead on certain particularly difficult times in my life. The time I was horribly depressed, when I rode my bike without a helmet in a kind of passive-aggressive attempt to hurt myself. While resting at the top of a big hill, I looked up and there, right across the street not ten feet away was a large hawk, fixing me in its crosshairs. In that anguished moment, I thought of Grandma. I put on my helmet.

But she's not always in hawk form. She's in certain places, like my dreams, or I'll catch a glimpse of her across a busy street. When I look again, of course, it's someone else.

I can't separate memories of Grandma from thinking about the trip down to Brooklyn, where she used to live—a ride that was tight with traffic and tension. As we'd get closer to New York, the discomfort worsened, as roads narrowed and cars got way too close. My ears rang with the noise of horns and my dad would start to swear.

There was a startling drama as we got closer to Grandma's: The chiarascuro of sunlight disappearing into darkness as we entered the Battery Tunnel. The sudden sea of skyscrapers. The Cross Bronx Expressway, with its layers of curved concrete—it looked like a roller coaster to me the first time I saw it. Once we left the highway behind and dove beneath the elevated trains, I knew we were close. I don't remember much about her actual neighborhood, but I do remember the lobby of her building, dim and heavy with an oily cooking chickeny smell, so dense that the air seemed to have weight to it. Her world was so different from the clean fresh air of my childhood home in suburban Connecticut—so fleshy and close.

Intensity was what Grandma was all about. It drew me to her while repelling me at the same time. There was no one like her. Her hair bloomed from her head in a stiff blond bouffant. She used orange lipstick with the zeal of a toddler with a crayon. She wore gold mules that made her meaty feet puff out over the sides like a French pastry. Her favorite color was pink. Sometimes she felt like an octopus, with long wiggly arms that would frequently grab me and pull me onto her lap. She'd kiss me and kiss me but then she'd suddenly start talking about how I had to beware of strangers and not "go riding in no cars with no one." There was a whole litany of

*Grandma with my sister Laura and me, when we stayed
with her in the Catskills. I'm on the right.*

terrible things that could happen to me, apparently, and she was compelled to spew them every single time she saw me. Then, just as quickly she would spring back to shining her smile on me like sun from behind clouds—until I would break one of her gilded shepherdess statues. Her anger was fast and furious, sudden wrath-of-God style. But I was bewildered by the mood swing, always caught off guard because— what else could I, an active, impulsive child do? She had nothing else to play with in her apartment other than two bottle openers with walnut heads, a boy and a girl. I'm not sure why I didn't have my own toys with me on these visits. Needless to say, they were boring and tiring, until I—or Grandma—stirred things up. Then almost immediately after the yelling she'd be beaming at me. Then we'd eat the predictable dinner of chicken soup and roasted chicken.

Grandma's seder was a highlight of my childhood, a combination of the archaic, the bizarre, and the chaotic. The livingroom would be filled with a long table, so crowded that sometimes you could not fit both of your legs underneath. Grandma hosted her sisters and their families, as well as any friend who was alone for the holidays. She would simply force in one more chair.

The old men—the grandfathers and great-uncles—all in black, sat at one end. The kids sat at the other. The women usually stood and helped Grandma serve the many courses. It seemed like there was no beginning or end to the seder. There would be the constant rumble of the men muttering the prayers quickly, rocking and bobbing their yarmulkah-ed heads while we laughed at them and the strangeness of the Hebrew. My sister Laura and I created a code that we shared with the cousins there, to alert them covertly about something funny one of the old people was doing. Maybe Uncle Joe was moving his toothless mouth up and down. We'd say "Jisha," the code for " look at Joe" and erupt in illicit laughter.

One particular seder, my cousin Randy—the oldest of the kids—piled horseradish onto a piece of matzah and then washed it down with wine, causing him to turn bright red. I didn't eat the burning horseradish that was part of the seder, but the grownups ate it with Grandma's gefilte fish. Those odd pale fish balls were something I only saw at Grandma's. She made them herself, something the adults made a big deal of. But they smelled like stale air and had a wiggly gold jelly clinging to them— the schmaltz, or fat. None of the kids would eat them.

In the 1970's, Grandma moved to Fort Lauderdale, and I saw her a lot less. I didn't care at that time, because I was in my teens and a bit self-absorbed in the normal teenage way. I visited her once a year, flying down with my sister for the hot weather. My other grandmother lived nearby and we stayed with her, much to Grandma's dismay. We'd see Grandma for a meal a day, but that was it.

"What's she got over there, the Brooklyn Bridge?" Grandma once asked. Then, with a sigh she said, "Well, if I'm only gonna get a crumb, I'll take a crumb." Laura and I looked at each other, trying not to laugh, just like when we were kids.

It wasn't until I became a mother myself that I stopped laughing at Grandma. I knew something was wrong with Nat, my firstborn, but I could not put my finger on it. No one else saw what I saw, not even the pediatrician, and so I thought I was crazy. But Nat was not acting at all the way babies were supposed to act—no interest in toys, no functional language, no curiosity in other children. My days were filled with a nauseating, lonely worry.

Eventually we learned that Nat had autism, and nothing was the same after that. I had to figure out how to be a mother, how to take care of a very complicated little person, how to give my entire self over to him. I badly needed support, and my family rose up in force, fully embracing Nat, and all that he brought. I guess I started seeing people differently, perhaps more compassionately. Including Grandma. Suddenly she was an actual person, rather than a cartoon. A passionate woman who loved with a sloppy, juicy love and was not afraid to show it. She was so real. And I needed that kind of force in my life.

Grandma, of course, was up to the task of loving Nat. My beautiful Nat, who looked like my Dad as a baby, was her first great-grandchild and had completely captured her heart. "He's just a little slow," she'd say, batting away the scary diagnosis. It wasn't exactly true, yet it did comfort me to see Nat in this more benign, forgiving light. I clung to that simple, elemental love. I started feeling closer to her, appreciative of her color, her noise, her emotional heft. I started writing her letters, sending her little presents.

I visited her in Florida, bringing my children with me so she could know them. And that was all she needed, it seemed, to be happy. I remember her looking from Nat, to his baby brother Max, just drinking them in, saying, "My millions! One, two." And then she remembered I was there and said, "And you're the thoid." I laughed but now I was on her side as much as she was on mine. She was so unabashedly in love with us. And now that I knew how it felt to be torn wide open by children, I could only imagine how joyful great-grandchildren must feel.

When Grandma was 92, I got a call from my mom telling me that Grandma was slipping away. My heart seized up and after I hung up I said aloud, "No! Not yet, Grandma!" My whole body felt like it was fighting for her. And she did hang on, for another year, but with some alarming falls and bouts of congestive heart failure. I made arrangements to visit her in Florida, in the assisted living facility where she had recently and reluctantly moved. Her nose was bandaged from her latest fall and she gestured to it, laughing at herself and saying, "Such an idiot." But I didn't want to hear it. I couldn't stand her making fun of herself. And I couldn't bear how diminished she was. Where was the big body? The helmet of hair? I looked at her shoes. She had on plain sneakers, of all things.

When I said goodbye to her, I knew it was really goodbye. I was crying. She snickered and said something in Yiddish, something like, "Look at this one." She died soon after that. This time we all made the trip down to Florida, for her funeral.

My Aunt Rhoda got up to say the eulogy for her mother. I listened in a daze, until I heard Aunt Rhoda saying "... and the year before she died, when we thought we were losing her, afterwards she told me she actually heard someone telling her to hang on, a voice saying 'not yet!'"

I felt chills. I looked around to see if anyone else was shocked by this. I whispered to Laura, "That was *me!* I was the one who told her not to die yet! She must have heard me somehow—" But I knew I sounded crazy.

And yet. Something big, incomprehensible, and wonderful had occurred—though not at the knowable physical level, but soul-to-soul. Maybe it had been happening all along, threads of Grandma slowly getting tied up with bits of me. After all, once she was gone, I was the one who took her china shepherdesses; I wear her rhinestone pin; I carry around her silver sequined purse; my favorite color is now hot pink; I never wear sensible shoes; I host the Passover seder at my own crowded table. And I now have Grandma's gefilte fish recipe.

My sister often laughs at me and my emotional excesses and says I *am* Grandma. Well, maybe. But not entirely. I watch my weight like, well, a hawk, because of course I take after that top-heavy side of the family. And my swelling stormy moods are controlled therapeutically.

Several years ago, my son Max, now 25, moved to Brooklyn. Tall, thin, easygoing, he lives there because it's even *more* hip than Manhattan. My parents shake their heads. Brooklyn, cool? But Max is a filmmaker from NYU, he knows cool. Max's neighborhood, though, is not quite hip yet, which is good because he can't afford that. Driving in to see him for the first time, we fought traffic for hours, it seemed. We parked near those same elevated trains. On the streets walked black-clothed Orthodox Jews, who likely mutter Hebrew at their Passover seders.

Max knows no Hebrew, and he barely remembers Grandma Esther Gross. But the first time I visited him, as I stepped into the lobby of his dimly lit apartment building, I swear I could smell Grandma's cooking oil and roasted chicken.

Ned –

Please forward this to Susan. I hope you are doing well.
Love,
Aunt Rhoda

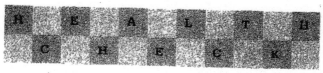

HEALTH
CHECK

<u>Gefulte Fish</u> – a la Grandma Esther

4 lb white fish
2 lb carp
2 lb yellow pike
6 med. onions, ~~2 carrots~~
2-3 carrots, 2 stalks celery
4 eggs
1 c. water
2½ tsp salt, ⅜ tsp pepper, 4 tsp sugar – motzah meal (1 cup), oil

(1) Put into pot - of warm water
2 onions, 2 carrots, bones, celery

(2) Grind fish, 2 onions, 1 stalk celery, 1 carrot

(3) In bowl add eggs + sugar salt pepper + ground mixture. Stir in motzah meal + ¾ c oil. Refrigerate

(4) form oval balls and gently put into boiling water (number 1) + simmer 2 hours.

(5) Remove are refrigerate balls + veggies – throw out bones

Served chilled with horseradish

Grandma's Gefilte Fish

GEFILTE FISH À LA GRANDMA ESTHER

INGREDIENTS

4 lbs. white fish
2 lbs. carp
2 lbs. yellow pike
6 medium onions
2–3 carrots
2 stalks celery
4 eggs
1 cup water
2 ½ tsp salt
3/8th tsp pepper
4 tsp sugar + matzo meal
1 cup oil

TO PREPARE

1. Remove bones from fish. Save bones.
2. Put into pot of warm water, the following: 2 onions, 2 carrots, fish bones and celery.
3. Grind fish with 2 onions, 1 carrot, 1 stalk of celery
4. In a bowl, add the following: eggs, sugar, salt, pepper, and ground (fish) mixture.
5. Add matzo meal and ¾ cup oil. Refrigerate.
6. Form oval balls and gently put into boiling water and simmer for 2 hours *(editors' note: the recipe card says "(number 1)" after the words "boiling water." The author and editors have no idea why.)*
7. Remove from pot and refrigerate fish balls and veggies. Discard bones. *(editor's note: MY Grandma Esther used to bury the fish bones in the garden for fertilizer. She had an awesome garden ~AB)*
8. Serve chilled with horseradish.

A Meal for All Seasons

by Lisa Grace Lednicer

Three months after graduating from college, I moved to a cramped apartment on the west coast of Florida. Somewhat improbably, I had landed a job at a great newspaper, and I was thrown immediately into writing about the minutiae of local government. My floundering efforts to understand budgets, police procedures and the concerns of community activists, who scolded me for doing a terrible job covering their town, left me constantly on edge.

The only place I managed to find relief from my first-job angst was in the kitchen. No one in my family would have guessed that I would find solace in cooking. I had left home with no culinary skills to speak of, because the kitchen was my mother's domain, and she shooed me away when I wouldn't follow her exacting instructions. As a teenager, I bucked her efforts to teach me how to cook, and we spent a fair amount of time yelling at one another. I was determined to have a career *and* a beautiful home *and* elegant dinners, and I just assumed that I'd figure out on my own how to do so.

And then I found myself far from home, wobbling in my career and desperately wanting to succeed at single life. I found a recipe for pastitsio, which I had sampled at festivals in the predominantly Greek community that I covered, and I started baking banana bread, braising swordfish, and blending chickpeas, paprika and lemon juice into hummus. The act of following a recipe down to the letter—I was too scared to deviate by even a quarter-teaspoon—and getting the same result every time was wonderfully reassuring, a way of telling myself that at least I was competent in *one* area of my life. Eventually I grew confident enough to start throwing small dinner parties, adding fish stew and cornbread to my repertoire.

But I found myself returning again and again to one particular dish: baked chicken with shell-shaped pasta. It was easy to make—a bit of seasoned salt, paprika, dried parsley, salt and pepper, butter—and it had been my favorite dish growing up, the one I always requested for my birthday. My mom fancied it up for guests by adding pats of jam to the top of the chicken before baking it, but I preferred the simpler original version. I made it a lot for myself in Florida, and it always tasted like home.

And then, suddenly, the job ended. Feeling adrift, I headed to southern Africa as a volunteer teacher in Namibia, two years after it had won its independence from South Africa. Volunteers got just three weeks of training before being sent to remote villages without phones or computers. I struggled to explain English grammar and sentence structure while my students laughed at my feeble attempts.

And then there was the matter of cooking: Meat was expensive and finding good-quality cuts was difficult. I had left all my recipes and cookbooks at home. Without them, I had no idea how to make a meal out of grains, beans and vegetables.

But my two-room house came with a plug-in camp stove, and I tried to use the few ingredients available to me during the rare times I was able to hitchhike to a grocery store. I plucked papayas from the tree outside my bedroom for breakfast and created a lentil stew with tomatoes, onions and rice. Every successful meal felt like a validation of my ability to survive in a new country. My increasing confidence in the kitchen led me to relax more around my students, and I organized a bunch of small English classes for adults, too.

But I still lacked a tangible food connection to home. For the second half of my stay, I had access to a real cooktop, and I started dreaming about making my old favorite, baked chicken. Yet without an oven I was unsure how to manage it. I wrote Mom a letter, and a week later I received her adaptation. It called for stewing the chicken in a pot instead of baking it. The dish tasted exactly how I remembered, the sharpness of the salt mingling with the smokiness of the paprika. Tears filled my eyes as I savored that meal, and that night my loneliness abated a bit. I made it only one more time during my stay, the night I invited a fellow teacher over for dinner as a way of thanking him for his support. We celebrated the end of the school year and his wife's pregnancy, and he told me that they had decided to name their child after me.

Years later, married and with a 2-year-old daughter of my own, I faced my toughest challenge yet. At the height of the Great Recession, and months before my husband was about to leave for graduate school on the other side of the country, I lost my newspaper job. With journalism work scarce and getting scarcer, I had to find a new career. As I sent out resumes and filed for unemployment, I lost interest in food. More precisely, I lost interest in eating. When concerned friends visited me, my husband took them aside and whispered: "Please, make Lisa eat."

Amazingly, within six weeks I had found a new job in a new field. Drew left for New York, and I was alone in Oregon with our daughter, Rachel. My job was an hour away from home, and we had no family in town. I took in boarders to help make the mortgage, but my overriding concern was how to fill the weekends without Drew around for family outings to the grocery store, the playground and children's theater productions. So I turned to something that took time: cooking. I resolved to stuff our weekends with people and food, and thus began an epic, ten-month stretch of dinner parties.

I invited former colleagues, Rachel's preschool friends and their parents, members of the chorus I sang with, colleagues at my new job. I made chocolate-chip cake, Cornish game hens, lamb stew, challah, and soups that took hours. Sometimes guests brought a dish or two, sometimes not. One group of young, childless women contributed a homemade pozole so magnificent that I haven't been able to bring myself to replicate it.

But the staple I always returned to was baked chicken. I pushed aside my doubts that it wasn't elegant enough for guests; it was, after all, just chicken and pasta. It seemed almost churlish to offer something so basic. But amid all the changes in my life—an absent husband, one career shattered, another one launched—the familiarity of that dish comforted me. At the same time I was feeding my guests, I was also salving my wounds.

Six years later—in a turn of events that surprised me—I'm back in journalism. When Drew returned from grad school, we moved to the Washington, D.C., metro area. I've had to adjust to a faster-paced life, both in my career and as a mom. Again I find myself searching for comfort in food. The dinners I make on weekends now are pretty simple—roast beef, lamb chops, brisket, shepherd's pie—with the occasional experiment to persuade my daughter, now eight, to try something new. After more than two decades of cooking in kitchens of all sizes around the world, I trust myself to deviate from recipes: adding more chocolate, omitting the cayenne, replacing onions with leeks, shrugging when I don't have the full cup of flour or sugar that a dish requires.

Sometimes my daughter joins me as I'm cooking. I love to watch her graceful hands crack eggs and measure out baking soda. And one of the first things I taught her to make was baked chicken and shells. It's her favorite dinner, the one she requests for her birthdays and end-of-the-school-year celebrations. I preheat the oven and sprinkle the salt; she scatters the paprika and parsley. I haven't told her yet what that meal represents to me: overcoming insecurity, tamping down loneliness, willing myself to start over. Right now, it's enough for me to demonstrate that I'm no longer cooking through adversity. Instead, I'm cooking by heart.

CHICKEN AND SHELLS

INGREDIENTS

3½-pound cut-up chicken
Lawry's seasoned salt
Paprika
Dried parsley flakes
4 tbsp. butter
salt and pepper to taste

TO PREPARE

1. Preheat the oven to 375 degrees.
2. Wash and pat dry the chicken parts.
3. Sprinkle both sides of each part with Lawry's seasoned salt. Do the same with the paprika. Add salt and pepper to taste. Sprinkle parsley over everything.
4. Put the chicken in the pan, taking care not to let the pieces touch one another (use an additional pan if necessary), and fill about a quarter to halfway up the pan with water.
5. Cut each tablespoon of butter in half and place each piece on top of the chicken.
6. Bake 45 minutes to an hour.
7. While the chicken is baking, start the pasta: Fill a tall, deep pot with water, cover with a lid and bring to a boil.
8. Put about half a box of pasta in, then cover partway with the lid until the pasta is al dente.
9. Remove pasta from the pot and drain.
10. Spoon the gravy over the pasta and serve at once with the chicken.

The Terrified chef

I WASN'T FEEDING MYSELF, METAPHORICALLY OR OTHERWISE. UNTIL I DID. IT STARTED WITH A COOKING CLASS AT THE INSTITUTE OF CULINARY EDUCATION.

PLEASE SPLEET INTO GROUPS OF FOUR.

BUT I DON'T EVEN KNOW HOW TO BOIL WATER!

(THIS REALLY HAPPENED.)

THEN FOLLOWING SIMPLE RECIPES.

BEFORE LONG, I WAS ACTUALLY GETTING COMPLIMENTS ON MY COOKING.

EVEN IF I WAS JUST MAKING THE SAME THING OVER AND OVER.

THAT EARLY RECIPE FOR CHICKEN POT PIE, BORROWED FROM A CHILDHOOD FRIEND, TAUGHT ME HOW TO ~~FEED~~ **LOVE** MYSELF AND OTHERS.

APRIL 2006 STARTED HOSTING DINNER PARTIES

SEPTEMBER 2013 BECAME A SINGLE MOTHER BY CHOICE

JUNE 2014 MET MY GUY AND HIS FOUR, WONDERFUL GLUTEN-FREE KIDS.

Summer 2014

NOW I COOK EVERY NIGHT. AND CHICKEN POT PIE — ALBEIT THE GLUTEN-FREE VERSION — IS STILL THE MOST POPULAR ITEM ON THE MENU.

CHICKEN POT PIE

COURTESY OF JENNY ROSENSTRACH'S DINNER: A LOVE STORY

3/4 TO 1 CUP CHICKEN BROTH
1 SMALL SWEET POTATO, PEELED AND CUT INTO CUBES
1/2 CUP CHOPPED CARROTS
1/2 MEDIUM ONION
CHOPPED LEAVES FROM 1 SPRIG OF THYME
SALT AND PEPPER TO TASTE
1/2 CUP MILK MIXED WITH FLOUR (could substitute GLUTEN-FREE FLOUR)
1 CUP COOKED CHICKEN, SHREDDED OR CUBED
HANDFUL FROZEN PEAS
1 9-INCH PIECRUST (REGULAR OR GLUTEN-FREE)

PREHEAT OVEN TO 425°F. BRING BROTH TO BOIL IN A SAUCEPAN. ADD POTATO, CARROT, ONION AND THYME AND SIMMER FOR 15 MINUTES. STIR THE FLOUR MIXTURE SLOWLY INTO THE VEGETABLES AND SIMMER, STIRRING, UNTIL IT IS THICK. REMOVE PAN FROM HEAT; ADD CHICKEN AND PEAS. ADD FILLING TO 9-INCH PIE PLATE. COVER WITH CRUST; CUT A FEW SLITS IN THE SURFACE. BAKE FOR 25-30 MINUTES.

Mom's Tacos

by Val Breiman

I love to eat. I've always loved to eat. When I'm alone at home and nobody's watching, I eat like a starving hobo in a Preston Sturges movie. Food and I have a sick, dysfunctional, co-dependent relationship. Which brings me to my mother.

Two things got my mom through an extremely shitty childhood—food and humor. I know all about her shitty childhood because she never let any of her five kids forget how bad it had been.

After ten years of I-AM-NOT-MY-MOTHER!!!! therapy, I realized I was feeling bad for HER during MY shitty childhood. Not fair! But I digress…that story doesn't mix well with the preparation of food.

My mom is funny. Her brand of comedy is wicked. Whenever any of us would walk into a room she was in, she'd have her head back on the couch with her mouth and eyes open, tongue out, pretending to be dead. Not believably dead, just comically dead. Sometimes she'd even drool.

She was a single mom, who supported all five kids, taking jobs that varied from typist to court reporter to Executive Assistant. She sewed our clothes and helped guide us into our various hobbies and future careers, all while going back to school in her forties and getting her Master's Degree.

Oh, and she'd also cook. She didn't cook fancy stuff. She made tuna casseroles, hamburgers, "weenies and beans," and some mysterious stews. The one dish that stuck with me were her tacos. They were somehow both greasy and crispy, and they looked awful, but they were insanely delicious. They will forever be imbedded in two of my most vivid childhood memories. Memories that marked my first experiences with FUCKS: Familial Unrelenting Comedic Kinder Sadism.

Memory #1: I was five. Right before dinner I pricked my index finger with a thumb tack. A teeny, tiny spot of blood came out, and it totally freaked me out because I'd never seen my own blood before. I was a frail kid with yellow, wispy hair. I looked like I had a tiny Trump comb-over and my skin was so pale you could see my veins through it. Here is photographic evidence:

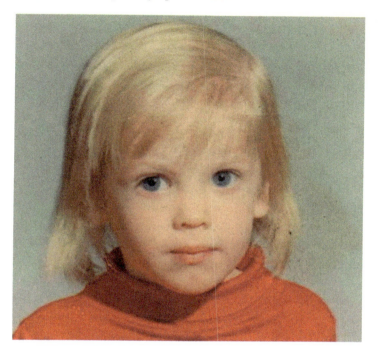

The smell of Mom's tacos filled the house. She and my four ruthless siblings were already sitting down when I ran into the dining room screaming and holding my finger up with the tiny spot of blood on it. "I'm bleeeeeeeding!"

One of my brothers acted horrified. "Oh, my God! Val's bleeeeeeeding!" My mom told me to come over so she could take a look. She stared for a long time, then got up. Because it was the 70's, she *dialed* a number on the phone. Everyone was silent, as my mom waited a couple of seconds. "Hello? Is this the hospital? Good. Yes, my daughter pricked her finger and it's bleeeeeeeding. Uh-huh. Yes, a lot. On her finger tip. WHAT?" She looked horrified. "Are you sure? One hundred percent sure? Okay. Thank you." She hung up, grim, then looked right at me. "I'm sorry, honey, the doctor says you're gonna die."

I screamed and my siblings burst out laughing. At first I thought they were happy I was dying, then I realized I was being teased and cried as hard as I could. Since I was so fair, my blonde eyebrows were invisible, and, for some cruel reason, nature gave me eyebrow ridges that turned bright red when I cried, so my siblings launched into the Red Eyebrows song. "Red eyebrows! Red eyebrows! Look who's got Red eyebrows!" My mom did step in and stop the chanting part of the torture then told me they were all just teasing. "You're not gonna die any time soon. I'll be dead LONG before you are. One day you'll look back on this and laugh. Eat your tacos."

Memory #2: Christmas Eve. I was seven. We were raised with no religion, so Christmas was only about presents. Mom made her tacos for dinner. The family tradition was to get all the goodies stuffed in our stockings first, eat dinner, then try to sleep until morning when it was time to rip through our presents like rabid dingoes. The stuff in the stockings was usually candy and a cool little gift. One year I got a mini plastic horse.

The aroma of Mom's Tacos filled the air as we all grabbed our stockings. Each one had a little note addressed to us in a tiny envelope. I tossed the note aside, reached into my stocking and pulled out a crumpled ball of newspaper. I reached in again and pulled out another one. The entire stocking was packed with newspaper. Everyone's was. Being the youngest, I was pretty upset. My older siblings thought it was hilarious. Mom said, "Aren't you gonna open the note?" Thinking something good would be in the note somehow, I grabbed mine and tore it open. It read: "Santa forgot you this year!" I was horrified. My siblings were reading their notes aloud and laughing. "Rudolph hates you!" "You shouldn't have picked your nose so much. Better luck next year!" After I started crying—which then led to another humiliating round of the Red Eyebrows song—my mom said she was just kidding around. "I forgot to get candy at the store yesterday. I had to do SOMETHING!"

We all went to the dinner table. I was still sniffling when my mom smiled at me. "One day you'll look back on this and laugh. Eat your tacos."

Looking back as I write this, it's almost like my mother planned to have tacos every time there would be some kind of family torture session just for me. I'm surprised that I don't get anxiety every time I see or smell tacos. But the truth is, it's exactly the opposite. I love tacos.

Please enjoy the taste of my childhood!

MOM'S TACOS

If you want the original tacos, these are the ingredients. If they no longer exist, replace with modern, healthier alternatives. I suggest going the full 1970s white-trash route.

INGREDIENTS (FROM THE 70S)

1/2 cup Wesson Oil or Crisco Vegetable Oil
1 pound ground beef
1 packet of McCormick taco seasoning mix
10 corn tortillas
Taco Boy hot sauce
Iceberg lettuce
1 cup tomatoes
1 cup chopped white onions
1 cup grated cheddar cheese

TO PREPARE

1. Chop and mix the lettuce, tomatoes, onions and grated cheese in a bowl and set aside.
2. Put half of the oil in a frying pan. When it gets sizzling hot, put the corn tortillas in one or two at a time. When they get semi-hard, use tongs to fold them into a taco shape. Flip a few times until you have soft, yet crunchy taco shells. Watch out for spattering grease!
3. Put the shells on a plate with paper towels.
4. Add the rest of the oil to the pan and cook the ground beef with the taco seasoning mix.
5. When meat is cooked, start stuffing the taco shells. Meat first, then the mixture.
6. Top each taco with the Taco Boy hot sauce and enjoy!

Thanks, Mom!

The Thing in the Freezer

by Maiya Williams

It was the summer of 1974, and my sister and I were spending two weeks without our parents at Grandma's house in Leavenworth, Kansas. Stranded along with us were two of our cousins, Kathy and Connie. Kathy was fourteen and the oldest, and therefore our leader. My sister was next at thirteen, then me and Connie at eleven. Also there was Bonna, our ninety-two-year-old great-grandmother. I think the point of our stay was for us to get to know Grandma Williams a little better. We didn't know Grandma very well, but what we did know made us nervous.

What we knew was that Grandma was strict. Her resting face resembled the stone-faced subjects in Matthew Brady photographs. Sure enough, as soon as we arrived, she laid down the rules. Certain rooms in the house were off limits: her bedroom, Bonna's bedroom, the living room, and any room where Bonna was sitting, because she didn't want to have to put up with our nonsense. If you were inside, you had to be quiet so that you didn't wake Bonna, who seemed to sleep twenty-three hours a day. Chores were to be carried out quickly and without complaint.

If you broke any of these rules, you would be hit with a glare so sharp it could cleave lumber. If the glare wasn't bad enough, the ever-present threat of a whipping hung in the air like humidity. We knew Grandma had whipped our fathers when they were boys. In an act of twisted genius she would make my dad go out to a bush and cut a switch for her to whip his brother, and then Uncle Joe did the same for my dad. Grandma never explicitly threatened to beat any of us, but she didn't have to. We knew what she was capable of.

At dinner, before we could eat, Grandma made us each recite a verse from the Bible. Whoever went first always chose the easiest and shortest one: "Jesus wept." If you didn't know another verse (and we didn't), Grandma would provide one, saying it slowly so that you could repeat it. Dinner then commenced without conversation except for polite requests to pass the salt and pepper. Also, Grandma insisted you finish all the food on your plate.

Every morsel.

My father was born in 1929. He grew up during the Great Depression. He told us stories about how his family survived those hard times, how his father, the rare black pharmacist who owned his own pharmacy, had to close up and get a job as a guard in Leavenworth prison. How he and his four siblings all had to sleep in one bed. How sometimes the only meat they got was whatever they could gnaw off a chicken's foot. How neighbors would drop by with a sack holding whatever they'd hunted that day—squirrels, rabbits, opossums—offering to share what they had with Mrs. Williams and her five kids.

I should note here that I am a black person who was not raised eating "soul food." In our household we ate classic white-bread American meals made from bloodless meat packaged antiseptically on white Styrofoam, sometimes mixed with Hamburger Helper, other times Shake-n-Bake, supplemented with frozen or canned vegetables. In between meals, we ate a wide variety of snacks packed with sugar, salt, and artificial flavoring, all brought to you in bright, fun packages with brand mascots. My father's Depression diet of weird animals and their innards astonished and disgusted my sister and me. What we didn't realize was that the cuisine grandma developed and perfected during the Depression had become her permanent go-to recipes.

We found this out one night, when we were served something we didn't recognize. Kathy, being the leader, was also the bravest. She asked Grandma what it was, and Grandma responded tartly, "Well, what does it taste like?" When Kathy answered, "Chicken," Grandma nodded and said, "That's right, it tastes like chicken," and didn't say another word about it. Immediately all kinds of alarms went off in my head. Grandma was clearly being cagey. We all exchanged worried glances but the rule was that you had to clean your plate, so we did.

Later we found out it was rabbit.

Rabbit?! What the hell? Rabbit was not available in grocery stores packaged on Styrofoam!

That was just the beginning. With a little detective work, we figured out the sausage Grandma was mixing in the scrambled eggs wasn't sausage at all—it was brains. And she was putting kidneys and god knows what else in the gravy. And that weird-tasting chicken that wasn't chicken or rabbit was sometimes opossum.

It got to the point where we were afraid to eat anything but vegetables, but even those had this and that thrown in for "flavor." What kind of flavor does a chicken heart add to broth that couldn't be equally satisfied with good ol' salt and pepper, I ask you? Answer: none. But still we were expected to finish everything on our plate.

Every morsel.

Because in this house we don't waste food.

My sister and cousins managed to choke down their meals, but not me. I'd wait until Grandma wasn't looking, then hide the offending substance in my napkin and throw it away.

This was the beginning of my lifelong refusal to eat wild animals. I don't care for exotic meats—bison, ostrich, alligator, snake—and it saddens me when I see them on a menu. Moreover, the idea of eating organ meats, the parts of an animal that have a purpose beyond moving the skeleton around, makes me a little sick to my stomach (braised esophagus, anyone?). Frankly, the idea of eating any animal flesh at all disturbs me, and yet I do eat it, night after night. I'm one of those irrational people who disassociates the meat in the supermarket from the animal who provided it. I fool myself into pretending I don't know where it comes from, like gelatin, which is also kind of gross if you think about it, as are eggs and cheese. If I didn't like In-n-Out cheeseburgers so much I'd go full on vegan. But I digress.

We went along like this for a couple more nights, when one very boring day, after spending the morning trying to make homemade raisins by setting grapes out on the searing hot pavement, we decided to cool off with some Minute Maid lemonade. The four of us trooped into the kitchen, got out the glasses, found the powdered drink mix, and then my sister screamed. She was standing in front of the open freezer, about to get some ice. We rushed over and saw what she was staring at: a monstrous, bulging meat-thing, wrapped in plastic. Kathy grimly removed it, turning it over in her hands. We floated ideas as to what it could possibly be: a giant slug, some big animal's stomach, an elephant penis? There was no way to tell because it wasn't labeled.

Immediately we began making plans to run away, but just as quickly we realized there was nowhere to run to; Grandma lived out in the sticks. The liveliest social center was the laundromat, where there was a coke machine, and even that was a forty-five minute walk from Grandma's house. Moreover, if we resorted to camping, "living off the land" so to speak, we'd be faced with the same bad selection of meals that we had at Grandma's. Also, did I mention the constant but unspoken threat of whippings? I'm sure I did.

We brooded over what we should do, until Kathy finally said she was going to confront Grandma at dinner, which was in an hour. As the minutes ticked by, we faced our next meal with no small amount of excitement and trepidation.

As we sat at the dinner table waiting to see what would be served, and anticipating the explosion when Kathy complained, to our great surprise and relief my grandmother brought out a platter of catfish. Catfish! An involuntary cheer rose from our lips, and then we all fell out laughing. Grandma looked at us like we were crazy, momentarily forgot about the Bible verses, and exclaimed, "What's gotten into you girls?" It all came out in a rush: how we found the thing in the freezer and were afraid to eat it, and how we were afraid to eat most of her dinners because we didn't like game animals and organ meats.

Grandma pursed her lips like she always did and told us the thing in the freezer was just a beef tongue. Hadn't we ever had beef tongue sandwiches before? I didn't say what I was really thinking, that the idea of biting into some other animal's tongue was absurd, but we all made it clear right then and there that we were unused to, and wary of, many of the things she prepared. Grandma shook her head and said that if all we wanted to eat were hamburgers, hot dogs, and chicken, then that was all she'd make. She said it like a threat, but those words were music to our ears. (Yes, I know hot dogs contain all the things I just said made me queasy, including perhaps elephant penis, but at the time I didn't know. Hot dogs were just…well…hot dogs.)

Here's the funny thing. After that night, we did get to know Grandma better. Our confession broke the ice. Grandma started telling us stories about what it was like raising our dads, which of course was endlessly entertaining. Then she told us about the years when Bonna owned a pie shop. Apparently Bonna—her real name was Susie Fields—owned a very popular bakery, where she produced all kinds of cookies and cakes and pies. In fact, she had a pancake recipe that was so good, it was bought by a company that paid her a great sum of money, which she then used to embark on an extended trip to South America. All this time we had been avoiding Bonna, afraid of annoying her, and here she was a renowned cook!

If there are any lessons to be learned from this, it's, first, that you should have the courage to be honest, and, second, there is always more to people than meets the eye. It's almost always worth digging to find those treasures.

Grandma wasn't Bonna though; she didn't make us any pies that summer. But she did make us some homemade peach ice-cream using an old fashioned bucket with a crank, rock salt, ice, fresh peaches, sugar and cream. It's the thing I remember most fondly about that trip, and to this day I've never tasted better ice cream anywhere. Unfortunately for you, dear reader, that's not the recipe I'm submitting.

ROASTED OPOSSUM

INGREDIENTS

1 opossum
1 cup of salt
Stuffing:
1 large onion
1 Tbsp fat
Opossum liver
1 cup breadcrumbs
1 dash Worcestershire sauce
1 hard boiled egg, chopped fine

TO PREPARE

1. Catch the opossum and kill it. I'm not sure how to do this, check YOUTUBE.
2. Skin and dress the opossum. Again, check YOUTUBE for instructions.
3. Wash opossum carcass inside and out.
4. Cover carcass with water to which has been added 1 cup salt.
5. Brine overnight, or for 10 hours. In the morning drain off the salted water and rinse carcass well.
6. Set oven to 350 degrees.
7. Make stuffing: brown onion in fat. Add finely chopped opossum liver and cook until liver is tender. Add breadcrumbs, Worcestershire sauce and egg, salt to taste and add water to moisten.
8. Stuff stuffing into the carcass. Sew the opening shut or fasten with skewers.
9. Roast in roasting pan with 2 Tbsp. water until tender and richly browned, approximately 1 ½ hours, basting every 15 minutes.
10. Remove from oven, undo the stitches.

SERVING SUGGESTIONS

Don't. Please don't serve this. If you do, provide plenty of napkins and a nearby garbage can. Or, simply refuse to tell your guests what it is. When they ask, stubbornly say, "it tastes like chicken."

Comfort Jiaozi

by May-lee Chai

When I was twelve, my world changed dramatically—my family moved from the New York City metropolitan area to a small farm in rural South Dakota. My parents were tired of the crime and drama of New York City in the 1970s and decided they wanted a more bucolic and "simpler life," as they put it. The 70s had been a rough decade for the city: there were tong gang wars in Chinatown, the bankruptcy of 1975 (remember the *New York Daily News* headline: "Ford to City: Drop Dead"?), the blackout and subsequent looting, the Son of Sam. I now understand how my parents felt in a way that I did not when I was twelve.

My father taught at the City College of New York and commuted to the city from our house in the suburbs of New Jersey. For me, however, the problems of the city were an abstraction. New York City meant for me first and foremost my paternal grandparents. Every Sunday my father drove us to Manhattan so that we could have dinner with Ye-ye and Nai-nai at their favorite Chinese restaurant, Chun Cha Fu at Broadway and West 91st.

I loved those Sunday meals. Our extended family gathered together—my uncles, aunt, cousins, grandparents, my parents, and me—in our own room, partitioned by sliding wall panels, complete with a round table topped by a spinning lazy Susan. My cousin, my brother and I often had our own table. There could be new unexpected guests every week, people my grandfather met and invited to our "Chinese banquet" and their kids would join our table, the more the merrier.

My grandfather always asked the owner, Mr. Lee, what was fresh, what was available, and they'd confer, heads together, leaving the menu behind. We'd have lion's head meatballs, bamboo steamers of xiao long bao soup dumplings, plates of fresh sautéed vegetables, platters with a whole fish—head attached. Every meal ended with a soup—sometimes with little bird claws at the bottom (pigeon I think) or tiny heads or tentacles, mysterious things that came up unexpectedly in our glass spoons. My brother, cousin, and I giggled, shocked at the newness. Even if we didn't always dare to eat the solid parts, we enjoyed the broth, which was always delicious.

My grandparents and father and uncles shouted at each other loudly in Chinese; my mother and aunt conversed in English, since neither of them was Chinese; and my brother and cousin and I played *Star Wars* after dinner, running around the room pretending to shoot invisible Stormtroopers with our fingers pointed like blasters.

After we moved, the family meals stopped, of course. We were too far away.

In fact, Chinese food ceased to be a part of our life.

There was no Chinese restaurant in the small town nearest our farm in South Dakota, and the next nearest town 28 miles away had a tiny chop suey place that served the local population, but wasn't what we were used to. That first year my parents took to driving long distances, 130 miles round trip to Sioux Falls, or 80 miles to the south to Sioux City, Iowa, in search of a Chinese restaurant, but the food was not the same, and the blizzards in winter made such long-distance treks in search of food impossible.

We lost more than access to Chinese food, however.

My parents had not realized that our family would be controversial in this community. As it turned out, we were the first mixed-race family with a Chinese man married to a white woman that this town had ever seen, and many people stopped and stared at us when we walked together as a family down the tiny town's Main Street or shopped in the grocery store or walked in the drug store. Kids at school were more blunt. They said that mixed-race children were against God's will and we were a sign of the One World Government that would mark the Devil's Reign on earth. I'd never heard such nonsense before in my life, and in the beginning I told the kids off and said this was stupid. Sometimes I laughed.

Then men started driving by our house in the countryside and shot our dogs. They hurled racial slurs out the windows of their pickups.

The following year, my parents tried to sell the farm but no one who wanted to buy our farm was given a loan by the local banks. Potential buyers who liked our place could get loans to buy other properties, just not ours. This continued for years. (In fact, no one would ever get a loan to buy our farm. It would sell eight years later only after people whom my mother had hired to clean the carpets once won the Iowa State Lottery and paid cash for our property.)

My father took a job in a different state and commuted to work. My mother, brother, and I continued to live on the farm fulltime.

I hated the farm, I hated the town, and, due to the bullying, I hated myself.

And I learned to hate food.

My mother wanted us to raise chickens; she thought since we lived on a farm, we should have a farm experience, but I hated eating the animals that I cared for. Watering and feeding them every day, I knew their every move, their bucks and clucks, their quirks and odd habits, this chicken who was a good broody hen and liked to sit on her eggs until they hatched versus the contemplative hen who liked to perch on the edge of the roost and bathe in the light of the sun that seeped into the coop from the tiny window. Even after they were dead and plucked and frozen in our freezer, I could recognize the chickens by the shape of their bodies. Some were lumpier than others, some longer, some squatter. I could picture them with their feathers. Eating them felt like eating pets. My mother could not understand my squeamishness and I could not understand her callousness.

I took to eating peanut butter sandwiches and granola bars, and with that diet, combined with the labor of farm work, caring for the animals, all the chores every day, I grew very thin.

By the time I was eighteen, I was ready to leave the farm by any means necessary.

My father, being of the generation of men that didn't involve themselves in the raising of their children in a hands-on way, let my mother raise my brother and me as she saw fit while he worked to earn the money that supported our family.

I came to resent his detachment. Sometimes I argued with him when he came from his job in the other state. I'd try to tell him about the violence at school, the white boys who attacked my brother, something awful someone said in class, a racist joke uttered by a teacher, and he'd say, "You don't know how to get along with people." Sometimes we'd shout at each other for hours. Sometimes I'd refuse to speak to him at all.

I can understand now as an adult the kind of pain my father must have been going through then, every statement out of my teenage mouth proof that he could not protect his family, but nothing I said then could get him to admit the role that racism played in our lives. He wasn't trained to talk about race. Neither was my mother for that matter. Their generation, born in the 1930s, children of war, had learned to bear the hardships of life without talking about them.

Nothing changed in the dynamic of the family until I was almost eighteen years of age and an extraordinary opportunity to travel to China arose.

My father had been invited to an important academic conference in Beijing. It was 1985, six years after the U.S. and China had re-established ties. My father had not been back to the Mainland since he and his family had left at the end of the Chinese Civil War in 1949. They'd gone to Taiwan first, and then my father had come to America on a college scholarship, followed by the rest of his family in the 1950s. Only after Nai-nai had already died did the family in America start hearing from relatives on the Mainland. Now here was this opportunity to visit.

My father was excited but also nervous. There was a lot of pressure on him. As an American scholar of Chinese heritage who'd been born in Shanghai, he was uncertain how he'd be treated on the Mainland. Would the government be upset about his publications as a political scientist who did not skew to the Communist Party's ideology? It was so early in the new relationship between America and China that he didn't know what to expect. Meantime, Ye-ye wanted him to meet up with family, bringing gifts and re-establishing ties. Nai-nai had died by this time, and Ye-ye was eager to re-connect with the family remaining in China. He wanted my father to report back on everything: what had happened to cousins and nieces and in-laws, was the family house still standing, what did everything look like?

My father wanted our whole family to go with him, but my mother and brother were afraid to fly. The years of violence directed at us on the farm had only exacerbated their anxieties, and they just couldn't do it. However, I announced I would go with him.

My parents were shocked. I'd gone from arguing with my father all the time to now wanting to travel with him on a nineteen-hour flight halfway around the world?

Yes, I said. I'd go.

And so, shortly after my eighteenth birthday, my father and I traveled together to China.

At first my father was overwhelmed by all the changes. He'd left China as a sixteen-year-old and his memories were of war and fear. Walking the streets of Beijing where all the signs were written in the unfamiliar simplified script that had been adopted in the 1950s, meeting with relatives who'd suffered during the Cultural Revolution, listening to their tales of suffering compounded his emotional wounds as a child of war. He yelled at me when I couldn't understand our relatives.

"Why can't you speak Chinese?" he once exclaimed angrily, after I'd asked him to translate for me.

"You never taught me!" I reminded him.

When it was time for him to attend the conference meetings, he told me I had to wait for him in the hotel room. "Don't go out! Stay here!" he commanded. But I knew those meetings could last for hours, and I wasn't going to waste my precious visit sitting inside.

The moment after he left, I left, too.

At first I stuck to the most familiar street near our hotel, Chang'an Boulevard, which I knew from the hotel map led to the Forbidden City and Tiananmen Square. As I walked on the wide sidewalk, I marveled that no one here stared at me, while back "home" in South Dakota people still stared at my family every time we went out. I grew more confident. I enjoyed for once blending in. My shoulders felt less tight, the knot in the pit of my stomach loosened. Finally, I dared to wander down a side street, following throngs of Chinese shoppers, and was delighted to find stalls of all varieties, selling everything from newspapers and magazines to bamboo bird cages and household sundries to watermelon, eggs boiled in tea, and bamboo steamers full of baozi.

And then I saw the zongzi!

A street vendor was selling them out of a pushcart, from what looked like a giant rice cooker covered with a damp, canvas cloth. The cloth was not clean but I figured they were hot, how dirty could they be? And how charming to look at! How could I resist?

Thick green bamboo leaves tied with a string. Inside: a pyramid of steaming sticky rice with a center of spiced meat.

Before I headed back to the hotel, I bought a white mosquito net, a paper fan, and three zongzi, which were hot and moist, as long as my palm.

My father had expressly forbidden me to eat food sold on the street.

But in my hotel room, I knelt on the floor next to my bed and unwrapped the bamboo leaves. I'll just taste a little, I thought. I put my tongue to the rice, and then I couldn't resist. I gobbled the rest of the zongzi—the salty rice, the spicy center, the flavors blending in my mouth, irresistible, bite after bite. I hid the remaining two in the mini-bar so my father wouldn't know what I had done.

I was eighteen and just beginning to disobey my father.

That fall, when I enrolled in college, I decided that I would begin studying Mandarin. Both my parents were opposed to this idea. My father was afraid I was going to study something too narrow, something that would make it hard for me to find a job. Perhaps he was reacting unconsciously to the prejudice and violence we'd faced on the farm, which still hadn't sold. He couldn't articulate his anxiety in those days, he could only shout at me, trying to make me understand with volume instead of words, as though he could protect me from prejudice with the force of his voice, but he couldn't control what I studied, and so I enrolled anyway. My mother wanted me to focus on my writing—she had worked as a journalist before she married and thought this was a good, solid career—so I started writing for the school newspaper, but I kept up the Chinese classes as well.

By the time I was a senior, I had applied to a study abroad program in my grandmother's hometown of Nanjing and was ready to go to China on my own.

In August, Nanjing was filled with watermelons, small green mountains of them piled on the sidewalks. People gathered in clusters to eat the fresh fruit, sat on wooden stools under the shade of the plane trees, fanning themselves, trying to cool off in the muggy late-summer heat. I enjoyed walking the sidewalks around Nanjing University, watching people, stopping for watermelon, practicing my Mandarin. But most of all,

I enjoyed not being treated as though I were a freak. Most people assumed I was completely Chinese and were surprised that I had a funny accent when I spoke. After I explained that I was from America, people were friendly and curious. They peppered me with questions, and sometimes they told me about their own dreams for traveling abroad. No one called me any names or told me that I should never have been born—the things that I'd been told ever since we'd moved to the farm.

Then autumn arrived with slightly cooler temperatures, and mooncakes appeared in street corner vendor's stalls, in large government-managed department stores, in towering displays of metal tins and pink paper boxes tied with red strings.

Mid-Autumn Festival was coming and everyone was giving the hockey-puck-shaped cakes as gifts.

In addition to taking Chinese classes at Nanjing University, I also taught English at a local night school. My students gave me boxes of mooncakes, their parents, too, other teachers, friends. I was treated with respect and kindness, included in the local customs in preparation for the Mid-Autumn Festival.

In America, I was used to the two brands available in Chinatown back when we lived on the East Coast: the red bean paste and the yellow bean paste, both dry as fruit cakes and just as unappealing. But in Nanjing there were pumpkin mooncakes, coconut, kumquat, lotus seed, as well as the old standards—sweet red bean and sweet white bean but moist! Some came single-yolked or double-yolked, with golden goose and duck egg yolks baked into the center like a secret sun. I ate two at a time, six in a day. I couldn't eat them fast enough. I ate mooncakes instead of meals. Once I ate three at a single sitting. Soon I couldn't button my pants anymore and had to buy a new pair. I bought green People's Liberation Army pants, one-size-truly-fits-all, wide as a door, made to be cinched and belted at the waist.

Then all at once it seemed, the air turned cooler, the leaves from the sycamores turned orange, then brown overnight, falling off the branches, littering the sidewalks like so many brown crabs, crunching underfoot.

I huffed and puffed on my tiny pink Swan bicycle around the city as the cold wind blew the leaves away, leaving the dull concrete exposed. My nose wouldn't stop running.

And one day all the mooncakes were gone.

Autumn was over.

With winter's arrival, I discovered the pleasures of jiaozi, the boiled, meat-filled dumplings that soon became my favorite food.

My go-to stand was run by a family of women outside the large stone gate to Nanjing University.

Giant metal vats of boiling water bubbled in the back, stirred by one red-cheeked woman with a large metal ladle, as the dumplings bobbed to the surface.

There was no heat allocated by the central government for cities south of the Yangtze, and Nanjing sat on the southern bank of the Yangtze, barely a Southern city at all. It rarely snowed but the temperatures hovered just above the freezing mark. Riding my Swan around the city, the cold metal between my legs, the handles burning through my gloves, I felt the frigid wind freezing the skin of my face. Inside my four-story stone dormitory was even worse, somehow colder than the outside. My roommates and I bought a goldfish bowl from the Confucius Temple Market at the beginning of fall, and one morning in December we were horrified to discover the water had frozen solid over night, our poor dead goldfish caught in the very center of the ice.

The jiaozi dian (dumpling shop) offered welcome respite. Patrons crowded together around the three wooden tables, the more the merrier, the warmth of our bodies mixing with the steam of the dumpling vats, the air filled with the sound of slurping. My friends and I went for jiaozi almost every day. I don't know which I loved more, the delicious dumplings or the joy of eating with friends—Chinese and Americans and other foreign students—who accepted me as I was, and who enjoyed my company.

"Ji liang? Ji liang jiaozi?" the owner called out as soon as we came in the door.

We held up our fingers: five, six, seven, eight. . . the orders increased as the temperatures fell. Each liang was approximately five dumplings. When I first arrived at the university, when the temperatures soared and the humid heat of summer made me sweat day and night, I could barely eat a bowl of five. But after the first frost, a bowl of thirty-five was a satisfying snack, the hot broth settling in my stomach like a personal heater, giving me courage to leave the warmth of the small tables and venture back out into another wintry night.

By the time my semester was over, I'd learned to love to eat again. Living in China I learned not only to eat to live but also to relish food, to savor the taste, to feel strong and powerful in a way that I had not felt since I was a child before we'd moved to the farm.

When I got off the plane back in America, my mother was waiting in the airport, but she didn't recognize me. I walked right up to her, but she continued to look past me, scanning the passengers spilling out of the gate. I'd changed that much.

Not only had I gained weight, but I'd gained a new confidence. I wasn't the shy and timid girl I'd been. The racism that I'd internalized was rooted out. I stood taller, I smiled more broadly so that all my teeth showed. I wasn't going to apologize for my appearance or my existence or let anyone boss me around anymore.

No longer the obedient child, I was well on my way to becoming the woman I am today. I had found my way home.

JIAOZI

INGREDIENTS

2 packages gyoza wrappers (using store-bought wraps is fastest) *
Filling:
1 pound ground meat
1 teaspoon sesame oil
3-4 cloves garlic (minced)
1 teaspoon fresh ginger (minced)
1 cup bok choy, finely chopped
½ cup white mushrooms, finely chopped
Salt
Pepper

DIPPING SAUCE

½ cup soy sauce
1/3 cup rice wine vinegar
pinch of la jiao (ground hot red pepper)

TO PREPARE

1. Mix the flavorings, cabbage, and mushrooms into the ground meat, but not the dipping sauce. Save that for when the jiaozi are done.
2. Take a teaspoonful of the meat and place in the center of the wrapping. Be careful not to overfill or the dumpling will explode while boiling.
3. Put a little water on the edge of half the wrapper. Then fold the wrapper in two so that it's a semi-circle. Pinch the edges, pulling the dough forward a bit with each new pinch. (Look online to see what this is supposed to look like. Don't just fold the dough in half or it will not be as stable a dumpling.)
4. Bring a large pot of water to a boil.
5. Place the first batch of dumplings into the water.
6. Add a cup of cold water. Stir so the dumplings don't stick together.
7. When the water starts boiling again, add another cup of cold water.
8. Once the water has boiled three times, the dumplings traditionally are considered done, but cooking time will vary depending on the size of your pot and how many dumplings you cook at a time. You may want to test one dumpling to make sure the meat is thoroughly cooked. If not, add more cold water and bring to another boil.

Serve with dipping sauce. Add la jiao to individual taste. (Warning: Chinese ground red peppers are very, very hot!)

Traditionally, dumplings are made to celebrate holidays like the New Year (Spring Festival) so it's best to make them with a group of friends. You can all share the wrapping duties or else this wrapping process will be very time-consuming.

*if you want to make your own wrappers
½ lb. of flour
½ cup of water (you may need more)

Mix flour and water by hand, keep kneading, should not be overly wet. Add a little more water if the mixture is too dry and crumbly. Add more flour if it's too wet and sticky. Shape into a ball and keep in a bowl under a wet rag while you are rolling out the dough. Take a handful of the dough and roll it into a log. Cut the logs into ¼ inch thick slices. Roll each slice into a circle. Repeat with another dough log. When you have enough circles to make your first batch of jiaozi (about 24), you may want to start wrapping the jiaozi and wait before you roll out more wrappers lest they become dry.

Funeral Casserole

by Kate Fuglei

"Who died?" my three brothers would yell as they threw baseball equipment down on the kitchen floor. They had spied the telltale silver pan of leftover funeral casserole on the kitchen table and were salivating at the thought of its ground beefy-cheesy-corn-flakey goodness.

It was 1965 and my mom was the head of the Our Redeemer Lutheran Church Women's Auxiliary. It was her responsibility to oversee the preparation and serving of the lunches after funerals. The menu never varied and I suppose this was part of the comfort factor for those who were in grief. If you died, and if you were a member of Our Redeemer Lutheran Church in Omaha, Nebraska, here is what your survivors got: funeral casserole, three bean salad, ambrosia and apple brown betty. Watery lemonade and coffee. Iced tea if it was June, July or August. You could bet anything on this. That was the way it was.

What my brothers saw on that table was the result of an entire morning of preparation beginning at 7AM. For an 11AM funeral lunch, my mom and I began browning the six pounds of ground beef early. We'd put a stack of our favorite musicals on the hi-fi in the dining room, beginning with Doris Day's "Hooray for Hollywood." We'd crank up the volume. After Doris Day came *The Music Man* with Barbara Cook, and by the time she was singing "Till There Was You," the beef had turned from pink to greyish brown. We used two large frying pans and drained the juicy meat in a gigantic silver colander. *Oklahoma* was next, and as I grated cheese, I gazed at the burnt orange album cover with the luscious Shirley Jones sitting in the surrey with the fringe on top. Her golden curls were perfect, peeking from her lacy bonnet. I told my mother that when I grew up, I wanted to be just like Laurie. It is no coincidence that when I started acting and singing professionally two of my go-to audition songs were "I Cain't Say No" and "Out of My Dreams."

At the time, I was only five and had no idea what Broadway was. I had no conception there were theatrical productions or films attached to these songs. I just made up stories as I grated. Sometimes Laurie and Curly got along and sometimes they didn't, just like Aunt Carolyn and Uncle Ed. (I had overheard my mom telling my dad Uncle Ed was a "skirt-chaser." I wondered why Uncle Ed would want to chase only skirts. What about dresses? And why chase at all?)

Mom usually took the boys to baseball practice before we cooked, so we could sing along with impunity. *South Pacific* followed *Oklahoma*, and we mixed the whole casserole concoction as Mary Martin belted out, "I'm In Love With A Wonderful Guy."

The Sound Of Music (also with Mary Martin) was last. I put wax paper over mounds of corn flakes and crushed them with a thick encyclopedia, and, as we sprinkled the crunchy topping over the casserole, we sang along to "Edelweiss."

Mom and I carried the pans to the car so she could drive them to Our Redeemer, just four blocks away, and put them in the church ovens to bake. When she returned, we'd put on Doris Day and drink lemonade on the back porch. I didn't know exactly what Hollywood was but the idea of Max Factor being able to make even a monkey look good sounded wonderful to me. I would ask my mother what it is that Will wants to do that Ado Annie can't say no to or what exactly it was that he did when he went to Kansas City on a Friday. And why was Curly singing about Judd's smelliness at his funeral? Wasn't that disrespectful? What did the mourners eat at Judd's funeral?

There were industrial-sized ovens in the basement kitchen of Our Redeemer and they were needed in order to fit the huge baking pans. The women's auxiliary lived in sheer terror of "running out." This never happened, as, no matter how old or how small the grieving survivor party, the Women's Auxiliary always put together enough grub to feed an entire platoon. The massive silver pans in which the food was prepared and presented took up half a card table. They were dented and blackened with age and looked as though they'd been around since the days of the Vikings, or at the very least since an earlier generation, in which they were used for Nebraska barn-raisings and times when whole communities gathered.

There were four women on the committee and when the call went out, they operated with lightning efficiency. They had to. Most of them had children, busy domestic lives and full-time jobs. My own mother had six children and ran the kitchen of a hospital in Omaha. She got up every day at 4AM to get to Nebraska Methodist Hospital, where she worked until 2PM. Then she came home and took care of her school-age children. She took the day off when there was a funeral.

Edna Concannon made the ambrosia. She had three children and taught first grade. We called Vesta Dobson (three-bean salad) an "old maid"; she was our piano teacher and the choir director. Mrs. Dale made the apple brown betty. She was the Youth Director and smoked cigarettes behind the church. She introduced us to *Jesus Christ Superstar* and let us play the album endlessly on the portable record player in the pastor's office. We adored her.

There were no maintenance men at Our Redeemer to do the heavy work. On funeral days, the women commandeered their children or husbands to set up the huge fold-out tables, or, if there was no help available, they did it themselves, hoisting the tables on their sides, cranking out the iron legs and flipping them up and over. Metal folding chairs were screeched into place. Pans of food were pulled out of the backs of old station wagons. Tablecloths were whipped up like sails and snapped down to cover the fading brown linoleum tabletops. The pans were placed next to one another with one giant metal serving spoon next to each pan. White napkins went at one end, with clumps of silverware and stacks of thick white plates at the other. There were no flower arrangements or color-coordinated anything.

These women were the daughters of midwestern farmers and the granddaughters of pioneers. Their parents and grandparents had come to Omaha to work at Union Pacific or at the stockyards. No matter how tired you were, how many kids you had, how hot it was or how deep the snow, if someone died and you were in the Our Redeemer Women's Auxiliary, you showed up and brought what you were supposed to bring. You contributed. You never knew when it might be you. And besides, the leftovers were taken home and could often feed your family for days.

After the mourners had gone, we picked up napkins, washed and dried coffee cups and folded the metal chairs, stacking them along the wall near the choir robe cabinets. We piled the crusted pans into the car and, if Mom seemed in a good mood, we'd sing "Poor Judd Is Dead" at the top of our lungs on the way home.

FUNERAL CASSEROLE

INGREDIENTS

1 lb ground beef
4 tablespoons butter
1 small onion
2 cloves garlic
One 30-oz bag hashed browned potatoes, thawed
One 10.5-oz can condensed cream of chicken soup
I cup sour cream
¼ cup grated Parmesan
1 ½ teaspoons kosher salt
½ teaspoon ground black pepper
2 cups shredded cheddar cheese
1½ cups lightly crushed corn flake cereal

TO PREPARE

1. Preheat oven to 350.
2. Brown ground beef in skillet and drain.
3. Heat 1 tablespoon of butter over medium heat in a skillet.
4. Add the diced onion and cook, stirring, until soft. Stir in the garlic and cook until fragrant and softened.
5. Mix with the ground beef.
6. In a bowl, toss together the ground beef, cooked onions and garlic, hashed browns, condensed soup, sour cream, Parmesan, salt and pepper and 1 ½ cups cheddar cheese.
7. Spread the mixture in a 9 by 13 inch buttered casserole dish.
8. Melt the remaining 2 tablespoons butter.
9. Top the casserole with the remaining ½ cup cheddar cheese, corn flake cereal and melted butter.
10. Bake until it bubbles around the sides, about 1 hour.
11. For funeral gathering, make at least six pans.

SPREAD 'EM
(AND SAUCE 'EM)

Uncle Benny's Barbecue Sauce

Not Lena's Pimento Cheese Dip, But Close

Pesto

Liquid Smoke

by Bernadette Luckett

My mother wasn't the best cook. (I'm being nice.) To her, cooking was about putting food on the table, not the quality of the food that was put there. I remember summer evenings in Berkeley, in our little pink stucco house, the back door open to inhale fresh air into our kitchen, swirl it around with the stink of my mother's cooking, then exhale it out the open window, into the streets, where it collided with the tantalizing smells of fried chicken, pot roast, pork chops, all emanating from our neighbors' homes.

You always knew what everyone was cooking in our neighborhood. I'd ride my bike down the street, salivating, while breathing in the smoky fragrance of meat cooking on a nearby grill, only to come home and betray my expectant stomach with a depressing dinner of boiled hot dogs and creamed corn. My mother was the worst cook. (I'm being honest.) I was ten, and I believed that fried liver was supposed to be hard as leather, picked up with both hands and gnawed on like a dog with a chew toy. I believed spaghetti was best made by pouring ketchup on pasta, then sprinkling canned corn on top. I believed that chili was made by first burning the beans, then adding a watery tomato sauce that allowed burned black flecks to rise to the surface. The menu never varied. The ingredients seldom changed. My culinary palate was installed with the default setting at LOW.

Whenever we'd have company for dinner, my mother would pull out the fine china that she bought at an auction. But the food disasters on top of the plate never rivaled the grandeur of the china itself. It doesn't matter whether you put manure on antique bone china or a Melmac dinner plate—it's still manure.

My mother worked full time. She'd rush home every night and start opening cans. All manner of pasty, pale-colored fruits and vegetables came in cans. She bought them all. The most disgusting was creamed corn, the closest visual cousin to real vomit on your plate. Second most disgusting was French-cut string beans. What was the big deal about cutting string beans diagonally? Ooo, quel genius! A French cut didn't help eliminate the de-vitaminized metallic stench, or the lifeless, rubbery texture. It's the only food I ever ate that squeaked when you chewed it.

My mother was obsessed with canned foods. *I* was obsessed with the electric can opener—the whirring sound, watching the gears turn and spin the cans. It was an amusement park ride for food. Vegetables were having their last bit of fun before being eaten. I'd step too close to the dangling, razor-sharp lid and my mother would yell, "Get back! You'll cut yourself and get lockjaw!" That scared me. I spent a large part of my youth in constant fear of getting lockjaw—Lockjaw. Rabies. And TB.

TB was the scariest. Having a TB test threw me into three agonizing days of anxiety; a weepy girl, eyes glued to the inoculation welts on my arm, convinced I had it. I'd lie awake, imagining my life in a sanitarium, my mother bringing me cans of Campbell's Chicken Noodle soup, which she believed healed everything. I'd sleep in a ward full of TB orphans, all of us hacking bloody disease-carrying phlegm projectiles onto the faces of the spinsterish nuns who dedicated their lives to caring for us. (I hate nuns.)

For dessert, my mother opened cans of fruit cocktail. I loved fruit cocktail. It had uniformly diced pieces of fruit in a sticky-sweet syrup. My skinny fingers swam through the liquid goo, fishing for the faded cherries, which I'd eat first. Then I'd pick out the grapes, the peaches, and the pineapple, leaving unidentifiable, white mushy cubelets spread out on the bottom of my bowl. Needless to say, I never saw any fruit that came directly from a tree or bush. The nutrition fairy rarely visited our house.

One of the saddest memories I have of my mother's cooking is when she discovered a mysterious food additive called "Liquid Smoke." A company had attempted to come up with a way to take that salivatin'-creatin' outdoorsy, charcoaled aroma that arises from the dripping of animal fat in fire, and put it in a bottle. Not only did it not smell like the heavenly barbecues that emanated weekly from my Uncle Benny's grill, it was closer to the stench of a burning, heavily-lacquered end table —a smell I knew well, thanks to my cousin Bobby's short-lived dalliance with a woodburning kit.

Uncle Benny lived two blocks away. Every Sunday, all the aunts, uncles, and their kids, went there for a barbecue. The parents sat around, talking, laughing, drinking beer. The cousins, about a dozen of us, ran wild all over the house. Uncle Benny held court in the backyard next to his oversized brick barbecue pit, wearing a white bib apron and a chef's hat. Sweat dripped down his face as he flipped big slabs of ribs, mopping them with his magical tangy-sweet barbecue sauce. No one could resist anything that sauce was on; sucking it off bones, licking it off plates, shoving every sloppy-sauced finger into their mouth and pulling it out clean. That's how good it was. My mother always made sure to bring home a jar of Uncle Benny's sauce, which she'd slather over meatloaf. It's the only meal we got excited about. So whenever my mother, father, sister and I sat down to eat on Meatloaf Night, everyone was in a good mood—even my father's ever-present knitted brow was relaxed. He wasn't one to comment much about food. He ate what was put in front of him without question or expression. To him, it was just food. "It all comes out the same way," he'd say. But he seemed a little happier on Meatloaf Night.

I drowned my meatloaf in extra barbecue sauce, then arranged the food on my plate so that the sauce trickled down onto my Betty Crocker Instant mashed potatoes and Green Giant canned peas. I stuck my fork into a huge chunk of meatloaf and shoved it into my mouth. Mmmm...Wait! Something was different. The sauce. Uncle Benny's barbecue sauce had a strange lingering aftertaste.

My mother looked at me. "How's the meatloaf?"

"Good!" I lied. I didn't want to hurt her feelings. Any effort on her part to do something extra begged to be appreciated.

"I got this seasoning at the store and put it in the barbecue sauce," she beamed. "It's called Liquid Smoke." Liquid Smoke had a hickory flavor. But it was more like sucking on a hickory stick that's been lying in dirt and run over by a couple of oil-dripping diesels during a chemical downpour.

My father nodded his head in approval and continued to eat, so I did too. No one said much for the rest of the meal except Walter Cronkite, whose voice droned on from a portable TV squeezed into the kitchen corner.

Since we all seemed to enjoy it, I guess my mother felt she had found a way to elevate all of our meals, because she started putting Liquid Smoke in everything— hamburgers, steaks, chicken, casseroles, tuna salad. It started creeping its way into Betty Crocker's mashed potatoes, into the creamed corn, onto the French cut string beans. The odor was inescapable. It'd stick to my fingers. It'd get in my hair, on my clothes, on the curtains, the bedding. At school, I'd avoid standing close to other kids for fear they'd get a whiff of my smoky funk. I didn't want to run the risk of being stigmatized for life as the 'stinky kid.'

It was Hamburger Night. Daylight Saving Time had ended, and the clocks were set back. It was dark outside and the air had a chill in it. On the table, flattened meat patties reeking of Liquid Smoke sat on slices of Wonder Bread topped with iceberg lettuce, tomatoes and Miracle Whip. My father recited his usual rote blessing, took a couple of bites of his hamburger and grumbled, "Y'know, I don't like this smoke stuff."

That was all. He just kept eating.

My mother's face dropped.

Walter Cronkite's voice devoured the silence in the room.

She never put Liquid Smoke in our food again.

My mother lives alone now. I went to visit her recently, and when I walked into the house I was slapped in the face with an unforgettable odor that sent me hurtling back in time. She was making hamburgers and asked if I wanted one. I said yes. We sat at her kitchen table eating our burgers. Anderson Cooper droned on in the background. "I put Liquid Smoke in them," she announced. "Remember when you kids were little, I used to cook with that all the time? I don't know why I stopped. It tastes good."

I gave myself a second.

"Yeah, it does," I lied. "It tastes really good."

UNCLE BENNY'S BARBECUE SAUCE

Uncle Benny was very secretive about his barbecue sauce recipe. He'd give you a few ingredients but leave others out. He'd say the key to making the sauce was in how you put it together. But he wouldn't tell you how he put it together. Or the amounts. So he ended up taking his secret recipe with him to that big brick barbecue in the sky. I've tried to reproduce it dozens of times and I'm close.

Here's what I think was in it.

INGREDIENTS

Ketchup
Worcestershire sauce
Tabasco sauce
Lemon juice with peel
Onions
White Vinegar
Brown sugar
Salt
Pepper
Optional (VERY optional): Liquid Smoke

TO PREPARE:

1. Mix all ingredients in a saucepan and cook till boiling.
2. Cover and let simmer on low heat for 1/2 hour.
3. Let stand overnight.
4. When the meat is about ¾ cooked, start mopping that sauce on. Don't be stingy!

Family Recipe

by Wendy Kout

Women's relationship with food began with Eve noshing on that forbidden apple. And, like our first female, I too insist on trying what's new and tempting. For me, food is fun, adventure and moan-out-loud pleasure. But I also have a problem related to food. Fortunately, it's not an eating disorder. My hereditary condition is a cooking disorder.

This aversion to anything "kitchen" began with my maternal grandmother, Lena "Never call me Grandma!" Weiner. While most women of her generation wore aprons and aspired to be Harriet to their husbands' Ozzie, Lena was a bling-wearing widow and ran Miami Beach hotels... which were fronts for a gambling syndicate. Later, in her eighties, having outlived two husbands, she remained a rule-breaker, rocking red lipstick, turquoise eye shadow, and a Holly Golightly cigarette holder while hitchhiking to Temple. Jewish grandmas are "Bubbe." Mine was "Bubbles"— not literally, but she did bubble with life.

Lena loved show business. She escaped her woes not by perfecting pie-crust, but by devouring Hollywood gossip rags. She never forgave Eddie Fisher or Richard Burton for leaving their wives for "that hussy" Liz Taylor. And, as a child, I never forgave her for being more interested in celebrities than her own granddaughter. But with time came perspective and empathy for what few choices she had as a woman of her generation. Who would she have become had she been born in my time? Would she have gone to college? Been married? Had children? Owned hotels instead of managing them? And would she have turned her homemade pimento cheese dip into a million-dollar product on "Shark Tank"? Yes, Lena hated being in the kitchen but everyone loved her signature dip... a recipe she never wrote down or taught.

My mother, like her mother, had a hunger for show business and a distaste for cooking. A cheerleader in high school, Betty was a great beauty who could sing (mostly show tunes) and dance (preferably tap). She imagined herself on stage, never at stove. But lacking the confidence to try to be a Broadway baby, she married young and had a baby named Larry. Eight years later, she divorced, even though back then it was a shanda (Yiddish for shame or disgrace). She and Larry moved in with her parents, and Betty went to work as a cigarette girl in a fancy beach hotel. One day her brother introduced her to his friend Norman, a thoughtful, handsome and impoverished law student. One look and she was in love. Norm felt the same, but he couldn't afford a pastrami on rye, let alone a wife and child. Betty begged but Norm refused to marry her. She retaliated by wedding a multi-millionaire named Leonard. If she couldn't have love, she could at least have a full-time chef! But during her Acapulco honeymoon on Leonard's yacht, she couldn't stop thinking about Norm. So she annulled the marriage and promised Norm that if he would marry her, she would work for the rest of her life. He did, she did, and that is how my parents began... and I began. With my Mom giving up the material world for her authentic heart.

Back to the dreaded kitchen for Betty. But despite her cooking disorder, Mom insisted that we have a homemade family dinner every night. No eating in front of the television or frozen dinners. No Chinese or pizza delivery. (Hard to imagine that kids now text parents their takeout orders.) Our family caught up at that dining table. Shared our day. Made each other laugh. So kudos to Mom for creating that every night. What did she create every morning? Nothing. Nada. Bupkus. My brother and I have no memory of Mom ever making us breakfast. Larry claims he didn't know what an egg was until he slept at a friend's house. School lunches? Tuna or PB & J. Fast. Easy. Done! That was Mom's motto. So there was no homemade chicken soup for this Jewish girl when I was sick. It was out-of-the-can Campbell's Cream of Tomato with crushed saltines on top. Fast. Easy. Done!

Like Lena, Mom also had a signature dish or two. Larry's favorite was her broiled lamb chops with spaghetti on the side. Franco-American, of course. My favorite was her rarely-made but spectacular donuts. I was given the grave responsibility of shaking them in a paper bag filled with powdered sugar. "Hurry. They have to be eaten when they're hot!" Mom instructed. Again the recipe was not written or taught, but sitting at our kitchen table, gorging on sugar-coated fried dough and cold milk with Mom, remains, literally and figuratively, one of my sweetest childhood memories... and may explain my obsession for donuts to this day.

So yes, I, the daughter of gifted and gorgeous Betty and the granddaughter of Lena-never-call-me-Grandma, inherited their cooking disorder and grew up not knowing a sieve from a spatula. But while the culinary arts were not valued in our home, the creative arts were highly encouraged... and a love for them was definitely inherited. I sang and danced for Lena's hotel guests and in our Temple talent shows. My Crayola drawings hung with Louvre-like honor on our kitchen wall. My improvised plays were met with parental "Bravos!" Mom was no cook, but she fed me praise and positivity and that nourished my confidence. By the age of six, I understood that my imagination could create great joy for others and myself. So I didn't see our weed-filled back yard as the sad fact that my folks couldn't afford landscaping—for me, it was early Egypt. And the eight Garcia kids next door were the Jewish slaves of mean Pharaoh who made them pick those weeds. I was Moses, of course, who freed my people... to celebrate with popsicles from the Good Humor truck. Seeds of a future screenwriter/playwright were planted among those weeds.

Who would my singer/dancer Mom have become had she benefited from the encouragement and confidence she gave me? Would her portrait grace the wall at Sardi's? Would a Tony, Oscar or Emmy have replaced Larry and Wendy? My mother's dream may have been deferred but it lived on in her daughter. In my freshman year at UCLA, I declared my major in Creative Writing, focusing on American Literature and film. Ever-cheerleader Mom waved those pom poms and cheered me on through college and beyond as I struggled to find my writer's voice and my way to a shot in television. How many trees did I kill with those unbought spec scripts?

I was beginning to question whether I was talented or just tenacious. Then in a moment, everything changed... as it often does for good or bad in life. In this case it was for good: I landed a job as a staff writer on *Mork and Mindy*. Ear-shattering screams and tears of joy from Mom for both of us. Her dream had also vicariously come true.

My grandmother's response? "That's nice, honey, but I was hoping for *Three's Company*. I'm crazy for that John Ritter!" Lena would have loved that, years later, John was my Co-Executive Producer on a series I created.

As for my own love life, my college boyfriend, a law student, found my role-defying "I don't do windows or cook" declarations endearing. We got engaged and his always-impeccably-groomed mother presented us with a porcelain teapot. To celebrate, and to commemorate my very first experience with brewing, I made tea for her by putting the pot directly on the stove. It exploded, of course, as did her hopes for me being a dutiful wife to her star-of-the-family son. Ten years later, we divorced. But it wasn't because my only culinary achievement was browning meat for Hamburger Helper.

Being on my own for the first time in my life was exciting. My thrice-married mother understood my divorce, but was petrified. "You're going to end up alone!" she warned. "Please, God!" I prayed.

Year two on "Mork and Mindy," and I meet a bright, boyish, studio executive. He was fun and good to my family. Mom was thrilled and so was I. We bought a big old house, remodeled the kitchen, which I never used, and adopted a mutt from the pound we named Babey. During hiatus we took terrific trips and every night dined in L.A.'s hottest restaurants. There was no time for home cooking, though I did once cook a Thanksgiving dinner for family and friends. Correction. *Attempted* to cook. I basted the turkey for six hours... but forgot to turn on the oven. The relationship also lost its heat when I found myself metaphorically asking, "Where's the beef?" Working hard and playing hard can be empty calories. After eight years we parted. He kept the old-new house. I kept the dog.

Strike two—and I was done with pursuing a committed relationship. I was happy without one, committed to writing and hanging with friends, family and my fur girl, Babey. But poor Mom had emotional whiplash, vacillating between pride of my professional life and fear of my personal one. Imagine her kvell (Yiddish for joy and pride) when I get a call that ABC has picked up my pilot, *Anything But Love*.

I was asked who I wanted to help steer the show and I immediately blurted out, "Dennis Koenig," a respected writer/producer on *M*A*S*H*. We met rescuing a comedy pilot titled *My Sister Sam*. Dennis was married at the time and I was living with that studio executive. I liked this Dennis. He was calm, kind, intelligent, secure and hilarious. Exactly the kind of mensch you want to be with in a foxhole. Three years later, Dennis became my show partner. He was no longer married and I was now a confirmed bachelorette.

Knowing how little free time I would have once the series was in production, I invited my parents to meet me for lunch at the studio commissary. I wanted them to see that I was okay and had solid support from this Dennis. My parents, as always, split a tuna sandwich—and I thought nothing of the fact that Dennis and I were *also* splitting a tuna sandwich. Heading back to our offices, my dad was walking ahead, joking with Dennis, and my mom whispered, "How does it feel to finally meet the right person for you?" I exploded: "This is a professional relationship, Mother. I have no time for this argument, let alone a man in my life." Mom backed off but annoyingly kept smiling.

The series ran for four years and won a Golden Globe, ASCAP Film & Television Award and two Viewers for Quality Television Awards. Dennis's and my run is still going strong after almost three decades and the rewards are daily and beyond measure. Mom knew before I did... and she didn't have to worry anymore.

Like my mother, I found love. Unlike my mother and grandmother, I actually began to reverse my cooking disorder. How did I break the anti-culinary chain? When Dennis and I were producing the series, what we cherished most wasn't our high ratings, but our private time together. So we began a ritual: every Saturday night, unless we had to work or there was an event to attend, we would stay home, cook dinner and watch films. We honor this ritual to this day. I'm still writing and still not a great cook, but I can brew tea and make a turkey now. And like Mom, I now understand the importance of a home-cooked dinner... or a deep-fried donut.

Take time to connect. Create something together and taste the moment. Count blessings, not calories.

My mother and grandmother did not record or pass on their signature dishes. They left no family recipes. But from Lena, I learned to be my colorful self and break the rules when necessary. From Mom, to sing my song, find the funny and follow my heart. From both, I learned to not be defined by a domestic identity, but to create my own signature life. They're gone, but alive and kicking in my delicious memories, and I dedicate this essay to them.

Betty Kout and her daughter, Wendy.

NOT LENA'S PIMENTO CHEESE DIP, BUT CLOSE

INGREDIENTS

2 cups shredded sharp Cheddar cheese
8 ounces cream cheese, softened
1/2 cup mayonnaise (life is short, use the real stuff)
1/4 teaspoon garlic powder
1/4 teaspoon ground cayenne pepper (optional)
1/4 teaspoon onion powder
1 jalapeno pepper, seeded and minced (optional)
1 (4 ounce) jar diced pimento, drained
salt & black pepper to taste

TO PREPARE

1. Place the cheddar cheese, cream cheese, mayonnaise, garlic powder, cayenne powder, onion powder, minced jalapeno, and pimento into the bowl of a mixer.
2. Beat at medium speed, with paddle if possible, until thoroughly combined.
3. Season to taste with salt and black pepper.

Serve chilled with crackers, crudité or toasted baguette slices... and enjoy! Thanks to allrecipes.com for this.

THE PESTO CHRONICLES

Nina Laden

IN THE SUMMER OF 1982, AFTER MY JUNIOR YEAR IN ART COLLEGE, I WAS A WAITRESS ON MARTHA'S VINEYARD. I WORKED IN A PLACE IN OAK BLUFFS CALLED THE BRASS BASS, SERVING SEAFOOD AND OCCASIONALLY DUMPING CLAM CHOWDER ON A HONEYMOONING COUPLE.

I'M SO SORRY!

SLIPPERY FLOOR ↓

THEY STILL GAVE ME A TIP!

I WANTED TO WORK AT THE FAMOUS RESTAURANT, THE BLACK DOG, WHICH I ATE AT WHEN I WAS A CHILD, WITH MY ARTIST PARENTS, BUT I DIDN'T KNOW THE RIGHT PEOPLE.

TAVERN

I DREAMED OF EATING AT THE BLACK DOG AGAIN.

ON ONE NIGHT OFF I DECIDED TO TREAT MYSELF. HERE I WAS, IN VINEYARD HAVEN FOOD HEAVEN STARING AT THE MENU.

IT WAS ALL SO EXPENSIVE.

The Black Dog Tavern

LIGHTER FARE

I GREW UP LIVING BELOW THE POVERTY LEVEL FROM AGE 11 ON WHEN MY BIPOLAR FATHER RAN OFF WITH MY BROTHER'S FIRST GRADE TEACHER. MY MOTHER COOKED LIKE SHE PAINTED = ABSTRACTLY. FOOD WAS A HORRIBLE EXPERIENCE IN OUR HOME.

WHAT IS THIS?

OH, SOME OLD MEATBALLS, SOME TOMATO SAUCE, SOME GRAPE JELLY FOR COLOR...

I USUALLY FED OUR GERMAN SHEPHERD, SPARKY UNDER THE TABLE. IF *HE* WOULDN'T EAT IT, I KNEW IT WAS BAD.

ROCK-HARD MEAT-BALL

VEGETABLES CAME FROZEN IN BLOCKS AND WERE COOKED UNTIL THEY TURNED INTO MUSH.

SPINACH- WITH STEMS

MASHED POTATOES WERE JUST THAT. MASHED. POTATO. BAKED UNTIL A CRUST FORMED.

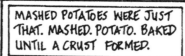
HAIR ADDED EXTRA PROTEIN.

I LIVED ON DANNON YOGURT AND RAISINS AND NUTS. BUT ON SOME SUB CONSCIOUS LEVEL MY SOUL WAS CRYING OUT FOR GOOD FOOD.

DANNON

AT THE BLACK DOG, THE CHEAPEST ITEM ON THE MENU WAS "MOUSTACCIOLI WITH PESTO." I HAD NO IDEA WHAT IT WAS, BUT I ORDERED IT ANYWAY.

I'LL HAVE THE MOUSE-TA-SEE-OH-LEE WITH PESTO.

MOOSE-TA CHELLY...

THE WAITRESS PUT A PLATE OF EMERALD GREEN PASTA IN FRONT OF ME. I WOULD SAY IT LOOKED LIKE GUACAMOLE, BUT AT THAT POINT IN MY LIFE I HAD NEVER HEARD OF GUACAMOLE.

I TENTATIVELY PUT A FORKFUL INTO MY MOUTH.

IT WAS A REVELATION.

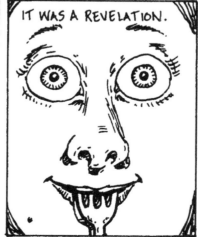

MY MOUTH AND MY STOMACH AND MY BRAIN HAD AN ORGASM - WHICH LASTED LONG AFTER THE MEAL WAS OVER AND I HAD PAID MY $7.95 PLUS TIP.

PESTO!

I WENT BACK TO SYRACUSE FOR MY SENIOR YEAR OF COLLEGE AND MOVED IN WITH MY BOYFRIEND, JACK. I WANTED TO IMPRESS HIM WITH MY COOKING PROWESS, SO ONE NIGHT I DECIDED TO MAKE PESTO. HAVING READ A RECIPE SOMEWHERE, I WENT SHOPPING AT PETER'S IGA. IT WAS WINTER. I WAS CLUELESS. I WANDERED AROUND THE STORE AND BOUGHT A GREEN CAN OF KRAFT PARMESAN CHEESE, SOME CHEAP OLIVE OIL, AND A BAG OF ANCIENT WALNUTS.

THEN I LOOKED FOR THE BASIL AND GARLIC. I FOUND THEM IN THE SPICE SECTION.

IN JARS.

DRIED AND POWDERED.

BACK AT MY APARTMENT I PUT ALL THE INGREDIENTS IN THE BLENDER, WHIRLED THEM TOGETHER,

AND MIXED THE PASTE WITH SOME COOKED PASTA.

IT WASN'T GREEN. IT WASN'T CREAMY. IT WASN'T GOOD.

THIS IS GROSS!

NEITHER WAS MY RELATIONSHIP.

YOU CAN'T COOK! YOU USE TOO MANY UTENSILS!

I DUMPED JACK, WHO WANTED ME TO COOK IN HIGH HEELS AND A BIKINI.

YOU NEED TO LOSE 5 LBS! YOU SHOULD WEAR HIGH HEELS - THEY MAKE YOU LOOK SEXIER...

BUT I DIDN'T GIVE UP ON THE PESTO.

LIVING IN ATLANTA AFTER COLLEGE, I DISCOVERED THE DEKALB FARMER'S MARKET.

Your Dekalb Farmers Market
A World Market

I ALSO DISCOVERED THAT BASIL WAS A PLANT

BASIL $1.99 BUNCH

OREGANO $1.99 BUNCH

AND THAT GARLIC WASN'T A POWDER. IT WAS A BULB.

ALSO, PINE NUTS DIDN'T TASTE LIKE PINE.

CREAMY! RICH! SWEET! NUTTY!

AND WHEN I DISCOVERED LOCATELLI SHEEP'S MILK ROMANO CHEESE I THREW AWAY THAT NASTY GREEN CAN OF PARMESAN.

LOCATELLI

IT TOOK A LITTLE LONGER FOR MY OLIVE OIL TO DISCOVER ITS VIRGINITY, BUT AS MY LIFE IMPROVED, SO DID MY INGREDIENTS.

MADONNA
LIKE A VIRGIN OLIVE OIL

WITH MY MINI KRUPS FOOD PROCESSOR I LEARNED TO WHIP UP PESTO AND MAKE PASTA TO TRY TO WOO THE GUYS I DATED. I THOUGHT THAT THE WAY TO A MAN'S HEART WAS THROUGH HIS STOMACH.

SADLY, MOST OF THE GUYS I DATED WERE MORE INTERESTED IN PUSSY THAN PESTO.

I DIDN'T REALIZE IT THEN, BUT I WAS SECRETLY SEEKING A MAN WHO WOULD SHARE MY OBSESSION FOR FOOD-ESPECIALLY

GARLICKY, NUTTY, CHEESY, BASIL-Y,

COMFORTING FOOD.

I MET THE MAN WHO WOULD BECOME MY FUTURE HUSBAND IN A BAR IN ATLANTA. HIS NAME WAS BOOTH. OUR RELATIONSHIP HAD TO SIMMER FOR A WHILE BECAUSE OF LONG DISTANCE AND SOME OTHER "ISSUES" LIKE: HE WAS GOING THROUGH A DIVORCE AND HE HAD THREE LITTLE BOYS.

ON THE POSITIVE SIDE, HE SOLD SEAFOOD TO JAPAN AND INTRODUCED ME TO INCREDIBLE SMOKED SALMON AND SUSHI - AND TO SEATTLE COFFEE.

I INTRODUCED BOOTH TO MY PESTO. PRETTY SOON WE WERE PUTTING HIS SMOKED SALMON ON MY PESTO AND HIS... OH, NEVER MIND.

OUR LONG DISTANCE RELATIONSHIP ENDED WHEN BOOTH LOST HIS BUSINESS AND HAD TO MOVE IN WITH ME IN ATLANTA. I HAD FALLEN IN LOVE WITH THE MAN, AND ALSO WITH THE COFFEE IN SEATTLE, SO WE DECIDED TO OPEN AN ESPRESSO BAR IN ATLANTA. THAT ALMOST SEEMED EASY COMPARED TO BECOMING AN INSTANT FAMILY: ADD THREE LITTLE BOYS, ONE PLANE RIDE, ONE CONVERTED ATTIC AND ROAST EVERYONE IN THE HOT ATLANTA SUMMER.

BRIAN

MOCHA

CHRIS

DOUG

AND OF COURSE I HAD TO FEED THEM. ENTER PESTO: PUTTING A PLATE OF GREEN FOOD IN FRONT OF LITTLE BOYS IS LIKE ASKING THEM TO EAT ALIEN VOMIT. ACTUALLY, THEY MIGHT HAVE LIKED THAT.

BOOTH DECIDED WE WOULD ADD SALMON ROE "IKURA" TO THE PESTO. TO MY SURPRISE THE BOYS LOVED IT. GREEN FOOD? FISH EGGS? WHAT WAS NEXT?

SALMON ROE
KETA SALMON

NEXT WAS SEATTLE. WE NEEDED TO MOVE BACK THERE. I SOLD MY HOUSE IN ATLANTA. WE BOUGHT A HOUSE IN SEATTLE,

TOTAL FIXER-UPPER

AND THEN A HOUSE ON LUMMI ISLAND. MANY THINGS HAPPENED, GOOD AND BAD, OVER THE YEARS, AND I LEARNED HOW TO GROW MY OWN HERBS, FRUIT, VEGETABLES, POTATOES, GARLIC...

DEER-PROOF RAISED BEDS

AND I BECAME A FORAGER: MUSHROOMS,

BLEWITS

CHANTERELLES

PORCINI

MORELS

& OTHERS

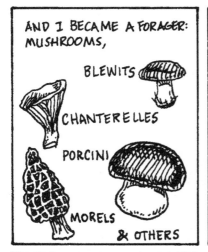

NETTLES,

THEY STING.

WEAR GLOVES. USE SCISSORS. BLANCH IN BOILING WATER.

WILD BERRIES.

WILD PLUMS, TOO.

SALMON BERRIES

HUCKLE-BERRIES

BLACKBERRIES

THIMBLE BERRIES

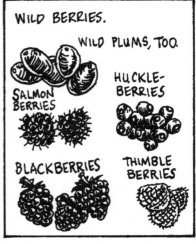

NETTLE PESTO IS AMAZING. OREGANO TAKING OVER THE GARDEN? MAKE OREGANO PESTO. GOT GARLIC SCAPES? MAKE GARLIC SCAPE PESTO.

GRATED LOCATELLI

SALT

EXTRA VIRGIN OLIVE OIL

GARLIC SCAPES

PESTO HAS GONE ON FISH. IT'S BEEN SWIRLED ON TOMATO TARTS. IT GOES INTO MY RISOTTO.

HALIBUT

TOMATO TART

SMOKED SALMON PIECES

RISOTTO

WE EVEN HAD A CAT, CALI WHO ATE PESTO.

PESTO HAS BEEN A CONSTANT COMFORT AND THE VERY GLUE THAT HAS HELD MY LIFE TOGETHER AND MADE IT SO DELICIOUS. PLUS IT IS SO EASY TO MAKE.

27 YEARS LATER...

AND THOSE THREE LITTLE BOYS ARE NOW MEN, AND THEY ALL ASKED ME FOR MY PESTO RECIPE. I SHARED IT WITH THEM, AND OF COURSE I'LL SHARE IT WITH YOU.

BRIAN IT GUY

CHRIS CHEF

DOUG ELECTRICIAN

PESTO

PESTO IS NOT AN EXACT RECIPE, BUT THE BETTER YOUR INGREDIENTS, THE BETTER YOUR PESTO. IT KEEPS WELL IN THE REFRIGERATOR, SO MAKE A BIG BATCH. I ALSO ADD THE POWDER FROM A VITAMIN C CAPSULE - (ASCORBIC ACID) TO HELP IT RETAIN ITS VERDANT COLOR.

PESTO INGREDIENTS:

A BUNCH OF FRESH BASIL LEAVES, CLEANED AND STEMMED
1 OR 2 CLOVES OF GARLIC, PEELED AND COARSELY CHOPPED
A SMALL HANDFUL OF PINE NUTS
ABOUT ½ CUP FRESHLY GRATED LOCATELLI ROMANO CHEESE
2 +/- TABLESPOONS EXTRA VIRGIN OLIVE OIL
¼ TEASPOON SEA SALT
1 VITAMIN C CAPSULE, POWDER ONLY

IN A FOOD PROCESSOR, PUT GARLIC AND PINE NUTS ON THE BOTTOM, AND THEN FILL WITH PACKED BASIL LEAVES. ADD THE SALT AND VITAMIN C POWDER, THEN ADD MOST OF THE GRATED CHEESE AND SOME OF THE OIL. START PROCESSING AND THEN STOP AND SCRAPE DOWN THE SIDES AND ADD MORE OIL AND MORE CHEESE UNTIL YOU GET A NICE, CREAMY, THICK, BRIGHT GREEN PASTE.

TOSS WITH HOT PASTA, AL DENTE, AND SERVE WITH SMOKED SALMON ON TOP, OR GRILLED CHICKEN BREAST,

ADD SOME FRESH STEAMED CORN KERNELS,

OR SOME SLOW ROASTED PLUM TOMATOES,

OR A SPOONFUL OF IKURA.

STIR PESTO INTO YOUR RISOTTO. MIX IT INTO POTATO SALAD.

PLAY WITH YOUR PESTO...

...AND DON'T FORGET TO FLOSS AFTER. IF YOU DON'T, EVERYONE WILL KNOW THAT YOU ATE PESTO.

MULTIPLE COURSASMS

Mustard Fish

Roasted or Grilled Vegetable Medley

Green Salad

Flourless Chocolate Cake

Blender Salsa

Pinto Beans

Tortillas

Tamales

The Elephant in the Room

by Claire LaZebnik

Question: How do you hide an 85-pound dog in your house?
Answer: Not for long.

My husband once said to me, "I'm well aware that if I died tomorrow, the house would be full of dogs and cats by the following week."

He's not wrong.

I don't want my husband to die, but there is something appealing about being able to bring home any pet I want, whenever I want, with no one to say no or be unhappy about it.

On the other hand. . .that could lead to a really exhausting life of way too many cats and dogs and poop and barf and barking and dead birds and irritated neighbors. I know this, because we currently have three dogs and one cat, and it's already a fairly exhausting life of poop and barf and barking and dead birds and irritated neighbors. So it's probably a good thing that I have someone in my life who says no when I want another pet. Which I always do.

Way too often, my daughter and I will decide to go to an animal shelter "for fun." My sons may or may not tag along. (They're the rational ones.) At some point, some furry little ball of wonder will paw at the cage and our hearts will melt on cue. "We can't just leave him/her here," we'll tell each other, close to tears. We decide we have to take it home. And then we call Rob, and he says, "No, absolutely not. No more pets." You can hear our hearts break in sync, as we slink miserably out of the shelter.

You're may be wondering how we even ended up with three dogs and a cat. Well, Rob does like cats—he grew up with them—and they don't bark, so he's fine always

· 164 ·

having one around. And our old yellow lab, Harvey, won his heart when, as a puppy, he was trotted out at a temple fundraiser to be auctioned off, and just quietly lay in people's arms without struggling. (He was and remains a Very Good Boy.)

Our little mixed-breed lapdog, Lula, though . . . getting *her* accepted was a tactical operation worthy of the Navy SEALs: Annie brought her home without permission; I pled for lenience since it was Mother's Day (which it was); and we both swore we were just boarding her for a few days. Lula was spayed that week, and I pointed out that we had to take care of her while she recovered . . . and by the time she had healed, I could honestly insist that she had proven herself a sweet and well-behaved dog and deserved a permanent spot in our household.

And Lula *was* a nice addition to our household. Even though he's never fallen as much in love with her as the rest of us, Rob doesn't harbor any resentment over her existence here.

Mabel, though . . . Mabel's a different story.

A story rife with tension, deception, sleuthing . . . and food.

It was the first day of summer vacation last year—my youngest had just gotten out of school, and so I took him and Annie and their older brother out for brunch to celebrate. We were having Rob's brothers over for dinner that night, and his sister-in-law and nephew, so I knew I'd have to start cooking in the late afternoon, but we still had several hours ahead that were deliciously open. (I try not to work when the kids are free—the luxury of being self-employed.)

It was, of course, Annie, who suggested we go to an animal shelter—one just happened to be around the corner from the restaurant.

"We don't need another pet," I said, pretending for one moment that I was a responsible adult.

"Just for fun," said the devil on my shoulder momentarily disguised as an eighteen-year-old girl. "Just to look."

The rest of the afternoon is a bit of a blur. At some point we saw Mabel's photo and then we saw Mabel herself—a Boxer/German Shepard mix with a gentle demeanor and evasive eyes. Annie and I instantly loved her. She seemed sweet but slightly damaged in a way that touched us. Johnny and Will were more cautious. It concerned them that she didn't always make eye contact. And . . .

"We should call Dad," Johnny said. More than once. Many times.

I fingered my phone but didn't place the call. I knew what would happen if I did. He would say *No, absolutely not*. And that would be the end of it. We couldn't adopt a dog once he had told us not to.

On the other hand, if I didn't give him a chance to *tell* me not to adopt the dog, I wasn't technically going against his wishes.

It was wrong not to call him and I knew that. But then there was Mabel . . .

The die was cast when I asked if Mabel was housetrained, and the shelter worker said, "It's hard to tell for sure, but she always keeps her kennel clean, which is a very good sign. The one time we didn't get around to walking her in the morning, she was so ashamed of having peed inside that she tried to lick it up." That was it for me: No way I was going to leave her there for that to happen again.

There was a flurry of activity and a lot of paperwork and a lot of waiting around—but eventually we found ourselves driving home with Mabel. The excitement of having a new family member was tempered by terror about what Rob would think. He still didn't know. He would come home eventually . . . and then what?

Meanwhile there was still the dinner at our house for my in-laws. I needed to start cooking. We got home with the dog, who was quiet but anxious in the car (no barfing though, which seemed like a good sign, and she was already cozying up to Annie, which also seemed like a good sign). As soon as we got home, I opened the back door, and she ran into the backyard. And she stayed there. Whether she was scared of us or just delighted to be outside and free, I don't know. Just that it was where she wanted to be. So I let her stay outside and went into the kitchen to cook.

As I started to move around the kitchen, gathering ingredients for my cooking (roasted vegetables and fish in mustard sauce; I wouldn't eat the fish—I'm a vegetarian—but the others would), I kept trying to figure out what I should say to Rob. I knew he wouldn't be happy to see a new pet in the house. To him, more pets meant more poop to clean up, more noise, and more mess. Some animals managed to charm him, but I wasn't sure Mabel would be one of those: she seemed pretty nervous around men.

Maybe since she was outside, he just wouldn't notice her for a while?

How long could you keep the presence of an 85-pound dog a secret?

As I cleaned and sliced mountains of vegetables, I fantasized about his *never* finding out. Maybe Mabel could just be an outdoor dog. She'd live happily in the yard, and when Rob was safely at work, I'd take her on walks and play with her. That could work, right?

He texted to say he was leaving work. I texted back, "Great!" and kept cooking. The dog stayed outside.

Rob came home. He parked his car in the garage, walked inside the house, greeted me cheerfully, talked about how dinner smelled good . . .

We had a nice conversation. I said nothing about a dog. Nothing. I just kept cooking. And then Rob started to clear off the table to set up for dinner.

"Wait," he said. "What is this? Why do we have something from an animal shelter?"

Oh, shit. I had left out Mable's folder. I opened my mouth but nothing came out.

"I don't understand," he said. "Who's Mabel? What's going on?" He looked all around, wildly, and then something caught his eye through the window. "Oh, no," he said. "Please tell me you didn't do this. Tell me you didn't get a dog today."

I'm going to gloss over the next few minutes. Suffice it to say that I've only seen my husband really furious at me maybe three or four times in our almost three-decade-long marriage. This was one of those times. The fact that his anger is so rare makes it absolutely terrifying when it emerges.

I had retreated to abject apology—"I'm sorry, I'm sorry, I know I shouldn't have, I'm sorry"—when the doorbell saved me. His brothers had arrived.

If you've ever been married or in any kind of longterm relationship, you know that there's an unspoken, unwritten, unacknowledged point system always in play. I had cost myself a *lot* of points—I mean, I was in the toilet. So I threw myself into making dinner as nice as it could possibly be. It was for *his* relatives. The better the meal, the nicer the time they had, the more I corrected the point imbalance.

And it *was* a good meal. The fish came out perfectly, the vegetables were slightly caramelized, and dessert was everyone's favorite: chocolate cake with berries and ice cream.

My in-laws sided with me: they thought the dog was cute and we should keep her. Rob smiled and chatted with them, but he avoided looking at me, and I knew he was still seething.

The relatives left. We cleaned up in silence.

The dog eventually came back into the house.

It's nine months later and we still have her.

She's an enormous pain in the butt—she barks way too much and she's skittish around strange men (we think she was abused at some point); she scares delivery people by lunging at the door when they come near; and she's a constant source of tension between me and Rob, who winces every time she barks. Sometimes I regret having brought her home. Life would definitely be easier without her.

But . . . Mabel loves me and I love her. She dances with delight when I come downstairs in the morning and comes running when I call her name. When I scratch right above her tail, she melts against me. Our little dog will curl up in anyone's lap, but Mabel's affection has to be earned and that makes it very precious.

Oh, also? She really *was* completely and perfectly housetrained. She's never had a single accident.

Rob's birthday came about a month after we had decided to keep her (in the end, he couldn't bear to disappoint the kids). I showered him with the normal boatload of electronics, books and games (we do birthdays big in this house), and after he had opened them all, I handed him one last small present.

He unwrapped it. It was framed note that said:

I promise never to adopt a pet without your full and enthusiastic consent from this day forward.

It was signed and dated.

He keeps it in a prominent place in his office, where we both can easily see it.

And I've kept my word.

So far.

Mabel dreams about being outside.

A MEAL TO MAKE WHEN YOU NEED
TO MAKE SOMEONE WHO'S MAD AT YOU
NOT SO MAD AT YOU

MUSTARD FISH

INGREDIENTS

One fish steak or filet for each eater, except of course the vegetarians, who will do just fine eating the vegetables, thank you very much
Crème fraiche or something similar, like Mexican crema or a mixture of sour cream and yogurt—basically it should be white and tangy
A few heaping spoonfuls or spoonsful of good mustard

Optional:
Chopped up onions
Capers

TO PREPARE

1. Mix up everything except the fish steaks or filets—put those in a pan and slather them with the sauce.
2. Bake at 425 until just cooked through. Don't overcook because overcooked fish is nasty. But, then, so is undercooked fish. Cook until just flaking.
3. Serve over rice.

ROASTED OR GRILLED VEGETABLE MEDLEY

INGREDIENTS

Go to the market and see what veggies look good. I heartily recommend:
Fennel
Carrots
Cauliflower
Broccolini
Onions
But you can try other ones too.

TO PREPARE

1. Clean the vegetables (peel if necessary).
2. Cut in similarly sized chunks, then roast in a 450 degree oven until softened and starting to brown. (You could also do bigger pieces and grill them but that's a lot of work, if you ask me—roasting is easier.)
3. Serve with slices of avocado and a dipping sauce. I recommend something that's creamy and smooth with lots of chopped up herbs, but if you like an onion-y dip or a ranch type thing or a tahini-based spread, all of those work.

GREEN SALAD

INGREDIENTS

Minced garlic (I usually use those little frozen blocks you can buy at Trader Joe's or the jarred garlic you can buy at Trader Joe's—I shop at Trader Joe's a lot)
Dijon mustard (Trader Joe's has a good one. Just saying).
Balsamic or white wine vinegar
Olive oil

TO PREPARE

1. Mix one teaspoon of minced garlic and one teaspoon of Dijon mustard
2. Add about a quarter cup of balsamic or wine vinegar and then as much olive oil as you want—I go light on the olive oil because my metabolism isn't what it used to be, but let's face it: the more olive oil, the yummier.
3. Whisk or shake, depending on whether or not your container has a secure lid.
4. Pour over a salad bowl full of arugula. Or baby lettuce. Or spinach. Toss well.

FLOURLESS CHOCOLATE CAKE

INGREDIENTS

1 full pound of bar chocolate (I have made this with all bittersweet and with a mixture of semi- and bitter, and I've even made it with milk chocolate—it works with anything, as far as I can tell).
2 sticks of butter
2 tablespoons of Kahlua—or any liqueur you like or no liqueur at all

9 large eggs, separated into yolks and whites, CLEANLY. No yolk in those whites.
1 ¾ cups of sugar

TO PREPARE

1. Preheat oven to 350.

2. Melt chocolate with butter in the microwave. Keep checking and mixing it so you don't overdo it or get any hot spots. I usually take it out when there are still small lumps of chocolate and let the residual heat melt those as I stir.

3. Beat egg yolks with sugar for a while (a stand mixer comes in handy). You want it to form "ribbons" when you lift the beater.

4. Beat the egg whites separately until they're stiff.

5. Fold everything together. This is a pain. Your arm will hurt. You'll wonder why you're bothering and you'll be tempted to just mix it all really quickly. So go ahead and cheat a little. Why not? Life's too short to fold in every molecule. But try to keep it as light and fluffy as possible.

6. Bake in a greased 10" springform pan until the edges have puffed and the center is still a little wobbly but not wet. (Somewhere around 45 minutes.)

7. Let cool. Chill it before eating and serve cold with whipped cream or ice cream and lots of fresh berries.

Toddlers and Tortillas

by April Salazar

When you're a shiny-haired, folic-acid-popping, under-forty woman married to a man who's beefy through the shoulders, it's easy to make a baby. Ogle those shoulders while he unloads the dishwasher. Involuntarily ovulate when he says, "I know you're on your period, but they're still your feelings." Purchase a bottle of Two Buck Chuck, throw in a backrub, and let nature take its course.

When that fails, there is always the surefire method: book a non-refundable vacation for exactly nine months from now. And when *that* fails, add saline water to a vial to reconstitute the fertility drug Menopur, inject the vial with a dose of Gonal F, draw the mixture into a syringe, pinch the fat on your belly, and sink that bad boy in. Try to avoid a spot on your stomach that has been bruised before by that needle. Laugh when your husband plays Velvet Underground songs on his iPhone.

Do this for several days, then stand in front of a mirror and inject yourself in the keister with a drug to induce ovulation. Ouch! Not from the shot, but from twisting your neck around like that. Set your alarm for 5am, sleep on it, and then wake your husband with a seductive hand job that is, per your doctor's instructions, aided by a bottle of mineral oil and only mineral oil. Try to avoid buying the bottle that says "intestinal lubricant"—unless you're into that.

Once you've procured the "product," place it between your boobs for the ten-minute subway ride to the fertility clinic. This is called foreplay. Go into an exam room and place your feet in the stirrups while a doctor inserts the now washed sperm into your barren womb. (Cross your fingers that it's a temporary state!) Laugh when your husband takes your hand and plays "Shake You Down" on his iPhone. If, on the way out, you recognize someone in the waiting room, pretend that you have never met.

Now the waiting. Try not to read too much into things. So what that it's your husband's 40th birthday. Try to imagine all of the things you're going to do with your child instead. Hold her. Teach her to smash the patriarchy. Share your family's Mexican traditions. Try not to imagine too hard, because if this doesn't work out it will just make you sad. Now repeat fourteen times.

After the eighth try, and safely in the second trimester, you think, "This is my reward for having such a difficult time conceiving. I get to have an easy pregnancy." You start to wonder what kind of little boy he will be and how you're going to raise him to be a good man: the kind who doesn't mansplain or take his privilege for granted.

When your husband was a child, he turned to his father and said, "When I grow up, I'll take my boy riding on his bicycle. And he'll take his boy on his bicycle. And that boy will take his boy. And we'll all go riding together." Your father-in-law died just a few years before, but your husband has held on to his yellow Schwinn. You imagine him placing your son on the seat behind him.

Find out in the second trimester that the baby has a rare birth defect and will suffocate right after birth. Choose to end the pregnancy. Be that rare couple who brings burial wishes to the abortion clinic, then place your son's ashes next to your father-in-law on a hill in the Hudson Valley. You know that he will look after him while the bicycle remains in storage.

No one ever told you it would be this hard. You believed that you and your husband were so crazy about each other that all you had to do was lock eyes to make a child. But eventually it does happen, and your daughter is born with your straight black hair. She is the most beautiful thing you have ever seen.

Now she is two and a half, sweet and hilarious. The straight black hair has given way to your husband's brown curls. She looks so white that all she's missing is a "Coexist" bumper sticker and a set of Crocs. You resist the urge to scream to every stranger, "SHE'S MEXICAN!" You vow that she will grow up learning how to make your grandmother's enchiladas, her chiles rellenos, and her flour tortillas. As God is your witness, your daughter will always recoil at store-bought salsa. In the meantime, a person who has campaigned on a platform of white supremacy—someone who has called your people criminals and rapists—has been elected president of the United States. Cooking with your daughter becomes more than sharing your family's traditions. It is now an act of defiance.

You have grand plans. You and your daughter are going to make Grandma Alice's tortillas on Christmas day. These are the tortillas her mother made in Baja California and later Tucson, after she fled the Mexican Revolution. These are the tortillas she made every day while your dad was growing up and that the Okie neighbors called "big ole flapjacks." She taught you how to make them when you were eight, and for as long as she lived she told everyone you looked so cute with flour on your nose. Now you get to have this kind of moment with your daughter. You'll commune with her and your grandma and all of your ancestors before her. All of those nights of jabbing that %#&$! needle in your belly—you did it for this.

You decide to warm up by making tamales together on Christmas Eve. "Together" is kind of a loose term when working with a toddler. You make the filling and do the assembling and steaming, but she helps make the masa by adding scoops of *masa harina* to the stand mixer, lowering its arm, and turning it on. As she's doing so, she smiles and says "making 'ma-les." Your heart grows by a million yards. Grandma Alice must be looking down and brushing a tear from her eye. That tear might be because your *pinche* vegan ass is using overpriced organic vegetable shortening instead of Rex lard.

Christmas Day comes and you are tired. You made the tamales *and* a batch of guacamole (which your daughter pronounces "macamole") *and* a batch of salsa, taking time to roast three different kinds of chilis on the stove's griddle (which you call the "fancy *comal*"). By 3 pm you work up the energy to ask your daughter if she wants to cook with you and she gives an enthusiastic yes. This is your husband's cue to ask if she wants to go to the playground. You have been *cookblocked*. He'll claim later that he didn't hear you ask about making tortillas and just wanted to give you a break. You spend the rest of the day fighting, because what kind of asshole tries to let his wife rest? The perfect moment on the perfect day has passed.

The next day, you start making the tortillas, but your daughter has no interest. Your husband takes pity on you and joins in. The stand mixer worked so well with the tamales, why not try it today, too? Pressing the vegetable shortening into the flour mix with a fork sounds too tedious. By the time you roll out your first tortilla and place it on the fancy *comal*, you see the problem with the mixer. Much like the expression "cool beans," the dough has been overworked. The tortilla is hard. You half-heartedly roll out a second one before tossing all of the dough into the trash. You devise a backup plan. Your dad will be in town in a few days, which means you and your daughter can make his mother's tortillas with him. Three generations in the kitchen—this is even more perfect than Christmas. In the meantime, your daughter looks up from Netflix long enough to walk into the kitchen, grab a tortilla off of the counter, and bring it back to the couch to eat.

Dad visits and the two of you make a long list of the foods you're going to make: Pinto beans with chopped raw onion, enchiladas, fideo, salsa, guacamole, taquitos, more tamales, and finally, tortillas. You cook the pinto beans all day in a big pot on the stove, seasoning them with salt, pepper, and vegetable bouillon instead of Dad's preferred ham hock. Your dad and stepmom make cheese enchiladas, taking care to soften the corn tortillas on the *comal* before drenching them in enchilada sauce. You make fideo seasoned with cumin, and so much salsa and guacamole that your daughter eats it by the spoonful and comes to expect it at every meal. Your dad and stepmom make taquitos filled with boiled potato and scallion and you sneak into the kitchen while they're frying to do "taste tests."

The kitchen itself is a family project. You renovated it last summer with your husband and father, stripping it to its studs before adding outlets, drywall, cabinets, and flooring. Dad, a retired bricklayer and mason, taught you how to spread thinset onto the wall with a trowel before placing tile for the backsplash. When it is time to make tamales, he is a pro at spreading the masa onto the cornhusk. You place a mixture of pinto beans and *comal*-roasted vegetables on top and then fold it.

A few days later, your dad and stepmom return to California. Once again, you have lost your perfect moment for making tortillas with your daughter. You're disappointed, but then it hits you. This will happen on its own schedule, not yours, and when it does, it will be beautiful, just like your little girl.

BLENDER SALSA

(Never Buy Store Salsa Again)

INGREDIENTS

1 medium onion
2-3 cloves garlic
2 tablespoons lime juice
1 jalapeno
6-8 plum tomatoes
1 bunch cilantro
Salt and pepper to taste

TO PREPARE

1. In a food processor, chop the onion, garlic, lime juice, and about ½" of the jalapeno. (Adjust the jalapeno quantity to your spice preference.)
2. Add the tomatoes and cilantro and pulse to chop.
3. Add salt and pepper.

NOTES

All ingredients are "to taste." Keep lots of teaspoons handy so that you can taste test and adjust quantities!

Chilies get spicier the closer you get to the stem.

BLENDER SALSA (CONT.)

This is a flexible recipe with lots of variations. You can:

◊   Hand chop all ingredients to make pico de gallo.
◊   Substitute tomatoes with 10-12 tomatillos to make salsa verde.
◊   Add to or substitute the jalapeno with serrano pepper, Anaheim chili, or poblano pepper.
◊   Substitute fresh chilis with peeled, seeded, roasted chilis from the *comal* (cast iron skillet) chilis.

PINTO BEANS

INGREDIENTS

1 pound dried pinto beans
8 cups vegetable stock
Salt and pepper to taste

TO PREPARE

1.   Rinse dried pinto beans, taking care to remove any stones, then cover with water, bring to a boil.
2.   Boil for one minute, then let beans soak for 1 hour.
3.   Drain and rinse all of the white foam off of the beans. This might take several washes.
4.   Add vegetable stock and simmer for about 3 hours.
5.   Add salt and pepper to taste after about an hour.

Garnish with chopped raw onions and scoop bites into flour tortillas!

TORTILLAS

INGREDIENTS

2 cups all purpose flour, plus ¼ cup
1 teaspoons baking powder
1 teaspoon salt
¼ cup vegetable shortening
1 cup warm water

1. Combine flour, baking powder, and salt in large mixing bowl. Cut vegetable shortening in with a fork or pastry blender until flour forms small beads. You should be able to press flour together to form a solid lump.

2. Mix in ½ cup water, then add more by the teaspoon until a soft dough is formed that doesn't stick to your hands.

3. Knead for about a minute or two.

4. Cover with plastic wrap and let rest for 30 minutes.

5. Divide dough into golf ball sized pieces.

6. Heat *comal* (cast iron skillet) to medium-high and sprinkle large cutting board with flour.

7. Brush hands with flour, and then flatten and roll out each golf ball, using quarter turns on the rolling pin until you have an almost paper-thin tortilla.

8. Heat each side on the *comal* for approximately 45 seconds. (Each side should have medium to dark-brown spots.)

TAMALES

INGREDIENTS

1 cup vegetable shortening
2 teaspoons baking powder
2 teaspoons salt
3 cups masa harina
2 cups warm vegetable stock
1 package dried corn husks
1 large onion
1 red pepper
8 white mushrooms
½ cup corn
1 cup pinto beans
1 zucchini
2 plum tomatoes
1 teaspoon garlic salt
1 teaspoon cumin
½ teaspoon chili powder
Salt and pepper to taste

TAMALES (CONT.)

TO PREPARE

1. Use mixer to cream vegetable shortening, baking powder, and salt.
2. Mix in all of the masa harina ½ cup at a time, then add 1 cup of the vegetable stock.
3. Cover with plastic wrap and then let rest in the fridge for at least an hour.
4. While the masa is resting, soak the corn husks in a bowl of water and dice all of the vegetables, except for the corn.
5. Season the vegetables with garlic salt, cumin, chili powder, and pepper, and grill on the comal. (You will have to do this in batches.)
6. Once the masa is rested, mix in the last of the vegetable stock.
7. Spread a thin layer of masa on each corn husk using a spoon or a tamale spreader, add a layer of the vegetable/bean mixture to the middle, and fold like a cheap suit—one side on top of the other.
8. Steam all of the tamales for about an hour. The dough should be firm and come off of the corn husk easily when done.

Enjoy with your homemade salsa!

WHO DOESN'T LIKE COOKIES?

Ammonia Cookies

Prince-Inspired Crispy Peanut Butter Bars

35-Second Chocolate Chip Cookies

Merrill's Guilt-Free Cookies and Cake

My Life in Six Cookies

by Nell Minow

Proust wrote seven books about his life, inspired by one cookie. My story is about six cookies that serve as chapter headings for my life. Really, there's nothing as delectable as a cookie, is there?

Chapter One: Pink Cookies (Age 5)

I grew up in Glencoe, Illinois, a small suburb north of Chicago on the shores of Lake Michigan. It was very much like the town Dick and Jane lived in with their dog Spot and their cat Puff in *Your Friends and Neighbors*, the first book I ever read.

My family lived a block from the business district, which consisted of one intersection with a couple of dozen stores. There, the three stops that were most important to me were directly opposite each other in a triangle. There was the public library and the Surprise Shop, a toy store whose birthday-party gifts were immediately recognizable from their candy-striped wrapping paper. And there was the Little Touch of Holland bakery, which had what were universally known as Pink Cookies.

Oh, the perfection of those pink cookies! They were big, flat, round sugar cookies with scalloped edges and a smooth glaze of powdered sugar frosting in a scrumptious pale shade of pink—except for the first two weeks of February, when they would be Valentine bright red, and all of October, when they would be orange, with piped chocolate triangle eyes and nose and a jagged-toothed jack o'lantern grin. The first way I learned to think about the passage of the seasons was watching for the change of the Little Touch of Holland cookies.

Chapter Two: Salerno Butter Cookies (Age 9)

We left Glencoe for two and a half years, when my father took a job in Washington. I was just starting fourth grade, and I learned for the first time not to assume that the rules in one place were the rules everywhere. My classmates and my new school were filled with surprises. Relationships, social structures, curriculum, and discipline were different. There was no PE class, just recess. Only boys were allowed to be patrols, supervising the children crossing the street. Until the Supreme Court ruled it unconstitutional, we said the Lord's Prayer every morning. And, most astonishing to me, we were served a half-pint of milk and a cookie every day at break. A cookie—in school.

And not just any cookie—one of my favorites. These were the daisy-shaped, light brown Salerno butter cookies with a hole in the middle. Not only were they delicious; they were an activity. How evenly could you nibble off the scallops when the cookie was strung on your finger, which you stuck through the handy little hole like it was a ring? Or should you open up the carton of milk and dunk?

If switching to a new school brought cookies, who knows what more adventures, gustatory and otherwise, were out there in the world to be discovered? The Salerno butter cookies served in school made me want to find out.

Chapter Three: Swedish Bark (Age 11)

We were back in Glencoe. My mother's best friend invited us to her house for a holiday tea. Paula was a lady of effortless elegance, grace, wit, and charm. She wore her hair up in a perfect belle époque poof. A friend once described her as looking like the queen of a small but very civilized country.

At the tea, she served us very, very thin, crisp, toasty-brown cookies on exquisite antique plates. We loved them, and Paula said that they were a cookie she learned about from her grandmother called "Swedish bark." They were brown, with a few crystalized red sugar sprinkles to suggest the Yule log. Not being Swedish or Christian, we were thrilled to learn of this exotic cultural tradition.

Paula's tea became an annual event for us, and over the years it grew to include dozens of lucky friends. Swedish bark was always at the center of the table, and my sisters and I were happy to show off our understanding of world culture by explaining about the cookies and the Yule log and Swedish Christmases.

When I was in law school, I attended another one of Paula's holiday teas, and as I was about to tell the story of the Christmas bark, she took me aside to explain that she had made the whole thing up. She had mis-measured the flour for a plain sugar cookie recipe, so in the oven they had all melted together and came out paper-thin.

We were about to arrive so she sprinkled on some sugar and came up with a story and a new tradition.

I still love Swedish bark, which taught me about aplomb, improvisation, and turning a mistake into a triumph, especially when there's a good story to go with it.

Chapter Four: Ammonia Cookies (age 15)

Our grandmother's friend sent us a tin of homemade cookies, and we all fell in love with them. I had never tasted anything quite like them. I recognized the ingredients of the usual sugar cookie: butter, flour, sugar, egg, vanilla. But the texture was crunchier and lighter than cookies made with baking soda. My mother called the friend to ask for the recipe and it turned out that instead of baking soda, they were made with a leavening agent that is found in Chinese almond cookies and some other ethnic pastries. The first time I tried a Pepperidge Farm butterfly cracker, I tasted it immediately.

At the time, there was only one place in Chicago that sold it, a pharmacy, and it came, thrillingly, in an unlabeled, unmarked brown glass bottle. It is called ammonia powder, so we call them ammonia cookies. They are still a family favorite. My sister had them at her wedding.

I learned from ammonia cookies how one small ingredient can be transformative.

Chapter Five: Oatmeal Lace (age 18)—and a Pink Cookie reprise

So, I met this guy. He was in my senior English class. And I liked him very, very much. I decided that a good way to impress him was to invite him over to my house and make ammonia cookies for him. That represented twenty-five percent of my culinary repertoire, along with popcorn, pasta (which we were still calling noodles), and steak. Note that the total ingredients for all of these recipes was nine and all had the same cooking instructions: heat and serve.

But I was sure that the combination of my cooking skills and the never-fail deliciousness of our special cookies would be just the thing to show him that he could not live without me.

He rode over on his bicycle, carrying a cylinder-shaped box of steel-cut oatmeal. He then sat me down in my kitchen, told me he was going to cook for me instead, and whipped up a batch of oatmeal lace cookies. I watched him cook with endless grace, confidence, creativity, generosity, and good spirits.

He was completely at home in the kitchen, as was, I would find out later, his father. I had never before met a father who was entirely sure where the kitchen in the house was.

The combination of the boy's cooking skills and the deliciousness of the cookies was just the thing to show me that I could not live without him. Now he more often makes actual oatmeal for me (steel-cut, and infused with chai tea) than oatmeal lace cookies, but I still love to watch him cook.

He grew up in Glencoe, too. Though our paths crossed many times in that magical triangle of bakery, toy store, and library, we did not meet until our senior year of high school. By then the Surprise Shop was gone, but we spent a lot of time together at the library and the Little Touch of Holland bakery.

The following fall, when we left for college on opposite sides of the country, he mailed me a pink cookie to help me get through my first week away from home. And seven years later, when he asked me to marry him, just a few blocks from the Little Touch of Holland bakery, and across the street from the house where Paula served us the Swedish bark, we celebrated with a shared pink cookie.

Chapter Six: Salty Oat (Now)

Every part of the country has its character-defining cuisine, but I have heard that only New York and Washington, DC are known for their cookies.

New York has the black-and-white cookie, which is okay, not great, but that's all right because they have the greatest variety of ethnic cuisines as cultural signifiers.

It is not, I am sure, a coincidence that I live in Washington, which has just one definitional food—the salty oat cookie. It comes in three varieties: regular (preferred by all persons of taste), chocolate, and chocolate chunk pecan, which would be worth getting if the original did not already exist. It is salty, it is oat-y, it is just the right amount of crumbly. The creation of pastry chef Terri Horn, the cookies are sold in Teaism tea shops, and the recipe has never been replicated.

The Washington Post tried and failed—and that's the paper that uncovered the Watergate scandal and busted Joe Klein as the "anonymous" author of Primary Colors. This gives the salty oat cookies a, well, tasty, tang of mystery.

Back in Washington, where Salerno butter cookies opened up the world of possibilities, the salty oat cookie reassures me that there is still more to discover.

AMMONIA COOKIES

INGREDIENTS

1 stick butter (soft)
¾ cup sugar
1 egg yolk
1 ¼ cups flour
Scant 1 tsp baker's ammonia powder (ammonium carbonate, available from King Arthur's or McCormick, use a pinch less than a teaspoon)
1 tsp vanilla

TO PREPARE

1. Cream butter and sugar. Add egg yolk, flour, ammonia powder and vanilla and mix well.
2. Roll into small balls and place on a greased cookie sheet. Make a shallow impression in each one with a finger.
3. Bake for 10-12 minutes at 350 degrees. They will be light in color—do not wait for them to turn brown.

Tip: store ammonia powder in the refrigerator after opening.

The Prince and The Peanut Butter

by Caissie St. Onge

Prince died. And much like the terrible way in which a person has to figure out what to do with the effects of someone they've lived with for years on the occasion of their departure from earth, so I had to fold up some vintage fantasies in acid-free tissue and file them away in my vault forever. Now I knew I would never get to see him sit down at a piano in an intimate setting to pour his heart, and everything else he had, into our overflowing glasses until all we girls and boys were taken, together, to another world of space and joy. I would also never, in said intimate setting, lock eyes with him in such a meaningful way that he'd send someone to fetch me backstage, where he'd propose that I pick up the dusty trumpet I hadn't touched since twelfth grade to go on tour with his band, ditching the suburbs and my family, who would, of course, totally understand. Finally, Prince would never be able to answer the one question I had longed to ask him for many, many, many years: *Do you like peanut butter?*

My feelings for Prince were love at first glimpse, when I was gawping at my Grammy's TV with my teenaged aunts, watching him stymie Dick Clark on American Bandstand in 1980. He wore gold pants, and said he was nineteen. I wore Garanimals and wouldn't turn eight for another four months. But when he sang "I Wanna Be Your Lover"—and without getting way more personal than a book of recipes perhaps calls for—let's just say it changed my little life forever. When you adore someone you don't actually know for that long and that hard, of course you imagine what you might ask that person if you ever met. "Do you like peanut butter?" was the one question I'd settled on if I ever found myself, say, sharing a taxi cab with Prince.

Why? Because, Prince was, at once, a wide-open book and an incredibly private man. He loudly told us everything he wanted us to know in his music and lyrics and movements and fashion and films and art, and the rest really wasn't anybody's beeswax. So, when I dug, as I did, the picture of him and me engaged in conversation, I couldn't fathom being bold enough to try to get him to give me more than he already had. Of course, I glanced at the gossip items and devoured the rare interviews he would sometimes grudgingly grant. I guiltily read rumors about him on the Internet, once that had been invented. But for every anecdote I've heard that was sort of wild, I would have much preferred to learn a detail that was mundane and mild. Like what a man put on his toast.

When you think of Prince, you might not think of him as a regular human who had to eat, or sleep, and indeed, he almost certainly did less of both than you or I. But, in 1985, Prince told Rolling Stone that when he was young, he didn't have any money, so he'd go to his local McDonald's and "just stand outside there and smell stuff." Multiple sources have confirmed that during business dinners, where plans for his first film, *Purple Rain*, were laid, Prince ordered spaghetti and orange juice. In the nineties, you were as likely to see Prince photographed publicly with a lollipop in his mouth as with lady candy on his arm. Also chewing gum. (If you want to send me into paroxysms of glee, send me a clip or GIF of Prince chewing some gum for my virtual museum.)

While Prince was known for loving sweets, he eventually lost his taste for meat, penning the pro-vegan and yet somehow very self-aware and not-at-all humorless tune "Animal Kingdom" for PETA in 1999, then going on to be crowned their "Sexiest Vegetarian" in 2006. And of course, in 2014, Fred Armisen famously told a story to Howard Stern about approaching Prince at an SNL after-party to tell him how great he was, to which Prince supposedly replied, "You know what I think is great? This mac and cheese," which Prince then continued to consume while, I assume, it was a good deal warmer than the reception he'd just served Fred. But in all I've ever gleaned about which foods were fit for my Prince, I never discovered the answer to whether or not he liked peanut butter. And now the question would stick in my craw, dry and unbudging, forever.

Why did I care so much whether or not PRN cared for PB? I don't know. Maybe it's because peanut butter has a lot in common with Prince? From the humblest origins, peanut butter is constant, smooth, astonishingly versatile, sometimes salty and often sweet. Peanut butter is fabulously rich and nourishing. It is beloved worldwide. Baby, peanut butter is a star! It would make sense that a poor American boy who grew up to be an enigmatic vegan genius rock god would probably at least be cool with peanut butter, but I just couldn't say for sure, and it was killing me, because I'm weird like that.

In the weeks and months following April 21, 2016, I mourned Prince's passing very publicly, across all social media platforms, with zero shame and plenty of patience on the part of my husband and sons. Every night, I went to sleep watching *Purple Rain* or *Under the Cherry Moon*, and the man I married and the boys I birthed never said boo about it. Every day, I listened exclusively to Prince's extensive musical catalog, while stealing moments to scroll through Instagram, gazing at photos of him posted by strangers who were obviously missing the man as much as I was.

It was in early October, during one of these Instaganders, that I saw a snap, uploaded by a stranger who'd attended the opening day of Paisley Park, Prince's former home, now a museum and monument to his life. And in that photo was the Paisley Park menu, created by Prince's chef, featuring some of Prince's favorite foods—and the answer to my question in the form of one dessert offering: a peanut butter-based Vegan Rice Crispy Bar that was "constantly stocked in his fridge" and "the perfect 4 a.m. energy snack." I'm not gonna lie: I cried. And my husband hugged me tightly, although I'm pretty sure he was also choking on a chuckle over my shoulder.

I was so happy, so relieved, to have this answer that appeared to me, like some kind of sign, and from such a reliable source, that I immediately took to Facebook, the forum I use like a teenager who is desperate for someone to pop the lock on her diary and read it. I could've written to the people in my secret Prince Facebook group about it (Hi, Purple Bananas!), but this information was so explosive that I just dumped my guts out about the whole thing on my public page with, as Prince sang on his first album, "love, sincerity and deepest care." And even though Facebook is how we communicate in the modern age, it also reminds me of the old mimeograph machines in school, minus the lovely lavender letters and delicious fumes. If someone enjoys what they've read, they can easily pass it on to everyone they know. Which is what happened.

I got a message from a wonderful friend, Sarah, who said she had shared it with a couple she knew, who ran a Prince website. And I was like, "Um, is the website Prince. org, Sarah? Because I know that website very, very well!!!" When she told me it was, I almost fainted. Then she asked if they could send me a little something in the mail. And I was like, "Good God, Sarah, yes!" I tried to play it cool as I watched the days on my calendar pass, waiting for that package to arrive. When it did, I opened it to find that Val and Ben, the founders of Prince.org and my new friends, had pulled some purple strings to send me a souvenir menu from Paisley Park, along with my very own perfectly prepared peanut butter-based Vegan Rice Crispy Bar! Just like Prince once enjoyed.

I was tempted to leave my treat in its plastic cling wrap forever, but like life and parties, Vegan Rice Crispy Bars weren't meant to last. So I ate it. You think I didn't? It was more delicious than its name implied and perhaps even more delicious than I was expecting it to be even considering that Prince probably wouldn't waste his precious time chewing something that was undelicious. Before I savored it, though, I took a pretty picture of my own and posted it to Instagram, like the social media trollop that I am. I suppose I was just looking for some likes, and the story could have ended there, but I got something even better.

Another social media friend, another Sarah, commented that her husband, Josh (a professional Internet personality your kids might know) had a recipe for a dessert that seemed similar to this, that had been passed down from his mother, who grew up in South Minneapolis near where Prince attended middle school. And they knew them as "Mrs. Nielsen Bars." Could Mrs. Nielsen Bars be close to what my Mr. Nelson loved? Further, Sarah said, after years of thinking it was some secret family specialty, Josh learned that they were a fairly common Minnesota delight, also known as "Scotcheroos," which, as names go, is about as adorable as Prince's childhood nickname, which was Skipper. Picture little Skipper scarfing a Scotcheroo after a long day at school practicing piano and jumping from atop that piano into splits! Okay, now stop before your heart bursts.

In both the original version, and Josh's improved version, the chewy, peanut-buttery, crispy rice base has a chocolate/butterscotch blend topping. And while there is some compelling evidence that Prince wouldn't have kicked butterscotch out of bed, I've omitted it in my version, because as far as I can tell, Prince's favorite iteration just had chocolate. I've also made some other adjustments. Not that I could ever know Prince's culinary business better than his personal chef! However, food, like music, is improvisational, and I would rather give you my interpretation than an imitation. Finally, my Prince-Inspired Crispy Peanut Butter Bars are not exactly vegan, but then, neither was he all of the time. Now, let's get nuts!

PRINCE-INSPIRED CRISPY PEANUT BUTTER BARS

INGREDIENTS

1 stick of unsalted butter, plus a little extra

2 cups light corn syrup (an entire 16 oz. bottle)

2 cups brown sugar

2 cups "natural" peanut butter (the kind without bad stuff in it, but not the super natural kind where you have to stir the oil back in) (an entire 16 oz. jar)

12-16 cups of crispy rice cereal (I keep it old school with Snap, Crackle & Pop)

12 ounces semi-sweet chocolate (chips, wafers, bars—you're gonna melt it, so it doesn't matter)

Sea salt, if you wish

TO PREPARE

1. Grease a 9x13 inch pan, all the way up! You can use Pam, she's a nice lady, but I prefer butter.

2. In a large pot, say 8 qt., melt, then gently brown, the stick of butter over low-to-medium heat. If you've never browned butter, it makes an already incredible substance sublime, and my general rule of thumb is, anything that's any good is always better when it's brown. Once the bubbles and foam start turning golden, watch it close, because it can burn in a second. Get it off the heat if it starts to turn too dark.

3. Add the corn syrup and sugar into the pot and cook over low-to-medium heat, stirring, stirring, stirring, until it comes to a boil. I like to let it boil for a moment because it's exciting and I believe in my heart it makes the final product more gooey, but don't let it go for more than a sec or your bars will be rock hard (in a funky place).

4. Remove the pot from the heat and stir in the jar of peanut butter. This is my favorite part because the brown swirls in the pot are so beautiful and hypnotic. Once everything is fully combined, the swirls go away and you can get on with your business.

5. Stir in your 12-16 cups of crispy rice cereal. I say 12-16 cups because it depends on what chewy-to-crispy ratio you like. I use closer to 12 cups, personally, and they still come out nice and thick like the ones from Paisley Park, but with plenty of peanut butter coating. I add a few cups at a time, but try to stir quickly before they start to set up. Your arms will get tired, but if Prince could play a stadium concert for hours, then go to a club and play for several more hours, you can stir some cereal into some syrup for a few minutes.

6. NOW! Turn it out…into your greased pan. I have tried spreading it with the spoon, but it's sticky like glue, so the best method, I think, is to put a piece of cling wrap over it, put a kitchen towel over that so you don't burn your hands, then press it into the pan until it's even. Peel off the cling wrap, then let it cool.

7. When it's no longer hot, all you have to do is top it with melted chocolate. You can melt your chocolate in a pan or double-boiler on your stove or in short 30 second bursts in a glass bowl in the microwave. If you have the time/energy/knowledge/higher-cocoa-butter-content chocolate, and you want to temper it so that it is sleek and glossy, by all means, do. But if you just have chocolate chips and you never even heard of tempering, just melt those and spread them in a layer on top. It won't be as cute, but chocolate doesn't need to be beautiful to turn me on. Then, before the chocolate hardens, you can, if you wish, hit it with a kiss of sea salt here and there.

8. Once everything has set, you can use a sharp knife to cut them into whatever size/shape pieces you desire. Prince often wished there were no rules and this seems like the perfect opportunity to forgo them.

Andy's Cookies

by Laura Shumaker

"Mom? Can I ask a huge favor?" Andy's thirteen-year-old voice cracked from low to high. "Can you help me clean up the house real quick? Luke and Greg are on their way over."

The last time my son Andy had friends over was four years ago, when his big brother Matthew, who is autistic, blasted the garden hose through the window and drenched a group of nine-year-old friends who were playing Battleship.

"He's trying to be funny," Andy told his friends apologetically, and in a way, I think Andy got it right.

From the time Matthew was three, he enjoyed running away impulsively, biting and hitting his brothers and classmates, and blasting them either with a hose or a super soaker. He liked to piss people off. Any of the consequences that followed were worth the thrill of getting people riled up. "Behavior is communication," his therapists told me earnestly, as if I hadn't figured that out already.

"Having a brother like Matthew will make Andy a better person," well-meaning friends had said when Matthew was first diagnosed with autism at age three. While their words were meant to comfort and encourage me, they implied that tough times were ahead for baby Andy, which strengthened my resolve to protect him.

Andy was five when I first noticed playmates in the park teasing him about his brother's hand flapping, and I flew to his side, ready to take on the little jerks.

"He has a brain problem," Andy was explaining to them cheerfully, "He can't help it." The boys nodded anxiously and backed away.

"Andy," I said with a lump in my throat, "I'm so proud of you. That was very loyal."

"Thank you," he said. "I'm proud of you, too."

It wasn't long, though, until the novelty of educating his peers wore off, and by the time he was seven, Andy's exuberant explanations started to turn defensive. I suggested some snappy comeback lines, but he never used them. My cheerful and outgoing son stopped having friends over. It was just easier that way, he said.

By the time Luke and Greg showed up at the door that day, Matthew had mellowed quite a bit since the Battleship incident, and was spending most of his afterschool hours with tutors and social skill coaches. But Andy was still nervous about having friends over again. He was out of practice.

"Tell you what. You work on your room, and I'll do the rest," I said, as I quickly heaved the mountain of laundry off the living room couch and carried it to my bedroom closet. I flipped on the oven in the kitchen.

Maybe I'd whip up a batch of cookies, or would that make it look as if we were trying too hard?

Within minutes, the clutter of the house was hurled into my room, the house was vacuumed and the toilets cleaned. The scent of Lysol still hung in the air from a quick wet-mop job, when the doorbell rang.

"Hi, guys!" I said, grinning like a modern June Cleaver. "He's back in his room."

They followed the sound of the electric guitar. Andy must have picked it up when he heard the doorbell ring, trying to act nonchalant.

I hid the mop and ran out to the yard to pick some roses. *What am I thinking? These are boys. But maybe their mothers do flowers. What the hell.*

After cutting a random assortment of roses, daisies, and salvia, I wondered if we had anything to eat. I ran to the kitchen, dropped the flowers in a vase, and threw open the cupboards. We had cereal, a few stale goldfish. No soda, only grape juice and milk. Popcorn? No.

Better whip up those cookies. But first I needed to change my shirt.

Andy thinks I look good in the blue V-neck.

Running to my room, I hear the boys laughing when I pass Andy's door, and my heart swells, my face warms. I hop over the laundry in my room and pull on the blue V-neck, brush my hair, put on some lipstick. I look fleetingly in the mirror.

Not bad.

Rushing back to the kitchen, I flip the oven on to 375, pull out the mixer and throw the ingredients together: a cube of butter, an egg, a splash of vanilla, the sugar, the flour, a little salt, a little baking soda and a cup of Chocolate Chips. Within thirty-five seconds, the dough is ready, and I pull out the cookie sheets.

Oh, no! Here they come! I try to look casual as I slap the dough onto the pans.

"Cookie dough!" crows Andy as the three slide into the kitchen. "My mom makes the best cookies. Can we have some dough?"

"Sure!" I say casually. This is not the time to give a salmonella sermon. Luke wanders into the family room and takes in our garden.

"Ooooo, Andy, your backyard is awesome!"

When my son thought I was perfect.

Andy flashes me a glorious, grateful smile. His eyes are shining. It's almost more than I can take. I hope his friends don't notice my goosebumps.

"Let's go, guys," says Greg.

"Mom, we're walking downtown. See you later."

"Thank you, Mrs. Shumaker," they say, dipping their hands once more into the bowl of dough.

"Have fun!"

And they are out the door.

Andy runs back in, shouting to his friends that he forgot something. "Thank you sooo much, Mom. You were perfect!"

I quickly wipe away the tear that's made its way down to my chin while Andy squeezes me in a hug. He grabs his Cal baseball cap and runs out, forgetting to close the door in his exuberance. I close the door, pause, and put the cookies in the oven.

They'll be back.

35-SECOND CHOCOLATE CHIP COOKIES

INGREDIENTS

1 stick unsalted butter, barely soft
1 ½ cups brown sugar
1 egg
1 teaspoon vanilla or vanilla paste
1 ½ cup unbleached flour
½ teaspoon baking soda
¾ teaspoon salt
1 cup Semi-Sweet Chocolate Chips

TO PREPARE

1. Preheat the oven to 375.
2. Put the butter and brown sugar in a stand up mixer and cream 20 seconds, throw in the rest of the ingredients and mix a little longer.
3. Put parchment paper on a cookie sheet and spoon the dough on it.
4. The cookies are best if they are on the small side, about a teaspoon of cookie dough.
5. Bake for 7 minutes, or until the kitchen smells good.

A World Without Cookies

by Merrill Markoe

Sometimes I think that all I have ever really wanted to do is eat cookies.

From the moment I got that stellar write up from my pediatrician in his book of baby statistics for speaking my first word at just six months old, I was clear about my intentions. That first word was cookie. After only 180 days as a resident of planet earth, I already knew enough about what I liked to ask for it by name.

No one in my family liked to give compliments. If they did, they delivered them upside down, and backwards, as in "Well…that's not too bad." Yet, from the time I was a toddler, there was one unqualified compliment that I knew how to get from my mother and grandmother. They'd both light up like a moonbeam when they said, "Merrill is a good eater." So I would proudly shovel in any amount of food they'd put in front of me, not yet aware that an aptitude for eating is one of the basic perks that get thrown in with just being alive, kind of like floor mats when you negotiate the purchase of a new car.

That was my understanding of the way life seemed to work, until *THE DAY THAT EVERYTHING CHANGED.*

I speak of an ominous day, which I recorded for posterity in the diary I kept in fourth grade.

This was the day that it dawned on me that unless I moved to Mauritania, where young girls are force-fed on fat-farms because obesity is sign of wealth and status, my mother and grandmother had been peddling a faulty narrative.

Food was actually my enemy.

Panicked, the first thing I did was ask my mother to buy me the little pocket-sized calorie counter I saw for sale at the supermarket checkout stand. If this were a scene in a movie, the score would now change to a foreboding cello solo in a minor key as I came face to face for the first time with the wonderful world of gender-based expectations my culture had in store. Not only were there only 900 calories a day

in a weight loss diet, but one 2 ½"x 4" chocolate chip cookie, all by itself, contained 480 calories. Cue the cello again as a flashback showed me eating not one but *three* chocolate chip cookies earlier that day.

That damn calorie counter contained fresh horrors on every page. A baked potato with toppings was 450 calories! A cup of peanuts was 862!

Then a ray of sunshine: a stalk of celery was a mere six calories!

Back to more frightening cello chords as I confronted how much I hated celery.

By high school, I was trying to eat only celery, three meals a day. In search of better dieting tips, I'd started frequenting health food stores, aware that a diet moored in maintaining good health came with a foolproof set of counter arguments I could use in the contentious mealtime fights I was now having with my parents. And so I devoured books with unsettling titles like "The Mucusless Diet," whose cover was memorably adorned with a black and white photograph of its author, glowering behind his meticulously waxed handlebar mustache and goatee. As I read all his harsh dietary edicts, I tried not to imagine how his facial hair might have looked before he got his mucus problem under control.

By college I'd become a vegetarian, which helped make my many new rules for eating more user-friendly. Now I refused to eat anything that, while alive, would have caused me to emit the sound AWWW—a word I was never inspired to say when looking at celery. This simple but effective system served me well until the advent of "nouvelle cuisine," when I began saying AWWW at the sight of miniature potatoes and carrots.

In my sophomore year, still yearning for cookies, I stumbled upon a packaged weight loss plan called Metrecal Cookies™ which supposedly provided a balanced 900 calorie diet via three small flavorless pasty "cookies" per meal. Cautiously I embraced them, usually eating only half of the suggested portion because, deep inside, I continued to suffer from the searing betrayal of the cookies of my youth. It was difficult to shake the feeling that any cookie could really be trusted.

And so, as the years passed, cookies were banished from my life entirely.

I became such a devoted acolyte of all things nutritious and low calorie that when offered a choice between a delicious fresh baked chocolate chip cookie and a sad plate of damp tofu, I would choose the tofu one hundred percent of the time. Yes! ONE HUNDRED PERCENT! These were the sacrifices I made willingly on the road to being slender and immortal.

Once the Internet came along, a day rarely passed where I didn't succumb to a slide show of eight (or twelve or thirty) important "super foods" I quickly incorporated into my life. When people got mad at gluten, I got mad at it too. In no time at all, I had so many containers of vitamins and food supplements such as glucosamine, astragalus, and non-colloidal silver that there was no longer room on my kitchen counter for food preparation. That was fine with me. In my view, cooking had become an anachronism.

I was, of course, starting my day with a combination of raw vegetable juices, every glass a 'powerhouse' of semi-palatable nutrients extracted fresh by my very own juicer. Looking back, the only thing I forgot to do was grow my own food. Well I didn't forget. Those eight organic pea pods I grew that one year didn't stretch nearly as far as I had intended.

That was how I rolled. Until one night last spring when extreme feelings of nausea and chills sent me to the emergency room.

The events that transpired as I waited to have my gall bladder removed were surreal. As I sat in my hospital bed, awaiting surgery, every nurse and doctor I encountered, having just had a look at the x-ray of my grotesquely infected gall bladder, asked me the same question: *"What kind of diet have you been eating?"*

"A lot of fried foods?" guessed the first nurse.

"A lot of hot dogs and pizza? A lot of sweets?" guessed the surgeon.

"**FOR CRYING OUT LOUD, MOTHERFUCKERS**, " I screamed at them all, "**How about FORTY YEARS OF SALAD? How about blueberries and kale and whole grains and fresh raw organic vegetable juices packed with super nutrients**?"

The craziest part was: I could see that they didn't believe me. And so I sat stunned as my dreams of immortality through health food shattered into pieces around me.

That night, after my surgery, I ordered chocolate layer cake for my dinner.

When I got home from the hospital, I was so disillusioned I fully intended to start eating junk food. But it turns out good habits are as hard to break as bad ones. After all those years of unprocessed foods, the empty sweetness of donuts and cake no longer seemed fun. I realized I was stuck for life in a "healthy" eating pattern even though I no longer really believed in what "healthy" even meant.

I could take only one lesson away from this experience. There was absolutely no reason not to eat cookies.

So I created an amalgam of other people's healthy cookie recipes and ended up creating the sugar-free low-calorie high-protein nutrient-dense cookie I am sharing below. I am not frightened by these cookies because I know what's in them. And they fulfill my essential cookie requirements as much as the commercial kind.

This recipe is basically a cookie improvisation. If you attempt it, realize that your Phase One end-game is a tasty dough-like substance that, when combined with heat, will turn into baked goods.

If you thin it out and pour it into a loaf pan, it will turn into cake!

If you make it thick and drop it by the spoon full onto a greased baking sheet, you will get cookies.

Many of the ingredients are interchangeable. You are trying to make dough or batter. Go ahead and use more or fewer eggs, or seeds. I generally do. Also, you can throw in nuts or raisins, or add cinnamon! If you add the carrot pulp that is left after juicing, the cake becomes more dense and moist. Same if you throw in some fresh frozen blueberries.

What I'm saying is: feel free to change the ingredients around, except for the flour and baking soda. If you want to replace the chocolate with almond extract or lemon, you have my permission to go ahead. Just don't try to convince me it's a good idea. After so many years of dieting, I will not be talked out of chocolate ever again.

MERRILL'S GUILT-FREE COOKIES AND CAKE

INGREDIENTS

1/3 – ½ cup almond flour

1/3 – ½ cup oat bran

1/3 cup flax seeds, chia seeds, any other stuff you like in cookies

1 tsp. baking powder

2 tbs. Olive oil

Erythritol or other sweetener you prefer

Some egg whites (or eggs). Or not.

Some almond milk

Unsweetened cocoa powder

Vanilla, cinnamon, blueberry, carrot…whatever

TO PREPARE

1. I usually strive for 2-3 cups of dry stuff….about a third oat bran, a third almond flour and a third flax seeds/chia seeds/any old kind of seeds or nut flours. (protein!)

2. Now add 1 teaspoon baking powder, 2 tablespoons olive oil, and about ½ cup of the Erythritol (or whichever sweetener you can stand) until you achieve the level of sweetness that you, the consumer, require. After decades of eating rubberized

health food, I don't require much.

3. If you're vegan you can ignore the eggs/egg whites. Then add a dash of vanilla, (and ½ cup of carrots or blueberries or whatever else you want.).

4. Stir it all up. Thicker makes better cookies. Thinner with more egg whites makes better cake.

5. If its too dry, add some almond milk till you get the consistency of the kind of batter you want.

6. Heat up a little almond milk in a pan, and when it is bubbling, combine 2-3 tablespoons of unsweetened cocoa powder with an equal amount of sugar free sweetener until it is a glistening chocolaty paste. You are going to stir this into the other batter till it's all blended.

7. But first stick your finger in there and help yourself to some. That's what I always do at this point. If you're grossed out, I will assume you're the kind of person who would also judge me harshly because my furniture usually has a light dusting of dog hair. If I just described you, you have my permission to close this chapter and read someone else's damn recipe.

PS: Perhaps you want ICING…Well then, here is a delicious icing cheat:

Simply mix no fat plain yogurt of some kind with the same amount of lo-fat cream cheese. Add flavoring like vanilla, chocolate, sweetener, etc. Voila: ICING that isn't bad for you!

SWEETS TO THE SWEET*
(*BUT NOT IN THE CREEPY OPHELIA'S GRAVE SHAKESPEARE WAY)

Rainbow Gelatin Cake

Barbara Jeane's Chocolate Sheath Cake

Apple Pie

Michele's Baked Alaska

Ima's Chocolate Walnut Cake

Something Jelled

by Claire LaZebnik

I just stood there, in the middle of the supermarket aisle, crying.

I felt . . . useless. Stupid. Frustrated. Wretched.

My son had just been diagnosed with Celiac Disease, which meant a lot of the foods around me were toxic to him and had been for years, even though I hadn't known it. His intestines were badly damaged because of foods *I* had fed him. Foods like toast, spaghetti, mac and cheese, pizza, birthday cake . . . So many good comfort foods. So many of my favorites. So many of his favorites. And all poison to his system.

This was 1998 and "gluten-free" hadn't yet become a household word. People weren't trying to keep it out of their diets yet. I had studied up and knew gluten was a protein found in wheat and related grains (that's an oversimplification, but let's go with it) but what I didn't know was how to be sure it wasn't hiding in the foods I bought. Gluten, it seemed, was a *lurker*, an unsavory character in a raincoat who waited down dark alleys so it could suddenly dart out and ruin your son's life when you least expected it, making him ache and vomit and stop growing. The doctor said even a trace amount of gluten could cause more symptoms, but back in the late nineties food labeling wasn't as precise as it is now, and there were still lots of ingredients that weren't clear about whether or not they contained gluten, like modified starches or those weird chemicals that I usually ignore at the bottom of the ingredient list.

My son was four years old and he was the size of a two-year-old. He'd be going to kindergarten in the fall, but he still only weighed twenty-five pounds, because I'd been poisoning him. Lovingly, dotingly, kindly poisoning him.

The last thing I wanted to do was continue to poison him. But as I squinted at label after label, my heart sank. I just couldn't *tell* whether or not these foods were safe. I was starting to understand why so many people online said you had to call the manufacturers and ask about every single item—a task that sounded about as much fun to me as going to the DMV. During lunch hour. When the lines are a billion feet long.

So I burst into tears.

Right there in the supermarket.

Then I stopped crying and got to work: I bought the things I felt were safe and wrote down the names of the ones I wasn't so sure about so I could research them later.

This was my life now. My new normal. I would figure it out because I had to.

Oh, there were bumps in the road, like the first birthday cake I made. I thought (incorrectly) that I could simply replace wheat flour with rice flour—I still remember a kind mother at Johnny's birthday party manfully choking down a few gritty bites while all the brutally honest five-year-olds made faces and pushed their plates away. Or the time—many years later—that I made tacos for dinner, using a new brand of "corn" tortillas that were remarkably springy and soft and delicious . . . and which made Johnny vomit all night long, because wheat flour had been added to give them that lovely texture.

But overall, I like to think I made Celiac Disease my bitch.

* * *

My mother and Johnny had gotten into the habit of baking together whenever she visited from Boston, but his diagnosis made that a lot more complicated—none of her old recipes worked anymore. So she did a little research and discovered that gelatin is gluten-free.

Now, personally, I don't eat gelatin. It's not a moral stance, or anything—although it probably *should* be, now that I think about it. I mean, I'm a vegetarian and gelatin's made from animals, right?

So let me rephrase that:

I don't eat gelatin. For moral reasons.

I'm a deeply moral human being.

Also? My mother used to make gelatin for us when we were sick. Bad stomach, sore throat, fever—whatever we had, we got served a dish of red gelatin. (That wasn't just the color. Red was also the flavor, as far as I could tell. Red-*flavored* gelatin.) I'd squish it through my teeth like mouthwash until it was liquid and then swallow it. It wasn't good but it was fun.

Unfortunately, being sick and eating gelatin led to a connection between the two things in my mind, and eventually just the thought of the stuff made me queasy.

(It doesn't help that the only time I make gelatin for myself now is when I'm prepping for a colonoscopy—it's the only solid(ish) food you're allowed. Yep, just the thing to bring it back into favor: celebrate the most fun day of your life—the one you get to spend entirely in the bathroom—with a big ol' bowl of green Jell-o. It successfully reminds me why I hate the stuff and should avoid it on that day and every other.)

Gelatin desserts and I were not, and would never be, friends, but I was glad my mother and Johnny had found something they could still make together.

I even bought a gelatin brand cookbook at the school book fair. It was filled with dozens of recipes of dishes I would never want to eat but which looked like perfect future grandmother/grandson projects.

Unfortunately, on her next visit to LA, my mother wasn't in the mood to do much cooking. She spent a lot of her time just hanging out at the hotel, turning down our invitations to come over. She said she didn't feel up to doing much and mentioned that her stomach was acting up a little. She seemed basically fine, though, and I felt annoyed—what was the point of my parents flying all the way from Boston to Los Angeles if my mother wasn't going to drive the extra ten minutes to actually spend time with her grandchildren?

When my parents got back to the east coast, the doctor decided my mother's stomach aches were probably gallstone-related and ordered an ultrasound to confirm.

That's when they found the cancer. Pancreatic. Stage IV. It had already spread everywhere.

We'd been through it with my grandfather a couple of decades earlier so we knew what that meant. He'd lasted twelve weeks. My mother didn't even make eleven.

* * *

I still had that stupid, unused gelatin cookbook, and in some weird way it felt like a connection to my mother, so one day I took it down and decided to try making some of the recipes with the kids.

Not everything worked out perfectly—I seem to remember an aquarium made out of blue gelatin that was a huge disappointment when compared to the photo in the cookbook—but then I stumbled across the rainbow cake recipe. (That's not actually what it's called. But it's what *we* call it.)

The rainbow cake requires a lot of dedication. You use five different colors of gelatin to make ten layers (five clear, five made opaque by the addition of a few tablespoons of sour cream). You have to build it slowly and laboriously, layer by layer. You have to know exactly when to pour the next color (the previous one should be firm but slightly tacky) and you have to keep the whole assembly line moving smoothly along so your gelatin's not too hot (which makes holes) or too cold (which makes lumps) when you pour.

When it comes out right, and you unmold and slice it, you get a cross-section of all ten colors. They shimmer and glow and look like stained glass—as beautiful as Gatsby's famous shirts. (And about as edible, in my opinion.)

The lengthy preparation time required for the rainbow cake means that while sometimes a child or two is willing to start making one with me, I always end up finishing it by myself. That's okay: I kind of like the way time slows down on those days. And it gives me an excuse to stay home, near the kitchen, which is where I'm happiest.

I make the rainbow cake every year now, for an annual party we throw. It's become a tradition. I pull it out at dessert time, and people come running to ooh-and-aah as I slice into it and reveal the shining layers (breath held that they're discrete and perfect). A few guests actually *eat* it.

Not me, though. Never me.

A friend actually featured my rainbow cake in a movie she wrote. True story. That's the kind of thing that happens when you live in L.A. Even your food can become a star.

* * *

My son—the one who has Celiac Disease—became president of his high school's Gay Straight Alliance his junior year, and ran it for the next two years. Under Johnny's governance, the GSA grew in members and attendance and sponsored some kick-ass events, including a yearly family potluck.

I needed to bring something to that first potluck and it wasn't hard for me to figure out what it should be.

The rainbow cake, of course.

I got a lot of compliments as I walked into the room and carefully added the shining, quivering circle to the other offerings. It *was* the perfect addition to the table. I mean . . . an edible rainbow for a gay rights event? Come on. Almost TOO on the nose.

What made me happiest was that I'd discovered that recipe in the first place because of my mother. I knew that if she had lived, she would have been very proud of Johnny, of how he had grown up to be the kind of kid who wanted to make a difference in the world, who was already making a difference in his small community.

And I'd like to think she would also have been awestruck by how expert her daughter had become at working with gelatin as an artistic medium. I mean, the dessert looked *gorgeous*.

You still couldn't get me to eat a bite of it though. Not then. Not ever.

My mother, Cynthia Scovell

RAINBOW GELATIN CAKE

INGREDIENTS

5 different colors of packaged gelatin
Water
Sour cream or yogurt

TO PREPARE

1. Decide what order the colors of gelatin would look pretty in, keeping in mind that the bottom will become the top and vice versa.
2. Mix the first box with 2 ½ cups of boiling hot water. Pour half of the mixture into a bowl and the other half into a large bundt cake pan. Set that in the fridge.
3. Meanwhile, whisk three tablespoons of sour cream or yogurt into the other half.
4. In about 15 to 30 minutes, check to see if the gelatin in the mold is set. It should

be mostly firm—just slightly tacky. If it's ready, pour the gelatin-sour cream mixture on top and put it back in the fridge.

5. Repeat these steps with the other four packages, alternating plain/clear layers with opaque/sour cream ones.

6. Let sit overnight until completely firm. Unmold by dipping in hot water for 30 seconds. (DO NOT DRIP WATER ON TOP OF THE GELATIN IN THE PROCESS OF UNMOLDING IT. I'm not saying I've done this. But I'm not saying I haven't, either. Okay, I've done it. It's gross. Learn from my mistakes.) Invert on a pretty plate. Make sure it's centered before lifting the pan because you can't move it after without leaving fingerprint indentations. Slice and ADMIRE. Or weep bitter tears because somewhere along the way, something went horribly wrong. Let the tears flow. They're cathartic. And gluten-free.

Barbara Jeane

by *Norma Safford Vela*

I was born in the early 1950s, when a woman couldn't get a credit card in her own name without her husband's signature, before legal contraception and definitely before legal abortion. If a woman worked outside the home, she was paid 60% of what a man was paid. A woman couldn't serve on a jury in all fifty states until 1973. I was the youngest child of four and my mother was twenty-four when I was born.

My mother, Barbara Jeane, was the first real-life feminist I knew. She, to this day, denies that she is a feminist. She didn't protest or burn her bra or that type of thing, she simply WAS. She believed that she had absolutely the same right as anyone else to do, say or be anything she wanted. She had the right to fair treatment and free expression. I learned that women's rights were human rights and human rights were women's rights, and she has shown me those beliefs every day of her life.

Barbara was the older of two sisters. I've heard different versions of how she felt about her mother, but marrying too early to get the heck out of her family home seemed the best indicator that the relationship wasn't working for her. She went to college, majoring in music, and often brought my older sister to class with her. Interesting that bringing an infant to class wasn't a real problem back then.

She had the remaining three of us—boom, boom, boom—while my dad finished school and found work in the oil business. His job took him to Europe a great deal, sometimes for an entire month, leaving my mom alone with four children under the age of seven. Somehow, she managed to find crazy fun in it all. I don't remember being yelled at or spanked by her—although I do remember my two older brothers holding me down and pretending to spit into my mouth... And apparently I managed to get outside, into the car and lock all the doors when I was two, but I don't remember doing it. I remember being awakened before dawn to hurry to Herman Park to search for a car key hidden by a local radio show: find the key, win the car! My mother had been following the contest avidly, listening for the clue, and she was sure this was the spot. We searched everywhere around one particular group of trees. We learned later—from the winner of the car—that the key was on a branch just above our heads. Even if we didn't win, it was a great adventure.

She took us all to New York to visit our grandparents. Four children. All under ten years old. In an airplane. From Houston to New York. I'm just saying... that's impressive.

My father's success allowed us to join a yacht club. Although we had no yacht, it had a terrific swimming pool and we kids could go into the bar, order Shirley Temples and say, "Put it on our account," like fancy people did. We swam and caught crab and ran wild while the Normal Mothers glared at us. We also said "yes, sir" and "no, sir" and strangers would stop at our table in restaurants to compliment my father on our excellent manners. The Safford kids had "restaurant manners." But Barbara wore a pastel pink "It's-Not-Fake-Anything-It's-Real-Dynel" wig to the pool and was the only woman at the club who I remember wearing a bikini. She was a hottie. The Normal Mothers glared at her, too.

We had a cleaning lady named Bessie, who became one of my mother's best friends. Bessie was older than my mom. She was also black. An upper middle class white woman being friends with a black housekeeper in Texas in the '50s was... let's just say it was uncommon. But Bessie was family. I was regularly sent two or three blocks down the street to the convenience store to buy Bessie a pack of Pall Mall cigarettes. I was five. Barbara would play Elvis Presley records and dance while Bessie did the ironing. And they would talk.

Finally, the reality of a husband being gone too often and for too long took its toll on Barbara. There was also my father's expectation that she be the Perfect 1950s Silent-And-Servile Housewife while he was clearly having affairs. They divorced when I was seven. He destroyed her in the divorce, paid friends to lie, and got custody of all four kids. He kept her piano but refused to let us play it. He even had the court order her to move to another city, when she kept violating the visitation agreement by waiting for us on the corner after school. She had lost her marriage, her home, her friends and her children. Now she even had to leave town.

Barbara moved to Dallas, where she got an entry-level job as a switchboard operator at a geotechnical engineering company. It was one of those switchboards like you see in the movies with all the plugs and cables. She studied shorthand in her spare time and worked during her lunch break as the cashier in exchange for free lunches.

Still the lover of adventure, she and her sister, also recently divorced, did their best to celebrate single life in Dallas. They spent one night during the Christmas holidays hysterically laughing as they piled Christmas trees stolen from the local Safeway into her car. They leaned one tree against each front door of half a dozen apartments in her building. As she tells the story, concert pianist Van Cliburn was at a bachelor party in one of those apartments and got a face-full of Christmas tree when he tried to leave.

At the switchboard, a field worker had to check in daily with his department head, and all of his calls went through Barbara. I'm guessing he didn't call just to check in with his office. He was a handsome physicist, eight years younger than Barbara, with crinkly, twinkly eyes. He asked her out one day when she was working as cashier at the lunch line. She says she knew "that instant" she would marry him. But she turned him down for the date, then hurried off to look at his personnel file to check him out. They were married within a year. I'm not sure when he learned that four children came with the deal, but he adored her and accepted whatever came with her.

They bought a little house with enough space for all four of us, even though we would only descend on them maybe three times a year. Barbara would haul us off to the Texas State Fair or the amusement park, or Shakey's Pizza. If we went to Six Flags, we were there when the park opened and they had to drag us out when they closed. Let me correct that: they had to drag my mother out. We kids were exhausted. As we got old enough, each of us moved out of our dad's house as quickly as we could. When my sister became engaged at eighteen, she and my dad had a huge fight. She moved out and I was "invited" to go live with my mom. It was the best break I ever got.

After seven years of being conditioned to silence and the acrid scent of platinum blonde Lady Clairol with my stepmother, I was returned to the rough and rowdy world of my daring and adventurous mother. She had finally gotten one of her kids back and was determined to spoil me rotten. I had clothes from Neiman-Marcus (bought on sale, because the combined total of my mother's and stepdad's salary was $750 a month). Shopping for shoes is my first real memory of her as a militant feminist. We had picked out a couple of pairs to try on, and waited, like you did in those days, for a salesclerk. After more than one clerk passed us by, my mother grabbed one of them and said firmly, "You go get your manager right now." I had honestly never seen her talk that way to anyone. She was furious and let that manager have both barrels. He could not stop apologizing, but she wouldn't let go. She showed me how to not be a passive victim, waiting to be noticed. She showed me how to grab someone by the lapels and *make* them pay attention. She was done being mistreated.

My mother bought me my first copy of *Cosmopolitan* magazine. She introduced me to Bob Dylan's music, and took me to see *The Graduate* when I was fourteen. She dragged me to the mall to see Tiny Tim tiptoe through the tulips in person and shoved me to the front. She received the phone call from my high school dean, who complained that I was not wearing a bra and the dean could see my nipples. "Well, she *does* have them," was Barbara's reply, and she hung up the phone. She never once made me think I couldn't do any idiot thing I had an idea to do. As far as she was concerned, I was unstoppable.

While my mother was fabulous in so very many ways, what she was not was a cook. She had her regular meals—mostly casserole recipes learned in junior high cooking class—but she was not the kind of cook that made you want to drag friends home for dinner. Christmas eve always included our version of the dinner from the movie *A Christmas Story*: my mother, my stepdad and me happily eating Chinese food at the local restaurant.

That said, Barbara did make the most spectacular chocolate cake, hands down. It was basically sugar, butter and chocolate with an egg and some flour thrown in to make it "healthy." It was simple and fabulous, and I wonder if it wasn't her version of "You want cake? Here's your fucking cake." I don't know. I don't remember it being any special occasion cake or reward or related to anything really; just every now and then, that heavenly cake would appear and all was right with the world.

Some years after I graduated high school and left home for college, my mother worked her way up to being Secretarial Assistant to the entire engineering department in her company. She was a really popular gal, loved to laugh and joke with everyone, and did an incredibly good job to boot. She worked on computers that you had to go into a "clean room" to use. She was still entering contests and won a paid-for lunch at the Playboy Club for her entire department. Other people noticed that while the engineers she worked for got the money and the credit, it was Barbara who juggled their half-done paperwork, handled all the phone calls from clients, wrote the sales quotes for customers and made the department run like clockwork.

One day, one of the guys from the printing department brought her a gift: a box of her own business cards. He decided that since she did so much of the work herself, she deserved them. She earned them. He left them as a surprise on her desk. One of the engineers found them as she came back from her break, showed them to her and said, "What the hell would YOU need a business card for?" and he threw them in the trash as she stood there. She had worked at that company for 22 years. She pulled the box of cards out of the trash, picked up her purse and walked out the door. And yes, every executive in the company called and apologized. But she never went back.

It's my favorite moment of her life. She just said, "No" and that was it. She said "No" to being treated as less than. She said "No" to being an ordinary mom and a silent, acquiescent wife doing ordinary, boring things. She said "No" to some court telling her when she could or couldn't see her children. She said "No" to being a victim. She even said "No" to jumping at a handsome young hunk just because he'd

Sheath Cake

Mix in large bowl
2 cups sugar
2 cups flour
     (Set aside)
1 stick butter
3 ½ Tbs cocoa
1 cup water
½ cup wesson oil
    (bring to boil)
Add this mixture to sugar and flour
½ cup buttermilk or sourmilk
dissolve 1 teas soda
2 eggs slightly beaten
1 teas. vanilla (Mix in with other ingredients

Cake recipe from 1965.

grease and flour 1 large pan.
Bake 350° for 30 min.
     Icing (Make during last 5
                minutes cake is
                in oven)
1 stick butter
4 Tbs cocoa
6 Tbs. sweet milk
Bring to boil
Add ⅓ box powered sugar

Ice cake as soon as it comes out of
oven..

Icing recipe from 1965.

asked her, until she had checked him out thoroughly. She said "No, I don't have to be a cook or a housekeeper or a homemaker or quiet or well-behaved or anything I don't want to be in order to be a woman."

She's 87 now and is busy saying "Yes" to life again, after her twinkly-eyed physicist died of brain cancer. She slept at his feet as he slipped away in the hospice. She said "yes" again to forgiving my father so that she could have daily phone conversations and comfort him as he dealt with his own terminal cancer. When he died, she was at his side, too, at the same hospice facility where her husband had died four year earlier.

My mother taught me that it was okay to say "No" any time I needed to. She taught me to say "Yes" to adventure, to staying up too late, to wasting money and making people laugh. She also taught me how to make that incredible cake.

BARBARA JEANE'S CHOCOLATE SHEATH CAKE

INGREDIENTS

2 cups flour
2 cups sugar
1 stick butter
3 ½ Tbs. cocoa powder
1 cup water
½ cup Wesson oil
½ cup buttermilk or sour milk
2 eggs
Baking soda
Vanilla extract

TO PREPARE

1. Into a large mixing bowl, add flour and sugar. Set aside
2. Into a saucepan, combine butter, cocoa, water and oil. Bring to a boil
3. Add boiled mixture to dry ingredients bowl
4. Add ½ cup buttermilk or sour milk
5. Dissolve 1 tsp. soda into mixture
6. Add 2 eggs, slightly beaten
7. Add 1 tsp. vanilla
8. Mix well

BARBARA JEANE'S CHOCOLATE SHEATH CAKE (CONT.)

9. Pour into large greased and floured pan
10. Bake at 350 degrees for 30 minutes

If you want to make icing, start it 5 minutes before the cake comes out of the oven.

ICING

INGREDIENTS

1 stick butter
4 Tbs. cocoa
6 Tbs. milk
Powdered sugar

TO PREPARE

1. Bring all ingredients—except powdered sugar—to a boil.
2. Add 1/3 box powdered sugar.
3. Ice cake immediately out of the oven.

Apples and Orange Polyester Castles

by Becky Hartman Edwards

At least I didn't projectile vomit this time.

In 1974, when I was twelve years old, my parents sat me down on our rattan couch and told me were moving from Berkeley to Israel in a month. About ten seconds after they broke the news, I threw up. Well, "threw up" makes it sound like a run-of-the-mill stomach flu. When they informed me that we were moving halfway around the world, I stopped breathing and then when I opened my mouth to gasp for air, it was not unlike the scene in *The Exorcist* that involved copious amounts of pea soup… (Don't worry, this essay doesn't end with a pea soup recipe.)

So two years later, when my parents sat me down on our rattan couch in our Tel Aviv apartment (they were big fans of wicker furniture), and told me we were moving to Boston, I didn't throw up. I just sobbed, told them I hated them, and ran into the closet-sized bedroom I shared with my sister.

The first year in Israel had been hard—intense Hebrew lessons for the first half of the day, sitting in a classroom not understanding a word the second half. But by the second year, I had a posse of friends from other English-speaking countries, my Hebrew was passable, I was even occasionally mistaken for a *Sabra* (native Israeli), and most exciting of all, I had my first boyfriend. A blonde-haired Brit named Paul, who was like a young Hugh Grant before anybody knew who Hugh Grant was. So when my parents told me we were moving back to the States and not back to the Bay Area, but to Boston, a place where I had no ties, no friends, and definitely no boyfriend with an adorable British accent,I was understandably unhappy.

We ended up in a Western suburb of Boston called Newton. Despite the fact that it was filled with beautiful Victorian homes and tree-lined streets and even had its own lake, I hated it. I hated it because I wanted to be back in Israel; I hated it because I was fourteen and hated almost everything my parents liked; but most of all I hated it because it meant starting at yet another new school. Weeks Junior High would be my *seventh* school in ten years.

My only solace was that I had the perfect first day of school outfit, an ensemble that was considered the height of fashion in my Israeli junior high. A polyester shirt with a landscape that featured a neon orange castle, brown clogs and bellbottom jeans with zippers all over that had double entendre patches that read "stop," "yield" and "slippery when wet." I walked into Ms. Imo's eighth-grade homeroom and immediately realized just how far Newton really was from Tel Aviv. Everybody in the class was wearing some version of a Lacoste shirt, Levis 501 jeans and topsiders. Well, there may have been a rebel or two wearing Tretorn sneakers, but the dress code was clearly conservative and preppy, not flashy and Eurotrashy. Two mean girls literally laughed out loud as I entered; most of the other kids just stared in disbelief.

And even though I quickly made a trip to the Chestnut Hill Mall and bought my own Lacoste and Levis, I was still very much the outsider. I discovered, much to my embarrassment, that in language class I spoke French with a Hebrew accent; I had no idea how to feather my hair; and, worst of all, I didn't wear lip-gloss. I was convinced this place would never feel like home. My only hope was that my parents would move again.

But by October the only excursion outside of Newton I made was on a class field trip to the Belkin Apple Farm in Natick. My bus buddy was Heather Gifford, who'd arrived in Newton the previous spring. She was waspy and quiet, and I assumed she sat in silent judgment of me like the rest of the Weeks Junior High population.

She didn't say much as we drove down Route Nine, but as an apple-picking novice, I had to ask why we all had to bring ten dollars to pay the orchard to let us do their work. I didn't get a response, but I did get a smile.

Once we got to the orchard, the Toughies (that was the incredibly disarming nickname kids in Newton gave to the kids who smoked, drank and had sex) headed behind the bus to light up, while the rest of us were handed baskets.

There was an awkward moment, when I wasn't sure if we were going to stick together or go our separate ways, and then Heather turned to me and said, "Bet you I get more."

Next to polyester shirts with castles on them, there's nothing I love more than a meaningless and random competition. I still claim that I won with three and a half baskets of McIntosh apples, but if Heather were writing this essay she'd claim that her three overflowing baskets actually held more apples.

What neither of us would dispute is that, while racing to yank as many apples off their branches as we could, we started to forge a friendship. Heather confessed that she moved to Newton the previous year because, after her parents' divorce, her mother fell asleep with a lit cigarette in hand and burnt down their home in Dartmouth. I confessed that I hated topsiders. At the end of the day she invited me over. Her mother picked us up from school and asked us what we planned on doing with all these apples.

We clearly hadn't thought that far ahead, but after a moment I blurted out that we were planning on making apple pie. So as soon as we got to Heather's house, we dug out her mother's Fannie Farmer cookbook and got to work.

We cut ourselves peeling the apples and had to make and remake the pie dough three times before we had something we could roll out that wouldn't fall apart, but by the end of the evening we had an actual apple pie that was only a *little* burnt. And it was the first time Newton stopped feeling like enemy territory and started to feel like home.

She's the one in the bikini who clearly didn't enjoy the apple pie as much as I did.

APPLE PIE

Double pie crust for a 9-inch pie
2/3 cup of sugar
½ teaspoon of salt
1 teaspoon of cinnamon
½ teaspoon of nutmeg
1 ½ teaspoons of flour
7 large firm tart apples
3 tablespoons butter

TO PREPARE

1. Pre-heat the oven to 425 degrees
2. Roll out one of the crusts and line the pie pan with it.
3. Mix sugar, salt, cinnamon, nutmeg and flour in a large bowl.
4. Peel, core and slice the apples. Toss them with the sugar mixture then heap them in the crust-lined pan and dot with butter.
5. Roll out the top crust and drape it over the pie. Crimp the edges and cut several vents into the top.
6. Bake 10 minutes at 425 degrees, then lower the heat to 350 and bake 30-40 minutes more, or until the apples are tender when pierced with a skewer and the crust is browned.

31 Flavors of Inspiration

by Michele Willens

Whenever I am asked when I knew I wanted to be a writer, I think back on my sixteenth year. I was still a year away from my driver's license and my introduction to French kissing. (Thank you, Jim McHugh.) But it was the year when I personally discovered that written words could have real impact.

It began with a letter to the Editor, my first, sent with impassioned zeal to *Life Magazine*. I complained about an article in the previous issue in which the author named the best ice cream in the country. Specifically, I criticized the *omission* of Baskin-Robbins' 31 Flavors. I had become seriously addicted to at least 28 of those, including Here Comes The Fudge, Peanut Cluster and Charlie Brownie. I ended my tiny tome by saying something like, "31 Flavors makes all the others on your list seem like chopped liver."

My first thrill was seeing the letter in print—sure enough, there it was, signed "Michele Willens, Los Angeles." I could have died happy at that point, but it turned out, that was just the prologue. A few days after publication, I received a phone call from my mother's best pal, Ernestine. It was about ten at night and I recall getting out of the bathtub to take what seemed like an odd call. I stood shivering and stunned as Ernestine said how amazing the "ad in today's paper" was. I, of course, had no idea what she was talking about.

"I can't be the first one to tell you!" she said. Per her instructions, I immediately found that day's *Los Angeles Times* and turned to a particular page of the Life section. There, in boldface letters, was a half-page paid message: "Michele Willens, who are you? WHERE are you? Please call us. Your friends at Baskin-Robbins."

Needless to say, I did not sleep much that night and I may have even grabbed a pint of Jamoca Almond Fudge out of the freezer. I had not been that excited since my brother and I won the entire Top 40 on KFWB for correctly guessing the following week's top ten. (Thank you, "All In The Game.")

The next morning, hands shaking, I made the call and heard an equally excited and relieved voice inviting me out to the B.R. factory in Van Nuys. I was speechless. (Think Ann-Margret picking up the receiver to learn she'd been chosen to meet Conrad Birdie.) I asked if my brother could come with me since he was my partner in all things gluttony.

When we pulled up to the block-long factory in a rather desolate area, we looked up to see an equally block-long banner reading "Welcome Michele." What followed was a meet-and-greet with all the top execs, and a private tour to watch the ice cream being churned, the fudge sauce being swirled, and the fixins being tossed. Did I mention the standing ovations from the employees every step of the way?

Once again, I could have died happy right then and there. But no, they then led the way to their on-site Baskin-Robbins store, and instructed us to fill the car with however much it (not to mention our freezer at home) could hold. I recall boxes of ice cream sandwiches, quarts and pints galore, and whatever else we could stuff in the car before stuffing it into our stomachs.

I was kind of a mini-star in my 'hood for a week or so: something I would be again five years later when I wrote an Opinion piece for *The Los Angeles Times* entitled "A Child Of The Sixties: From Mouseketeers to McCarthy." But I soon learned that those starry moments end quickly…the latter fifteen minutes of fame was superseded by Joyce Maynard's *New York Times Magazine* cover. (She was a year younger, the paper more prestigious, *and* she'd had a fling with J.D Salinger.)

What did we do with all that ice cream? I would like to report that we donated it to a homeless shelter but a: I didn't know of any in Santa Monica then; and b: We were far too greedy. My mother did try a ration system at one point, and then she and I found ways to use the winnings in recipes. I became a pretty good creator of frozen desserts after that, but I would argue that my Baskin-Robbins experience had even more meaning: it showed me the power my own words could have, both on readers and on my own life. It was at that point I laid down the spoon (well, sort of) and picked up the pen.

MICHELE'S BAKED ALASKA

INGREDIENTS

¾ cup flour
1 c sugar
7 tbsp cocoa
¾ tsp salt
½ tsp baking powder
2/3 c butter
2 eggs
1 tsp vanilla
1 tbsp corn syrup
2 pints Baskin-Robbins ice cream (choose your flavors)

TO PREPARE

1. Sift first five ingredients, then add the rest, except for the ice cream.
2. Mix and spread in greased cake pan. Bake 350 for about 30 minutes. (I like it fudgy)
3. While cake is baking, line a deep bowl with foil and spread the two flavors of ice cream on top of each other. Freeze.
4. When ready, flip ice cream mound onto cooled cake and cover it all with meringue.

MERINGUE

INGREDIENTS

2 eggs
Sugar
Vanilla

TO PREPARE

1. Beat two egg whites with 4 tbsp sugar and ½ tsp vanilla
2. Before serving, stick under broiler for a minute.

Bittersweet and Nuts

by Leslie Greenberger

My grandmother was formidable. She was nasty and critical and could find something negative to say about nearly every subject. She took up a lot of space, not because she was bigger than I was, but because she always made her disapproval known. Her default expression was a scowl.

We called her Ima (pronounced Ee-mah), and she came to stay with us for a month or so every year.

She had a beaklike nose, a hunched neck, and wide shoulders, capping a broad back. Her arms were burly and her elbows pointed away from her body, as if ready for a tussle. She had an ample bosom and a roundish belly, and the mass of her upper body was improbably supported by a pair of spindly legs, bony knees, and toes that pointed inward. Curiously, this only made her seem more imposing. As a child, I thought she resembled a giant, angry pigeon.

All this is to say she wasn't anything like your typical sweet old grandmother. But there was one way she showed her love: She baked. Cherry strudel, apple torte, apricot palachinka, but my favorite—the whole family's favorite—was her walnut cake with dark chocolate icing. It was an old family recipe that had been handed down through the generations on her mother's side. It was one of the few things she had left of her family. During World War II, she had lost both parents and both sisters, her sisters' husbands, and their children. She and my grandfather had narrowly escaped from Romania with my mother, then six or seven years old, and my uncle, an infant. They boarded one of three boats destined for Palestine—the only boat to make it. The other two were sunk by the Nazis with all passengers on board.

Ima seemed lighter, happier, when she was baking. In the process of teaching my sisters and me to shell and grind the nuts and beat the egg whites, she was patient, relaxed, seeming to enjoy the normalcy of a task she must have shared with her own

mother. But there were no measurements, no exact recipe. Ima did it all by eye. We looked on as she put in a handful of this and a pinch of that. Each time, the cake turned out a little differently, sometimes more spongy and light, other times heavy and dense. Either way, it was luscious.

Once it was baked, Ima's arthritic, gnarled hands cut the cooled, square cake in half, spread on the dark chocolate icing and stacked the layers, the result of which was a slightly misshapen (shall we say, "rustic-looking?") loaf. But, to me, to all of us, it was a thing of wonder and beauty; a decadent, rich, chocolaty and nutty treat that we would dream about for the eleven months of the year we didn't see her. It was the main reason we looked forward to her visits. From the moment she arrived, we would anticipate our first bites of the dark, bittersweet delicacy.

I remember dragging my fork across the plate to scrape up every trace of creamy chocolate and ground nuts. I'd have picked that plate up and licked it clean if Ima wouldn't have disapproved. She was very concerned with appearances, as though we were all always being watched and judged. Perhaps that was the legacy of having been persecuted.

She was actually only five-foot-two, and had been beautiful when she was young. But this was not apparent to me at the time. The only hint of her former beauty was her vivid sea-green eyes, once probably so full of hope, now hooded and haunted. Decades later, I can imagine the carefree young woman she'd surely been before the war, before the Holocaust, before she'd lost her entire family. Now, I look back at her with more compassion and understanding. I think we might have liked each other, if only history had been kinder to her.

IMA'S CHOCOLATE WALNUT CAKE

THE CAKE

INGREDIENTS

8 large eggs, separated
3/4-1 cup sugar
Pinch of salt
1 1/2-2 cups ground walnuts
1-2 tablespoons matzoh meal
1 teaspoon grated lemon zest (optional)

TO PREPARE

1. Preheat oven to 350°.
2. Beat yolks until light. Add sugar and salt and combine well. Add ground walnuts, matzoh meal, lemon zest (if desired), and mix well. Set aside.
3. Beat egg whites until they form medium stiff peaks. Stir one large spoonful of egg whites into the egg-walnut mixture to loosen it a bit. Then, gently fold the remainder of egg whites in.
4. Pour into a greased 13" x 9" pan and bake until inserted toothpick comes out clean, approximately 40 minutes.
5. Cool on a wire rack, then remove cake from pan and cut in half crosswise.

THE ICING

INGREDIENTS

3 ounces bittersweet chocolate
3 tablespoons margarine
3 tablespoons sugar
3 tablespoons water
1/4 teaspoon instant coffee

TO PREPARE

1. Mix all ingredients in the top of a double boiler. Melt over low heat while stirring.
2. Spread on cooled cake layers and stack.

HOT DRINKS FOR COLD TIMES

Saffron Hot Chocolate

The Perfect Coffee Moment

Bread and Tea, a poem

Spring

by Leah Krinsky

When I was in kindergarten, my parents kept my hair in a pixie cut. If I complained, they would say, "But don't you want to be mod? Twiggy has short hair." In 1965, that was all I needed to hear.

But it required regular trips to the beauty shop. That was my father's responsibility. We'd take the bus from our apartment in Queens, and we would make an afternoon of it, stopping at a coffee shop after my haircut, where we would sit at the counter and he would order us hot chocolate. I already knew that chatting in restaurants was something adults did, and I felt very grown-up sitting there with my dad. I made sure to sip my hot chocolate as slowly as I could to make the time last. We would talk about this and that, tell silly jokes, or engage in wordplay. He'd point to letters on my paper placemat and I'd tell him what they were. My father and I always enjoyed each other's company.

One day in late winter, we were walking from the bus stop to my hair appointment. Our route took us past an old stone church, and on this mild Saturday, the churchyard was filled with crocuses in full bloom, delicate little petaled cups in soft colors reaching out of the bare earth on short, pale green stalks. I knew what they were because we had learned about them in school, and my dad knew what they were because he knew…everything. They were packed close together, so close you couldn't even see the individual flowers, just masses of pale purple and bright orange, swaths of color. As we walked we exclaimed about all the crocuses. So many! So pretty!

It couldn't have been more than half a city block, but to a child captivated by the vividness of the colors and the novelty of seeing hundreds and hundreds of flowers all at once, it seemed to go on forever. It was thrilling to see so much beauty almost by accident, in the simple act of walking down the street. The rest of the day—the haircut, the hot chocolate—were all electrified by the spectacle of those crocuses. It has stayed in my mind always.

It's one of the happiest memories of my childhood. It's also one of the only memories I have of my father walking.

* * *

In 1960, the year I was born, my dad was diagnosed with multiple sclerosis, and by the time I was 6 it began to affect his mobility. Shortly after our crocus day, he started using a walker and could only manage short distances. He would fall occasionally, which was terrifying. Heat and stress incapacitated him. On the June day in 1968 when Robert Kennedy was assassinated, the weather in New York was sticky and hot, and when Dad got home from work he couldn't make it up the steps into our apartment building; he sat on a low brick wall in front and waited for my mother to come back from a nearby medical supply place with a rented wheelchair to bring him into the building through the basement. Soon after, we bought a wheelchair for him to use when his legs couldn't support him.

His disease essentially held my family hostage, casting a shadow over every aspect of our lives; it was the villain on which I, as a child, blamed all my family's heartache: my mother's abusive, screaming tirades; my brother's troubles at school; my embarrassment as my classmates stared at my father laboriously dragging himself up the steps to my school with his walker.

Every birthday cake, every Thanksgiving wishbone, every penny thrown into a well or a fountain, every ball of dandelion fluff blown away in just one breath—any opportunity I had to make a wish as a child and even into my adolescence—I wished for my father to get well. I made that wish, devoutly, fervently, because I wanted so badly for us to be a normal family instead of the strange, sad one we were.

A therapist once said to me, "It must be hard for you to imagine that anything might ever go well." Secondary-progressive MS, the type my father had, has one outcome. He died in 1997 at age 72. He had become quadriplegic and bedridden and, after the disease had finished ravaging his voluntary muscular system, it attacked his respiratory system, killing him in his sleep.

It's still hard to imagine that anything might ever go well. And a lot of the time it doesn't. But even then there are still some little purple and orange flowers sticking their heads out of the cold ground, and I make it a point always to allow myself to be enchanted by them.

And towards the end, when he had terrible bedsores and muscle spasms in his legs that kept him up all night, and his voice was barely audible, we still watched Warner Brothers cartoons together and swapped awful puns (ME: "You seem euphoric today." DAD: "Alas, euphoric, I knew him, Horatio."). I would read him the clues from *The Sunday New York Times* crossword and he would solve it in his head while I wrote down the answers on the grid. We would listen to Mahler and sigh. And sometimes, I would make us hot chocolate.

Dad wasn't one for exotic ingredients, so I kept it to milk and Hershey's hot chocolate mix. But because of him, hot chocolate always exists in my mind with crocuses, whose pistils I later learned are the source for saffron. So here's a recipe for saffron hot chocolate. It uses cocoa powder, which is much richer than hot chocolate mix.

SAFFRON HOT CHOCOLATE

For one serving

INGREDIENTS

8 ounces milk of choice
2 generous teaspoons cocoa powder
1/2 teaspoon cardamom powder
1 pinch of saffron, finely ground and dissolved in 1 Tablespoon of hot water
1/2 teaspoon of vanilla extract
Sweetener of choice (stevia, agave nectar, sugar, etc) to taste

TO PREPARE

1. Warm a non-reactive saucepan under low heat. Add in chocolate and cardamom powder, and lightly "toast" for 20-30 seconds over low heat to bring out the flavors.
2. Add in one-third of the milk and whisk until chocolate is lump-free and well-dissolved into the milk.
3. Add in the rest of the milk and whisk again. Do not boil, but cook on low heat until the edges of the milk start to bubble.
4. Stir in vanilla and saffron and remove from heat.
5. If using sweetener, sweeten to taste and enjoy!

I Heart
1,3,7-TRIMETHYLXANTHINE

by Barbara Horowitz

Seated shoulder to shoulder alongside 2500 other academic physicians in a packed hotel ballroom, I leaned forward, eager to hear the results of a crucial clinical trial.

Like many of the other cardiologists present, I had flown in on the red-eye the night before so that I could squeeze in a full afternoon of procedures and patients before leaving. I'd arrived at the convention center hotel at 4:30 am, collapsed on the bed, and was wake-up-call-startled out of bed a few hours later. Rushing out of my room to the venue with no time for a proper breakfast, I'd stuffed a dry bagel into my mouth and washed it down with a hotel concession juice box.

I found an empty seat near the front of the room and, breathless but relieved I'd made it in time, sat down to hear the latest. But now, as I strained to take in the cascades of Powerpoint-data that filled the room, I noted, suddenly, that my head hurt…and it hurt a lot. This was especially notable to me because I never got headaches. No migraines, no clusters or tension headaches. None. Never.

But there I was, seated in a darkened room with the first real headache of my life, one that was rapidly turning into what we physicians call "the worst headache of your life." And that scared me: When a patient reports 'the worst headache of my life" we treat it as an emergency.

Indeed, as I went from mild discomfort to absolutely agonizing pain, I recognized the seriousness of what was happening. I consoled myself with how lucky I was to be surrounded by top physicians, as I managed to stand and stagger toward an old friend and colleague I had spotted on my way in.

"Cheryl, I'm having the 'worst headache of my life.'"

She instantly understood the gravity of those words coming from another physician. She led me out of the presentation arena to a lighted area, where she pulled out her phone and made a call....one that I assumed was to summons an ambulance. I closed my eyes and waited for the rest.....a CT scan followed by a terrifying diagnoses: bleeding in the brain or perhaps even a brain tumor.

But instead of putting me on an ambulance, she administered a bolus dose of 1,3,7-trimethylxanthine. The drug acted immediately—within 90 seconds, I noticed relief...minor at first, but soon the viselike pounding started to truly subside until, within ten minutes, I was normal again. Completely normal.

Pharmacologists refer to the drug she administered as a powerful releaser of endogenous catecholamines that acts on the sympathetic arc of the autonomic nervous system to induce vasoconstriction, tachycardia, and innumerous other neurohumoral responses.

Most everyone else calls it caffeine.

* * *

Three very very happy coincidences in the fall of 1992 led me to my one and only true non-lifeform-based love. First, I was in my early weeks of a notoriously intense cardiovascular fellowship at UCLA. Second, a new company with a funny green logo opened up a coffee shop on the corner of Lindbrook Drive and Westwood Boulevard, two blocks from the entrance of the ER I staffed. And, crucially, "Starbucks" started serving at 5:15 am....only minutes before my first rounds began.

To call it love at first sip would denigrate the intensity of the relationship. The physical passion. The longing. The literal pain—a headache—of separation. The heart-pounding thrill of reunion. Had I enjoyed coffee before? In medical school and residency, I'd slogged down Styrofoam cups of hot and tepid black brews to wake me up. And it was from these early ersatz, tarry elixirs poured from orange- and black-handled coffee pots in the nurses' lounge that the chemical part of my addiction got rolling. But the pleasure? The connection? The emotional ride? It wasn't until Starbucks coffee came to Bruintown that the cravings, the fantasies, my sudden absences from and swift returns to rounds holding a long odd logo'd white cardboard cup began in earnest.

In ICUs, clinics, and on-call rooms, caffeine spiked my epinephrine levels, sparking creative associations and pleasing word combinations. The drug accelerated my thoughts, my mood, my retrieval and—I am certain—my diagnostic and clinical acumen.

I was training to become a cardiologist, learning to reverse heart failure, open arteries, and defibrillate, propelled by 1,3,7-trimethylxanthine, one of the most ubiquitous and powerful cardiac stimulants in the world. For some it was just a cup of coffee. For me it was clarity, focus, creativity, and even joy.

Did I overdo it in my days as a 'baby' cardiologist? Absolutely. The many moments—EKG in my left hand, coffee cup in my right. Coffee before rounds? Yes! After rounds? Yes! Coffee for a 3:30 am late night? Yes! Coffee for a 3:30 am early start? Yes!

Did I worry about my coffee intake? Did I consider cutting back or quitting? Occasionally I did. But for the most part I turned a blind eye to occasional reports of coffee-related health concerns and celebrated reports of coffee-related health benefits. Because, between the performance enhancement and pleasure, I could not really see the benefit of cutting back.

At least that was what I believed until that morning at the conference, when I had what turned out to be a "caffeine withdrawal headache." It turns out that when the brain becomes accustomed to the consistent presence of caffeine (and many other drugs), the sudden absence of that agent can result in dramatic and painful symptoms. My caffeine withdrawal headache was awful, painful, frightening and, in retrospect, entirely predictable. Fortunately for me, my colleague that morning was a wise and experienced doc who knew that 'when you hear hoof beats, think about horses and not zebras' and ordered me a simple cup of coffee instead of a CAT scan or a craniotomy.

That said, my love affair with coffee continued and continues—albeit perhaps without the same youthful gusto and unbridled indulgence. But the relationship has evolved from those early days of passion—when I wanted and needed it all day and much of the night—to a more mature arrangement in which I meet my beloved elixir merely twice a day—once in the morning and once at night—and three times on the weekend and my birthday.

THE PERFECT COFFEE MOMENT

INGREDIENTS

An early morning
Coffee app on your phone

TO PREPARE

1. A cool but not bitterly cold morning temperature (45-60 F) at 4:30 am.
2. A six-mile brisk walk from 4:45-6:45 am
3. Fast shower, dress and jump into car and drive towards hospital.
4. Perfect parking spot right in front of coffee store(!)
5. Jump out of car....temperature still low for LA (<65)
6. No line, no waiting: "Small coffee in a double cup, please"
7. Phone coffee app works!!
8. Hands encircling cup are warmed during walk to car.
9. Ignition. NPR.
10. Aaaannndd.... sip.
11. Ahhh....

Bread and Tea

by Annie LaZebnik

i once asked my friend what the exact moment was when
she knew she was in love with her girlfriend
she said it was when she watched her hands slice a baguette
she said she realized in that moment
that she loved those hands.

she asked me the same question
and i thought about it for a while
and i realized that i knew i loved him when he made me tea
he would steep me a cup every morning or
when I was sick or upset
and silently set down the mug next to me

i wonder why tea and baguettes
are how they show they care.

Editors

Ann Brown

Ann Brown writes about parenting and family life by mostly making up stuff about her own family. She has a parenting show on YouTube—"The Motherload—Not Your Mother's Parenting Advice"—where she doesn't use naughty words, and a blog—www.drstrangemom.com—where she does. Her Grandma Esther used to eat flowers straight from the garden, and her mother was a health food enthusiast back in the 1950s. Ann used to sneak kale and flax into her sons' peanut butter sandwiches until they got hip to her tricks. She and her husband live in Oregon where she needs to shave her legs only two months out of the year. Her essays have been heard on Public Radio International, as part of the "A Time For…" series.

Claire LaZebnik

Claire is the author of five novels for adults and five YA novels, including *Epic Fail* and *Things I Should Have Known*. With Dr. Lynn Kern Koegel, she co-authored the non-fiction books *Overcoming Autism* and *Growing Up on the Spectrum*. She has written for *The New York Times*, *The Wall Street Journal*, and *Self Magazine*, among other publications, and contributed a monologue to the anthology play *Motherhood Out Loud*. Please check out her website at www.clairelazebnik.com or follow her on Facebook, Instagram or Twitter.

Contributors

Davis Alexander

Davis Alexander, who holds a culinary diploma from Le Cordon Bleu, is the Recipe Tester and an occasional contributing writer for the Food Section of *The Los Angeles Times*. In the test kitchen, and throughout life, Davis continues to learn lessons about best intentions and imperfect outcomes.

Kim Allen-Niesen

After practicing trusts and estates law for eighteen years, Kim stopped to take a deep dive into culture and raise her two teenagers. Now that they've all survived, she leads museum tours, scouts galleries, and writes about her experiences.

K. Bidus

K. Bidus was born and raised in Philadelphia, and attended Kutztown University before moving to New York City, where she met her husband, artist Drew Friedman. Bidus is a published poet, and in collaboration with Friedman, has written illustrated humor pieces for *The New Yorker*, *The New York Times Magazine* and *The New York Observer*, among many others. For the last twenty years, she has raised champion show beagles. Bidus currently resides in rural Pennsylvania with Drew.

Valerie Breiman

Valerie Breiman is a screenwriter, director and recovering actress. Her independent film *Love & Sex* premiered and sold at Sundance back in 2001. Since that time, she's written, rewritten and directed multiple TV and film projects at every studio. She is currently vegan and writing cartoons for Disney.

Liane Kupferberg Carter

Liane Kupferberg Carter is the author of Ketchup is *My Favorite Vegetable: A Family Grows Up with Autism* (Jessica Kingsley Publishers). Her articles and essays have appeared in many publications, including *The New York Times*, *The Washington Post*, *The Chicago Tribune*, *Brain Child Magazine*, *Literary Mama*, and *The Manifest-Station*. A parent, cat wrangler, and Oxford comma fan, she lives in New York.

Kimberly Brooks

In addition to her starring roles as mother, wife and daughter, Kimberly Brooks is a painter and multimedia artist whose work explores subjects dealing with history, memory and identity. Brooks has solo exhibitions throughout the United States. Brooks founded the Arts Section of the Huffington Post and is the founder of Griffith Moon Publishing. Brooks has two books forthcoming: *Painting Lessons* and a coffee table book entitled *I Notice People Disappear* (Vivant Publishing). www.kimberlybrooks.com

May-lee Chai

May-lee Chai is an educator and author of eight books, including the memoir *Hapa Girl*, a Kiriyama Prize Notable Book, and the novel *Tiger Girl*, which won an Asian/Pacific American Award for Literature. Her short prose has been published widely, including in *The Rumpus, Seventeen, Dallas Morning News, San Francisco Chronicle, ZYZZYVA,* and *Christian Science Monitor.* You can find her on Twitter @mayleechai.

Liza Donnelly

Liza Donnelly is a cartoonist and writer for *The New Yorker* magazine, and resident cartoonist at CBS News. Author of sixteen books, Liza also contributes writing and artwork to *The New York Times* and *Medium.* She isn't cooking much right now, but loves eating.

Becky Hartman Edwards

Becky Hartman Edwards is a television writer whose credits include *In Living Color, Living Single, Larry Sanders, Sex and the City, Parenthood, Switched At Birth,* and *Pitch.* And in 1996, her apple pie won second place in the Spaulding Square Neighborhood bake-off.

Kate Fuglei

Kate Fuglei is an actress and singer whose one-woman show, *Rachel Calof,* is based on the memoir of a Jewish homesteader on the northern plains. The show won best musical at the United Solo Festival in NYC in 2015 and continues to tour nationwide. Kate's work can be seen in over thirty episodes of network and cable television as well as in indie films and features. Most recently she was honored to work on *Feud!, The Santa Clarita Diet,* and in the AFI short *Aloud.* She completed her first non-fiction book in 2016, *Fermi's Gift,* about the life of Enrico Fermi, and is at work on another biography about Maria Montessori. She has written and performed monologues about being a military Mom for Spark Off Rose. She is proud to be the mother of Jack LaZebnik, a US Army Ranger, and Ben LaZebnik, a current student at Columbia University. www.rachelcalof.com, www.katefuglei.com

Leslie Greenberger

Leslie Greenberger is a freelance artist, illustrator, and photographer. She lives in Los Angeles and enjoys writing and eating.

Barbara Horowitz

Barbara Horowitz, M.D., is Visiting Professor at Harvard's Department of Human Evolutionary Biology and Professor of Cardiology and Evolutionary Biology at UCLA. She co-authored the award-winning science book, *Zoobiquity: The Astonishing Connection Between Human and Animal Health.*

Wendy Kout

Wendy Kout is an award-winning writer/producer of theater, film and television. Theatre credits include *Naked in Encino*, which had its world premiere December 2014, at the JCC CenterStage in Rochester, NY, and *We Are the Levinsons*, which will have its world premiere at Minnesota Jewish Theatre Company, spring 2017. Wendy wrote the award-winning indie film, *Dorfman in Love*, starring Elliott Gould and Sara Rue and created the hit ABC comedy, *Anything But Love*, starring Jamie Lee Curtis and Richard Lewis. But Wendy considers her greatest accomplishment the laugh-out-loud life she shares with her favorite male writer, Dennis Koenig.

Leah Krinsky

Leah Krinsky is an Emmy-winning comedy writer and licensed psychotherapist. She currently writes for *CONAN* on TBS and her less funny work has been published in *The Journal of Behavioral Sciences.*

Nina Laden

Nina Laden is an award-winning, bestselling children's book author, illustrator and poet. The daughter of two mentally ill artists, she grew up in New York City and didn't meet a fresh vegetable until after college. Her latest books are *If I Had A Little Dream*, and *Peek-a Moo!* She lives on Lummi Island, Washington. You can find her on Facebook: www.facebook.com/nina.laden and she occasionally updates her website: www.ninaladen.com

Cathy Ladman

Cathy Ladman is from Queens, New York City. She's been a standup comic for 36 years and counting, both performing live and on TV, on *The Tonight Show*, *The Late Late Show*, HBO, Showtime, and more. She's also an actor (see IMDB) and TV writer (*Roseanne*, *Caroline in the City*, *King of Queens*). Her solo show, *Does This Show Make Me Look Fat?*, will eventually be performed somewhere. She loves her dog more than anything. (She also loves her husband and daughter.)

Annie LaZebnik

Annie LaZebnik is an English major at Lewis and Clark College. She's a bad enough cook to burn cereal, but loves watching her mom bake and write. Stationed in Portland, Oregon, she's excited to be a part of this project.

Lisa Grace Lednicer

Lisa Grace Lednicer, an award-winning editor and writer, works at *The Washington Post*. Her work has appeared in the *Tampa Bay Times*, *The Boston Globe*, and *The Oregonian*, as well as in *Glamour* and *American Heritage* magazines. She is the co-author of *Extreme Barbecue* (Chronicle Books) and edited an amicus brief filed as part of a U.S. Supreme Court case. Lisa has taught school in Namibia, sung in a top-ranked women's chorus and briefly grew corn in the Oregon suburbs, just to see whether she could.

Bernadette Luckett

Bernadette Luckett started her career as a professional model in New York, but her love of comedy led her to become a standup comic. She has performed all over the country and appeared on several TV comedy shows. Bernadette has been a writer/producer on the TV sitcoms *Living Single*, *Sister, Sister*, *The Tracy Morgan Show*, *Romeo!* and *Girlfriends*. She was a contributor to the comedic anthology *No Kidding: Women Writers on Bypassing Parenthood*, and co-authored the popular self-awareness book *21 Days of Enlightenments*. Most recently, Bernadette appeared in and co-produced the award winning documentary *Comedy Warriors: Healing Through Humor* which premiered on Showtime.

Amy Wang Manning

Amy Wang Manning is a writer and editor whose work has appeared online and in newspapers and magazines. She is a contributor to the literary anthology *Family Stories From the Attic* (Hidden Timber Books, 2017). She is based in Portland, Oregon, where she also reads, cooks, crochets, takes long walks, and does her best (OK, OK, sometimes just her good) to be a wife and mother.

Merrill Markoe

Merrill Markoe is a writer of everything. A longer more detailed bio than you could possibly require is available at www.Merrillmarkoe.com

Nell Minow

Nell Minow writes about movies, culture, corporate misdeeds, San Diego Comic-Con, and now, food, from Virginia, where she is living happily ever after with her high school sweetheart. She does not do a lot of cooking, but in 2016 she prepared Thanksgiving dinner for ten members of her family, with no overlapping dietary preferences/restrictions, and everyone seemed happy. Her movie reviews and features are at www.moviemom.com and on radio stations across the country, and she also writes for *The Huffington Post* and www.Rogerebert.com.

Carolyn Omine

Carolyn Omine was born and raised in Hawaii. She moved to Los Angeles to attend UCLA. She has studied and performed improv and sketch comedy with The Groundlings, Funny You Should Ask, and The Upright Citizens Brigade. She has been on the writing staff of *The Simpsons* for nineteen seasons and directs the vocal performances. She lives in Los Angeles with dogs, cats, fish and one human boy.

Asmita Paranjape

Originally from Hingham, MA, Asmita Paranjape moved across the country to study Computer Science and Linguistics at UCLA. However, while in college, she began pursuing comedy writing, earning the Diversity Scholarship at Upright Citizen's Brigade multiple times, and securing internships at IFC and Universal Cable Productions.

Claudia Reilly

Claudia Reilly wrote for the TV shows *The Facts of Life* and *Women in Prison*. She is the author of the novelizations for Beth Henley's *Crimes of the Heart* and Tom Topor's *Nuts*. Her play *Astronauts* won the Great American Playwriting Contest and is published in the book *A Decade of New Comedy*. Recently, she's published articles in *FourTwoNine Magazine* and *The Southampton Review*.

April Salazar

April Salazar is a writer and storyteller. She's written for *The New York Times* and has told stories on NPR's *Latino USA* and *The Moth Radio Hour*. She is ride or die to a very sweet toddler. You can find her at www.aprilsalazar.com and on twitter @AprilSalazarNYC.

Laurie Sandell

Laurie Sandell has written for *The New York Times, Esquire, GQ, Marie Claire, Glamour, New York, Real Simple* and *InStyle*, among other publications, and her cartoons have appeared in *Glamour, New York, Redbook* and *The Wall Street Journal*. Her graphic memoir,

The Impostor's Daughter, about her larger-than-life con artist father [Little, Brown, July 2009] was nominated for a 2010 Eisner Award in the "Best Reality-Based Work" category, and her second book, *Truth and Consequences: Life Inside the Madoff Family* [Little, Brown, October 2011] is currently being adapted into an HBO film. She lives in Studio City, CA, where she is at work on her third book, a nonfiction graphic memoir for teens.

Alice Scovell

Alice Scovell writes mostly for kids (novels, including *Engraved In Stone*, and *The Spirit of Chatsworth Mansion*) and about kids (articles for the online magazine, Real Mom Daily). She's very grateful for this rare opportunity to write for adults, about adults. A Manhattan resident, she finds the city noisy, crowded, dirty, smelly...and wonderful. She loves to cook—even in her tiny closet of a kitchen—but has a greatly reduced audience for her creations. All three of her beloved children live on the West coast.

Nell Scovell

Nell Scovell is a television and magazine writer, producer and director. She is the creator of the television series *Sabrina, the Teenage Witch*, and has also written for *The Simpsons, Monk, NCIS, The Muppets* and *Late Night with David Letterman*. As a journalist, Nell contributes regularly to *Vanity Fair* and *The New York Times Op-ed page*. She has worked wtih Sheryl Sandberg on both *Lean In* and *Option B*. Nell is currently writing her memoir *Just the Funny Parts* for Dey Street Books.

Susan Senator

Susan Senator is an author, blogger, journalist, and educator living in Brookline, MA with her husband Ned Batchelder. She has three sons, the oldest of whom is 27 and has fairly severe autism. Ms. Senator is the author of *Making Peace With Autism* as well as *The Autism Mom's Survival Guide* and now, *Autism Adulthood: Strategies and Insights for a Fulfilling Life*. A journalist since 1997, she has published pieces on disability, parenting, and living happily, in places like *The New York Times, The Washington Post, Tthe Boston Globe, Exceptional Parent Magazine*, NPR, *Family Fun*, and *Education Week*. Senator has appeared as a guest on *The Today Show*, MSNBC, ABC News, PBS, NPR and CNN. Her writings on Special Olympics took her to the White House in 2006, to a state dinner for Eunice Kennedy Shriver. Ms. Senator's blog, publications, and events can be found on www.susansenator.com

Jeb Sharp

Jeb Sharp is an editor and correspondent with the public radio program's "PRI's The World." She lives with her family in Cambridge, Mass.

Laura Shumaker

Laura Shumaker is a San-Francisco-based writer and the author of *A Regular Guy: Growing Up with Autism*. Her essays have appeared in many places, including *The New York Times* Motherlode, CNN, and NPR. Laura is also the author of a long-time autism and disabilities blog for *The San Francisco Chronicle*. She's married to Peter, and is the proud mother of three adult sons.

Marcie Smolin

Marcie Smolin is a writer, stand-up comic, director, actress, award-winning journalist & Artistic Director of The Actors Circle. Also she likely has too many dogs! As an actress/comic she has been in three TV series, numerous feature films, and last year at the very same time she was flown to Washington to receive an award for a story she wrote after the Orlando shootings. You could also turn on the television and see her commercial for lady peepee underpants...because this is her life.

Caissie St. Onge

Caissie St.Onge is an author, comedy writer and TV producer who has worked on *The Late Show with David Letterman*, *The Rosie O'Donnell Show*, *Best Week Ever!* and for Joan Rivers and Bette Midler, to name a few. She is currently a co-executive producer of *Watch What Happens Live! with Andy Cohen* on Bravo and lives in Connecticut with the three dreamboats who are her husband and teen sons.

Sarah Thyre

Sarah Thyre is an actor (*Strangers with Candy*), writer (*Dark at the Roots*), and the creator/co-host of Earwolf's "Crybabies" podcast. She is a voiceover artist and reproductive rights activist. She lives in Los Angeles with her husband Andy Richter and their two children, Will and Mercy. She hates mayonnaise and buttons.

Ellen Twaddell

Ellen Twaddell is a writer and social worker living in New York City. In her varied career she has been a waitress, teacher, associate literary agent, and speechwriter. She's working on her first book, a horror novel, and makes more soup than anyone wants.

Norma Safford Vela

Norma Safford Vela had a twenty-five-year career in producing, writing and directing television. She wrote for two of the Writers' Guild of America's Top 101 Television Shows: *Roseanne* and *St. Elsewhere*. In 2013, she left California for the thrills and spills of rural Maine where she lives on an 80-acre family farm and helps care for her two grandchildren, manages the marketing and media side of the farm and is a partner in a small homegoods business (TetherMade.com) with her daughter and son-in-law. She is a little shocked to be included with the amazing group of gifted writers and editors of this book, but, hey, that's cool.

Lunaea Weatherstone

Lunaea Weatherstone is a writer, editor, and teacher of women's spirituality. She's the author of *Mystical Cats Tarot*, *Victorian Fairy Tarot*, and *Tending Brigid's Flame: Awaken to the Celtic Goddess of Hearth, Temple, and Forge*. She lives in Portland, Oregon, and her prime motivation for cooking is to have leftovers to share with the cat.

Michele Willens

Michele Willens is a journalist and published playwright, and is currently a theatre commentator for NPR-owned "Robinhoodradio." She writes frequently about culture for *The Huffington Post, The Atlantic, The Daily Beast, The New York Times, and The Los Angeles Times.* She is co-author of *Face It: What Women Really Feel As Their Looks Change* (Hay House). She lives in New York with her husband, NBC News VP David Corvo, and their two children.

Maiya Williams

Maiya Williams grew up in New Haven, Connecticut and Berkeley, California. She attended Harvard University where she was the first black woman to be elected to the Harvard Lampoon. She moved to Hollywood to write and produce television shows, including *The Fresh Prince of Bel-Air, Roc, Mad-TV* and *Futurama*. Her first novel for middle grade readers, *The Golden Hour*, won best YA novel from the Southern California Booksellers Association. Other novels include: *Hour of the Cobra, Hour of the Outlaw, The Fizzy Whiz Kid* and *Kaboom Academy* (originally released as *Middle School Cool*). Maiya lives with her family in Los Angeles. She enjoys hiking, horseback riding, playing piano, cooking, and traveling the world. Visit her website: www.maiyawilliams.com

Anna Winger

Anna Winger was born in 1970, raised in Kenya, Massachusetts and Mexico, and has lived in Berlin, Germany since 2002. She is creator of the television drama *Deutschland 83* and author of the novel *This Must Be the Place* (Riverhead). Her personal essays have appeared in *The New York Times Magazine, Condé Nast Traveler,* and the *Frankfurter Allgemeine Zeitung*.

Acknowledgments

We cannot adequately thank the women who contributed to this book. We offered them nothing: no pay, no glory and no expectation of a future pay-off. All we said was, "This will be fun and we want you to join us." And these wonderful and talented writers and artists said, "Sure." A lot of them went even further and invited other women to join us too. The best part of this whole project has been the continuing conversation on Facebook and in emails with these sisterwritereaters of ours. The warmth, the humor, the support—it's truly been a delight.

We discovered halfway through this project that neither of us has any organizational skills, so Adam Parker donned his superhero cape and flew in to save the day. Thank you, Adam! We're so sorry you had to wrestle with middle-age brain fog before your time.

Thank you to Rob and Robin, our husbands, who thought this project was a great idea and couldn't wait to try out all the new recipes—until they realized we weren't going to make any of the new recipes. After a combined sixty years of marriage, they still haven't accepted that we are pretty much all talk and no action. Fooled them twice.

And we're grateful to our children who are still waiting for dinner (you'd think they'd never heard of Postmates).

Without Kimberly Brooks, our idea might never have become this beautiful book. Thank you to her for sharing our vision and bringing her artistic eye to our pages.

Share your stories and enjoy more of ours
www.sisterwritereaters.com

Recipe Index

Ammonia Cookies 186

Apple Pie 220

Baked Alaska, Michele's 223

Banana Chocolate Muffins 22

Barbecue Sauce, Uncle Benny's 147

Beef Tacos, Mom's 123

Butter Sandwiches 40

Chicken and Shells 117

Chicken Pot Pie 119

Chicken Soup, a la Bachelor 62

Chocolate Chip Cookies, 35-second 195

Chocolate Sheath Cake, Barbara Jeane's 215

Chocolate Walnut Cake, Ima's 226

Cinnamon Rolls, Warm, for the Broken-hearted 8

Crepes, Dessert 25

Crispy Peanut Butter Bars, Prince-Inspired 190

Crumb Cake 29

Flourless Chocolate Cake 170

French Toast, May Ladman's 14

Gefilte Fish 113

Green Salad 170

Ground Beef ("Funeral") Casserole 141

Guilt-Free Cookies and Cake, Merrill's 200

Jiaozi (dumplings) 136

Opossum, Roasted 128

Mustard Fish 169

Pasta with Potatoes, Jörg's 71

Pesto 161

Pimento Cheese Dip, Not Lena's, But Close 153

Pinto Beans 176

Pork "Turnip" Soup 54
Potato Soup, Christmas Eve 58
Rainbow Gelatin Cake 208
Ramen, Savory Bitch (with sardines) 75
Roasted or Grilled Vegetable Medley 169
Sabudana Khicidi 91
Saffron Hot Chocolate 232
Salmon, Steve's 106
Salsa, Blender 175
Scrambled Eggs, Mom's Secret (Mustard) 19
Spaghetti Carbonara 96
Spinach Pie Roll-Ups 87
Stuffing, Insanely Good 82
Tamales 177
Tortillas 176
Tuna Guacamole Melt, Robyn's 35
Tuna Sandwich, The Best Ever 44
Vegetable Soup, Gram's 66

CPSIA information can be obtained
at www.ICGtesting.com
Printed in the USA
LVOW05*1926040617
536901LV00016B/37/P